TIDES OF FORTUNE

To: Mansi Agarwal

TIDES OF FORTUNE

With All Good Wishes

Memoirs of
CHANG YUNG-FA

with a foreword by Margaret Thatcher

TIMES BOOKS INTERNATIONAL
Singapore • Kuala Lumpur

Frontispiece: Photograph of author by Yu-hao Tsai
English translation: Molly Mok Choon-lan

Project coordinator: KE Tan
Copyeditor: Colin Cheong
Designer: Loo Chuan Ming

Published by Times Books International
an imprint of Times Editions Pte Ltd
Times Centre, 1 New Industrial Road
Singapore 536196
Fax: (65) 2854871 Tel: (65) 2848844
E-mail: te@corp.tpl.com.sg
Online Bookstore: http://www.timesone.com.sg/te

Times Subang
Lot 46, Subang Hi-Tech Industrial Park
Batu Tiga, 40000 Shah Alam
Selangor Darul Ehsan, Malaysia
Fax & Tel: (603) 7363517
E-mail: cchong@tpg.com.my

Printed in Singapore

ISBN 981 232 097 0

About the Author

Chang Yung-fa, chairman of the Evergreen Group, was born in Taiwan in 1927. After leaving school at 18, he found work in a Japanese shipping company where he continued to pursue his studies by attending night classes. With a voracious appetite for books and an equally unflappable spirit, he was determined to upgrade himself, rising rapidly through the ranks to eventually become the captain of a vessel.

In 1968, Chang founded Evergreen Marine Corporation with one second-hand general-cargo vessel. Today, Evergreen is a dominant force at the forefront of the global container shipping industry, having successively established several pioneering records both within and outside of Taiwan. One notable achievement was the unprecedented round-the-world twin-services launched in 1984.

On the aviation front, Chang invested heavily in Taiwan's first private international airline with an eye to raising the standards of flight safety and customer services in the Republic. EVA Air took off officially on 1 July 1991 and with it, the Evergreen Group was transformed into a truly diversified global conglomerate with activities spanning the sea, land and air sectors.

Contents

Foreword

by Margaret Thatcher

Dr Chang Yung-fa's memoirs provide the reader with more than a description of a phenomenally successful business career: they offer too a unique insight into Taiwan itself. Who could have imagined fifty years ago, when the Kuomintang leadership withdrew to that island from mainland China, that by the end of the twentieth century Taiwan would have become one of the region's most astonishing economic success stories? Moreover, during the recent difficulties that the whole Asia Pacific zone has experienced, the Taiwanese have shown the solidity of their achievement. While other previously booming economies have stalled or indeed imploded, Taiwan has continued to grow, albeit at a somewhat more modest rate. The sound-ness of the Taiwanese legal and political system, which has also been demonstrated under these troublesome conditions, has played a major part in ensuring this progress.

But so too have the remarkable human qualities of the Taiwan-ese people that are amply illustrated by the extraordinary life of Dr Chang Yung-fa. Dr Chang makes it clear at the start why he is writing: "My compelling hope is that [the book] will inspire and encourage the young people not to face adversity with trepidation, but to accept life's challenges with courage, select the right course to advance themselves, and be masters of their own destinies". It certainly deserves to do so.

Chinese people are known the world over for their business acumen. But Dr Chang shows that such consistent business success requires a great deal more than mere entrepreneurial instinct. In building up Evergreen to become one of the two largest container shipping companies in the world, after starting in business with one modest, elderly general-cargo ship over thirty years earlier, Dr Chang had to overcome obstacles that would have deterred any lesser man. He had to persuade banks, beat cartels, survive generalised crises, motivate staff and, of course, win and retain the confidence of international customers. His underpinning philosophy throughout was essentially that it is only by pressing ahead, looking to future opportunities rather than resting on present achievements, that a business can continue to thrive. This was the conviction that underlay what he rightly describes as his "momentous" decision made in 1972, when he resolved that Evergreen would take full advantage of the "containerisation revolution" that was transforming the economics of marine transportation. Three years later the company's first full-container ship was launched. Within another decade Evergreen container services were criss-crossing the globe. And in recent years has come entry into the airline and hotel and other sectors.

But at heart, it is clear, the author remains a seaman. In theory, of course, there is no reason why a shipping magnate should be fascinated by ships, or an aircraft manufacturer be captivated by aeroplanes, or a wine-grower by vintages. In all these instances, a knowledge of markets and a head for finance should suffice. Yet for the really great business figures it is usually otherwise. Dr Chang believes that his early exposure to the rigours of shipboard life made a fundamental contribution to his development, and he expects his employees to spend time at sea as well. This helps provide the kind of human wisdom for which reading a balance sheet offers no substitute. And on Dr Chang the imprint of maritime life, as he notes with a trace of unmistakable nostalgia, remains deep. He recalls "the warm embrace of the infinite vastness of the mighty ocean [where his] dream was one of hope and promises for the future". So not surprisingly even today, he describes a ship as "just like one of my children" – a large enough family, you might think, since the Evergreen Group now owns 123 container vessels and has 15 more on order.

It would, of course, be quite understandable if Dr Chang felt that having achieved so much he could now relax, put his feet up and enjoy the benefits. But that attitude is simply not compatible with his philosophy either. As he puts it, towards the end of the book: "The more successful a person becomes, the more he should remember his origin; the more he must be thankful to, and repay, society for all that he has benefited from the community". For Dr Chang, this view – which is enhanced, as he explains in some fascinating passages, by religious belief centred on the concept of the Tao – has led him to support numerous training, educational, cultural and other worthwhile charitable projects.

There is, therefore, much to enlighten and encourage us in these enjoyable memoirs, whatever the reader's background. Oddly enough, I too can find here echoes of the values which I learned from my own upbringing in an English provincial town. In terms of moral, rather than physical, geography Grantham and Keelung are clearly closer than I thought.

Prologue

Friends have often asked me to consider publishing a memoir that would incorporate the fruits of my work and the insights gained from the human landscape that I have traversed. On the one hand, they told me, it will serve as an inspiration for the young people to advance themselves and become useful citizens of society, and on the other, to record for posterity the plain facts of my life's struggles.

Soon after I had made up my mind to write the memoir, I started out collating materials pertaining to my formative years and academic pursuits, my career, as well as the founding of Evergreen, to ensure that the accounts of my story are expounded with candour and clarity. I am sure the answers to many wild rumours and speculations regarding Evergreen's meteoric rise from obscurity can be found in this book.

Throughout the 70 years of my life's journey thus far, starting from my childhood days to my first job and to the eventual creation of today's Evergreen Group, I did not seem to be able to extricate myself from the oceanic realms, the bosoms of my entrepreneurial dreams. The saying "living for the sea" aptly reflects my undiminished passion for the majestic ocean.

Many people are quick to link Evergreen's rapid rise from virtually nowhere to global prominence to myths and miracles. But I can tell you that luck played absolutely no part in our success. Rather, it was the huge amount of time and painstaking efforts my colleagues and I selflessly put in, over and above an unwavering determination, that underpinned our achievements, something perhaps outsiders may not fully fathom.

I still vividly remember how I was at the end of my tether in the face of all the setbacks and obstacles during those start-up years; it was as if I was constantly buffeted by the towering waves, battered but not crushed. Notwithstanding the carefully evaluated and thought-out plans, unexpected hiccups would throw me off guard, forcing me to scurry around, looking for the right solutions. Many a time I was completely exhausted, yet there was still no light at the end of the tunnel. My feelings on some of these occasions could be best described as "wishing to weep, but having no tears left". Thankfully, I discovered the inner strength to hang on and triumph.

EVA Air ran smack into a constant barrage of malicious rumours and innuendoes when it was first launched. The situation, which made a mockery of the notion of free and fair competition, led me to contemplate withdrawing from the airline business at one stage. In the midst of all these difficulties though, I took comfort in the belief that perhaps Heaven had a purpose for putting me through all those trials and tribulations.

Although Evergreen Group's activities now span the globe, I did not actually set out at the beginning to take the business to such grand heights. I was contented with just doing a good job, running the company to the best of my ability. But I guess it was with the help of the heavenly realm and society's kindness that I was able to turn adversities into opportunities, thus putting Evergreen on the path to greater success.

Each time I encountered a setback, a worrisome thought invariably surfaced in my mind: Was it because of my inadequate spiritual attainment in my previous life that caused things to go awry no matter how hard I tried, or was it something else? But as I grow older and as our business expands through the years, I am beginning to view adversity in a different light. I have the feeling that Heaven is using life's predicaments to test my resolve and propel me forward.

I believe that human nature is innately kind. Therefore, while we are still around on this earth, we must express our inner goodness to the fullest extent. This principle applies as much to business as it does to life in general. Entrepreneurs, for example, must endeavour to provide a secure job and livelihood for their employees; they should not forget their humble roots, but must repay society by serving the wider interest of the community. These are virtuous and meritorious deeds.

In the book, I have detailed the insights gained and lessons learnt from the thrills and spills of my formative years, as well as those stemming from my working life. My compelling hope is that it will inspire and encourage the young people not to face adversity with trepidation, but to accept life's challenges with courage, select the right course to advance themselves, and be masters of their own destinies.

The vagaries of reality with all its disappointments, twists and turns lend credence to the saying that "one should never take things for granted for life is fraught with too many imponderables". It is my hope that those who find themselves in trouble do not despair, but have the tenacity to hang on and press ahead.

[1]

Born of the Sea

*My entire existence is seemingly intertwined with the seas.
The Japanese adage "living for the sea" is a fitting portrayal
of my life, the vicissitudes of which, much like the billowing
swells, are inseparable from the high and mighty seas.*

I have frequently been asked where exactly my hometown is: Penghu, Suao, or Keelung? Each time, I would instinctively reply that I am by all accounts a resident of Keelung. I reason that the place where one resides the longest should rightly be considered one's hometown by virtue of the deep feelings and fond memories it spontaneously evokes.

Though Keelung was not my birthplace, I had lived there since I was seven years old. Indeed, a good forty years of my life were spent in this fair-sized seaport growing up, working, getting married and starting my own family, making friends, and venturing into business. In fact, it was where the curtains of my life's many episodes were either raised or drawn. Naturally, therefore, I am particularly fond of Keelung.

Come to think of it, however, Penghu and Suao also have a special relationship with me. The fact that these three towns share a common characteristic of being located near the seas makes me wonder sometimes if I should after all call the alluring ocean my rightful domicile.

I am of the tenth-generation of mainland Chinese in Taiwan; my forebears had crossed the Taiwan Strait from the province of Fujian in China to settle down on the island of Penghu. My father used to work in the Penghu Postal Office. He joined Osaka Shosen Kaisha as a seaman when he turned twenty-five, following which he moved his entire family from Makung, the county capital of Penghu, to Keelung.

To my father, the resettlement at the time appeared to be a little more than a minor inconvenience in his personal quest for a decent livelihood. In retrospect, however, the event represented a major turning point that altered the fortunes of the entire Chang family, not least mine.

After a short and uneventful stint in Keelung, the company posted my father to work as a carpenter on board vessels plying between Suao and Hualien. The family was compelled to move again, this time to the tiny north-eastern town of Suao. There, my mother gave birth to me during the Japanese Occupation, on 6 October 1927, the second year of the Showa Period. The third child of the family, I had two Penghu-born elder brothers. Later, two younger brothers, followed by two younger sisters came along, making nine of us in the family.

In the early days, seafaring was considered one of the most perilous professions in Taiwan. But jobs were so scarce and life so harsh during the Japanese rule that my father had no choice but to go sailing despite the dangers, as there were several mouths to feed in the family. My mother was a capable woman in her own right as she went about managing the household expenses with thrift while daddy was away on board ship.

Because of the nature of my father's job, he understandably spent more time away than he did at home. But, according to my mother, he changed considerably soon after I was born; not only did he devote more of his time to the family from then on, he also doted on me.

My mother had a profound influence on my attitudes and conduct in life. She was a woman with a heart of gold and an excellent housekeeper who took care of the family practically single-handedly. Cleanliness was her second nature, as our ship-shape home would attest to. She cared for and educated her children with total dedication.

17

During the Japanese Occupation, the common folk suffered many privations and getting by each day was a daunting struggle. But my dear mother would still think of ways to scrape together some meagre savings so that she could buy her children some candies or stationery. Sometimes, she would give me two cents in pocket money which I would spend on stationery items, as well as treat myself to some salty crackers from the grocery store. All said, although we were not a well-to-do family in our childhood years, we have very fond memories of them.

But although our mother doted on us, she was nevertheless a disciplinarian, placing considerable emphasis on proper conduct and moral principles. She constantly reminded us of the importance of being honest to other people, and if we should tell lies, we would expect punishment from her. As a result of our strict upbringing, we all grew up to be confident, open-hearted and responsible individuals.

My mother also believed in karma and providential justice, a result of the influence of traditional religious beliefs on her life. She faithfully drilled into us, right from an early age, the virtues of being benevolent and charitable. Ultimately, my mother's instructions exerted a far-reaching effect on me and they formed the guiding principles of my life.

Childhood memories

I lived in Suao for a very brief period of time, spending happy, carefree boyhood days there. One unforgettable incident happened when I was six. That day, I went to play at the nearby "Rice Urn" brook together with my second eldest brother, our neighbour and buddy, Lin Tai-san, as well as some other boys. The bunch of us was trooping boisterously along the embankment, with me keeping up with the pace at the rear, when suddenly I slipped and fell awkwardly, knocking myself unconscious on some boulders.

Unaware that I had disappeared, the rest of them merrily marched on. When they finally realised that I was missing, they hurried back to look for me. Seeing that I had passed out, they quickly rushed me to a nearby hospital where I remained in a coma for three days and three nights before regaining consciousness. Strangely enough, after the accident, I began to develop a distinct loathing and revulsion for all kinds of seafood. The phenomenon had probably emanated from the shock I sustained during the fall. In fact, I later abstained from eating seafood altogether.

When I was seven, my father was posted to work on board ships berthed at Keelung Harbour. The whole family thus moved back to Keelung once again. As I was ready for school then, my parents enrolled me in "Shou Kung" primary school.

During the Japanese colonial era, schools attended by Taiwanese children were known as the "kung" schools, in which lessons for the first-graders were taught in both the Taiwanese and Japanese languages. Japanese students, on the other hand, attended the "hsiao" schools where their native language was the sole medium of instruction.

The Japanese attached great importance to both moral education and the spirit of excellence. Children were inculcated with the concept of right and wrong from a very young age. Although parents in those days were disciplinarians in their own right, teachers were by far the supreme authority. They were deeply revered by their students who understood the principles of respect and moral responsibility.

Parents welcomed this form of education, besides keeping a close eye on the conduct of their children. If, for example, their children were not back from school at the usual hour, they would go to great lengths to find out the reasons for the delay. The children could expect a stern dressing-down from their parents when they got home, especially if they had been naughty in school and had thus been detained and punished (made to stand or kneel) by their teachers. The children understood the meaning of shame and were inclined to feel an overwhelming sense of remorse.

The schools also encouraged strongly the spirit of learning in those days. Instead of ornate portraits of state leaders adorning the walls of classrooms, there were photographs of notable personalities who exemplified the essence of determination and moral correctness, thus

19

serving as good role models for the students. For instance, in one of the pictures portraying filial piety, the subject dutifully carried his infirm mother on his back to seek medical treatment daily.

I remember another photograph that depicted a Japanese student named Sontoku Ninomiya, who sought self-advancement with zeal in the face of hardships. Because of abject poverty in the family, he could not afford to go to school; instead he had to collect firewood from the mountains everyday. But this did not deter him from pursuing his studies in his own time. Despite being saddled with a heavy load of twigs on his aching back, he still found the energy and enthusiasm to read on his way home from the woods. This spirit of tireless self-improvement was indeed admirable and served as a useful reminder to those who were more fortunate to cherish their educational opportunities.

In stark contrast, some people in this modern age tend to be uncultured or even ill-bred despite the sophisticated education they have the privilege to benefit from. I consider such a system an absolute failure.

But although teachers in those days were very strict, they were equally conscious of the importance of physical education, as well as artistic pursuits and other extra-curricular activities. Among all the subjects my school had to offer, painting was my favourite. In fact, of my present collection of paintings done by local artists, a number of them are works of my elementary school art teacher, Mr Su Chiu-tung.

As a teenager, I was full of zing, with a particular zest for sports and games, from which I derived enormous pleasure and fun. I would invariably jump with joy whenever the teacher announced that she was taking us out on an excursion. Once, our class teacher brought us to the Yuan San Zoo and I was so excited on the eve of the visit that I stayed awake all night, waiting in anticipation for dawn to break.

Back in those days, because the transport system was less advanced, we had to board the train bound for Taipei from Keelung Station early in the morning. At Taipei, we had to catch another train headed for Tamsui, from which it was still a good long walk to the zoo. But the joy and satisfaction of being able to spend half a day at the zoo more than made up for all the hassles of commuting.

Things are vastly different in today's affluent society, as children are generally well provided for by their parents. Because it is so easy for the children to get almost anything they want, they tend not to cherish and value their possessions.

Most of my elementary school classmates lived in the same neighbourhood and we got along extremely well. We kept in touch with each other even after we had left school, meeting regularly at our "old boy" reunions.

First taste of working life

After graduating from the "kung" elementary school, I wanted to further my studies at the Taipei Commercial School. It was one of the most prestigious institutions at the time and admission criteria were much more stringent for Taiwanese than they were for our Japanese counterparts.

Many pupils from our school sat for the entrance examination, but none of us made the grade. As a result, I had no choice but to return to my alma mater to pursue an advanced course while I prepared to re-take the test the following year.

As our family was practically living from hand to mouth, and the situation was getting worse by the day, my second eldest brother urged me to abandon my studies and look for a job instead to supplement the family income. In any case, he explained, I still had to save enough money to support myself should I gain admission into the Taipei Commercial School later on.

My brother was at the time working in the Passenger Section of Osaka Shosen Kaisha's Keelung branch office. He told me there was a vacant clerical position at the representative office of the Minami Nippon Steamship Company in Keelung and that I should grab this opportunity. If I was intent on pursuing my studies, I could always attend night classes after work, he said.

I agreed after some pondering. But in the meantime I also sat for

21

the entrance examination, which I passed, thus allowing me to secure a place in the School of Commercial Practice, a supplementary school of the Taipei Advanced Commercial School. I attended classes in the evenings while I worked at the Minami Nippon Steamship Company during the day.

In order that I would not be late for my evening classes, my employer allowed me to knock off earlier from work so that I could catch the 4.30 p.m. train to Taipei. As soon as the class ended, I would rush to board the night's last train bound for Keelung. The train was the only mode of public transport available between Taipei and Keelung in those days. I recalled how restless I would get if the lecturer were to overstretch his time, lest I should miss the last train back to Keelung. Thus, at the first chime of the school bell, I would grab my bag and make a dash for the train station.

Japan attacked Pearl Harbour on 8 December 1941, which prompted America to immediately declare war on the aggressor, thus setting off World War II on a full-scale. Taiwan fell into a state of tension and uncertainty, which exacerbated what was already a difficult livelihood for the people.

Although constantly shuttling between work and classes was extremely taxing, I nevertheless, felt a deep sense of satisfaction that I was able to pursue my education even amid all the wartime chaos.

Apart from paying for my school fees, the wages that I earned at the Japanese company also helped defray the family's expenses. As food was scarce during the war, it was rationed on the basis of an absurd "class system". Depending on the "class" they were in, families were entitled to varying quantities of the basic staples. Japanese households, which were designated "A" class, were naturally the most privileged lot and received the biggest rations. Japanese-speaking Taiwanese families, whose members had adopted Japanese names and a Japanese way of life, fell into the "B" category and were given the second biggest amount of food. The ordinary Taiwanese families, who belonged to the lowly "C" class, received the smallest portions.

Out of sheer expediency, it was the aspiration of many poor

Taiwanese households to get themselves into "B" class, and we were no exception. Which was why we took on Nagashima as our family name, and I subsequently came to be known as Hatsu.

A memorable maiden voyage

Minami Nippon Steamship Company promoted me to a staff employee at the end of 1943 and sent me to work in the head office's Ship Department in Taipei.

Mr Yamamoto Tomao, head of the department, was very fond of me and often treated me to lunch at a restaurant called Kikusuiken (predecessor of the present-day Chushuiche Foods Manufacturing Company Ltd) in the city. As most of the Japanese male employees in the company had been conscripted into the army, there were only three of us, including myself as the only Taiwanese, in the entire office at the time.

Japanese shipping companies had long had a tradition of requiring male employees who had worked in the carriers for a period of time to serve a short stint on board a vessel. The aim was to familiarise them with the practical aspects of shipping, as well as to sharpen their professionalism, besides broadening their personal horizons. I was not exempted either, as I soon received a summons from the company to serve my apprenticeship at sea.

When my mother heard that I was going sailing in the midst of a raging war, she naturally became very concerned about my safety. Her anxiety was not exactly allayed by the fact that all the men in our family were engaged in shipping one way or the other: my father and eldest brother were seafarers, while my second eldest brother was serving ashore in a shipping company. But she was also aware that I could not defy the company's order, as I would otherwise be taken to task by the Japanese military police.

"Going to sea is far better than joining the army, mother," I said, trying my best to alleviate her fears. "I'll take care of myself, so please don't worry."

I knew my words offered little if any comfort at all, given the perils of wartime navigation. Strangely enough, I was not the least bit frightened myself; on the contrary, I somehow felt that the training was a good and glorious thing to do.

Soon afterwards, around early 1944, I received notice requiring me to work on a passenger-cum-cargo liner called *Kishu Maru* as a general clerk. Two days after reporting for duty, I boarded the ship for my first voyage out on the high seas.

It was not unusual for merchant ships to be requisitioned by the navy during wartime, and *Kishu Maru* was not exempted. It was inducted to ply between Taiwan and Hainan Island, transporting passengers and cargo, and replenishing supplies.

The South China Sea had at the time been designated a dangerous war zone in which US submarines were often sighted. To avoid being torpedoed, ships literally had to zigzag their way through these perilous waters. As a result, a voyage that normally required 10 days would often take up to one month to complete. Sailors were practically courting death under these trying circumstances; indeed, morbidly speaking, we never knew when our end would come.

Aware that the ship might be sunk any minute, the crew constantly braced themselves for any eventuality by donning thick warm clothing and life vests, no matter the season, so that in case the ship should sink, they could escape a freezing death.

The vessel on which my second eldest brother was working was sunk during her passage through the Taiwan Strait, and he was left to drift in the icy waters for three days and three nights. When rescue finally came, he was almost unconscious and his body had turned blue due to the extreme cold. It was only three to four days later in the hospital that he came to. Although my brother's life was spared, the incident took a heavy toll on his health.

The skipper of *Kishu Maru* was the elderly Hamada Daikichi who treated me like a son. He liked to call me "musuko" ("son" in Japanese). Then there was the first mate, Mitsuyama Toraichi, who was a brother-like figure to me. Last but not least was the purser, Tobu, from whom I learnt a great deal.

Looking back at my first taste of life at sea, seasickness was my biggest problem and a constant source of discomfort. I remember vividly my first journey on board *Kishu Maru*, which was to take us from Keelung to Kaohsiung, where we were to berth the next day, before setting off for Hainan Island.

As soon as I got on board, Mr Tobu asked me to help him fill up 18 sets of the cargo manifests and port entry forms, and to have them ready at the end of the day for inspection by the officials when we arrived at Kaohsiung.

Unfortunately, *Kishu Maru* bumped into gale-force winds shortly after leaving Keelung. The vessel rolled and pitched violently and I braced myself for a tough journey ahead. Putting pen to paper under these circumstances was an almost impossible task, as I felt extremely dizzy and nauseous. But the job could not wait, and in desperation, I tied a towel tightly around my forehead as I struggled to finish the chore as quickly as I possibly could.

As copier machines were non-existent in those days, I had to resort to using carbon paper to help me in my task. But because the forms were so thick, I could only reproduce a maximum of four sets at any one-time, which meant I had to repeat the tedious process five times in all to get the job done. But no matter how hard I tried, the seasickness still got the better of me. Because I failed to get up and move away fast enough on a number of occasions, I ended up puking all over the documents, thus compelling me to redo the forms. Even though I toiled through the night, deprived of sleep and rest, I was far from completing the 18 sets when we arrived at Kaohsiung at 10 a.m. the next day.

When Tobu came to inquire about the documents, I explained to him apologetically the difficulties that I had had, half expecting a scolding from him. To my bewilderment, he told me quite nonchalantly that it did not really matter. With that, he proceeded to pull out from among the pile of papers on my desk four sets of the forms, one each for the military police at the port, the coast guard, the customs, and the immigration officials. He then asked me to destroy the rest.

At that moment, a feeling of resentment and of having been wronged instantly welled up within me. Why make me fill up 18 sets when actually four would have sufficed? I really could not fathom why he should make life so difficult for me. It was only later when our vessel had reached Hainan Island that he summoned me to his room and told me the reason for his being deliberately tough on me.

"It's the only way to make you take your mind off the seasickness. You'll never get accustomed to life at sea if you have to lie down every time you feel dizzy," he explained in all earnestness.

The purser's words were a great encouragement and I was grateful for his kind intention to train me up properly in good seamanship instead of trying to make a lesser mortal of me just because I was new on the job. As time passed, my admiration and respect for him grew deeper.

Incidentally, it was common practice in those days for seasoned crew to make a fool of new recruits. One of the silly things they did, for example, was to cajole the newcomers to drink a concoction of muddy water from the ship's anchor. The "prescription", they claimed, would permanently rid sailors of their seasickness.

On another occasion, Mr Tobu told me to have an apprentice clean up a cabin that he thought was rather filthy. My job, he said, was to ensure that it was properly done. When Tobu San inquired about the matter later, I told him that it was spick and span. Then he led me to the room and taught me a thing or two about thoroughness. He proceeded to peer at some nooks and crannies, as well as the window-sills, places people usually ignore, before running his index finger along the still dusty surfaces. He admonished me for not being observant enough. In life, Mr Tobu said, we should always view things with a critical eye instead of taking them superficially at face value.

Understandably, Mr Tobu placed a great deal of emphasis on the training and instruction of his crew. He was also very strict with them. If any of the stewards should repeatedly fall short of his expectations, those originally assigned to serve in the first-class passenger-cabins would see themselves relegated to work in the third-class sections in no time.

On this my maiden voyage, I learnt a great many things from Mr Tobu, not least of which was his conscientious and no-nonsense attitude towards work, which in turn served as a good example for me to emulate. This exposure to life at sea certainly afforded me a wealth of new experiences and inspirations; it also enabled me to understand more deeply the company's goal, and the importance of seafaring training.

When I later established Evergreen Marine Corporation, I adopted a similar personnel training policy, which allowed our commercial staff to spend some time aboard a vessel. This was to enable them to have a better appreciation of the major aspects of the ship's operations, as well as to let them have a general idea of the port facilities and logistics support available in various countries around the world. That our business people should be made aware of the difficulties and constraints our operations side had to face all the time would, I believe, help promote unity and harmony within the entire company in the long run. Moreover, their attachment aboard the ship would enable them to have a closer feel of the market, besides broadening their knowledge and horizons, so as to offer the highest standard of services to the customers.

The death of my father

The situation on the Japanese warfront was looking increasingly grim. As most of the Japanese men in its office had been drafted to fight in the war, Minami Nippon Steamship Company suddenly found itself facing a severe manpower shortage. As a result, I was hurriedly transferred back to the Ship Division in the Taipei head office, although I had barely worked for one year at sea. Under normal circumstances, employees had to serve a two to three year stint aboard a vessel before they were eligible for posting back to shore.

Mr Yamamoto was very pleased to have me back in the office. He said he was happy to note that I had done well in my short stint at sea. He asked me to take charge of the crew's rosters and told me to report to him directly. To be assigned such a heavy responsibility at this young age gave me an enormous sense of pride and achievement. Hence, it was with added zeal that I put myself to the new task.

By then the war had already spread to most parts of Taiwan and many families were forced to evacuate helter-skelter, often compelling members of the same households to become separated. I packed my mother and younger siblings off to Kung Liao Village in Ilan, while I moved to Shijr together with my elder brother and his wife in view of my work commitments in Taipei.

Not long after our evacuation came the devastating news of my father's death. Japanese troops had by then overrun the American dependency of Leyte Island in the Philippines. *Shonan Maru*, the supply vessel on which my father was working at the time, was attacked and sunk by the Allied Forces in the vicinity of the island.

An eyewitness account told of how my father had valiantly swum ashore as the ship went down. But, unfortunately, guerrillas on Leyte Island mistook him for an enemy and shot him. The year was 1944 and I was only 18 years old.

My father left behind a meagre pension, while my elder brothers were both married and had family commitments of their own. In the event, the responsibility of looking after my mother and younger siblings was suddenly thrust onto my shoulders.

As war raged on, the Japanese government formed what it called Sempaku Unekai, an organisation that was vested with the wide-ranging power of requisitioning merchant vessels for the purpose of war. Jointly controlled by the occupation government and its military, Sempaku Unekai also required employees of all shipping companies to compulsorily register with and work under them. Since I was an employee in a shipping firm, I was compelled to join this organisation too.

On 15 August 1945, not long after I had started work in Sempaku Unekai, Japan declared its unconditional surrender to the Allies, thus bringing World War II to an abrupt end. In the wake of Taiwan's retrocession to Chinese sovereignty, many garrisons of mainland troops, as well as large numbers of government officials be-gan making their way to Taiwan to take back the territory from the Japanese.

The Japanese Occupation of Taiwan had by then lasted some 50 years, and I had grown up under its rule. As a result, I never had a chance to receive Chinese education, let alone learn how to speak the Beijing dialect (Mandarin). Thus, after Taiwan's liberation, I found myself temporarily unemployed as I could not find a suitable job because of my language problem.

I thought of moving my mother and younger siblings to our old abode in Keelung at the time. But when we got back, we discovered that the house had been completely gutted during the war. In desperation, we rented a place on Nan Rong Road in Keelung and relied on my late father's paltry pension to get by. Those were particularly trying times for the family.

My mentors and friends

My friendships with Lin Tai-san and Lin Tien-fu have had an enduring and positive impact on my life. Lin Tai-san and my elder brother were classmates in primary school. In fact, our families had had very close ties with each other since my childhood days. When Lin was studying in the Keelung School of Fisheries, he and his father often came by to visit us, and our bond grew even stronger.

Following his graduation from the Fisheries School, Lin Tai-san found work on a naval patrol boat, *Kainan Maru*, which belonged to the Office of the Governor of Taiwan. But monotony soon set in and he was yearning for a job in merchant shipping. My father was then working on *Kishu Maru* and he got along quite well with the shipmaster, Hashimoto Fumio. He put in a strong recommendation for Lin who soon found himself reporting for work as a third mate on board the vessel. Lin has remained in merchant shipping ever since.

During the war, every time Lin Tai-san and the ship's first mate, Mitsuyama Toraichi, were on standby duty, they would stay over at our house. We were like brothers to each other. Lin Tien-fu and Lin

Tai-san were classmates as well as pals at Keelung School of Fisheries. The school ran a training ship called *Nanho Maru* on which both gentlemen were serving their apprenticeships. I often dropped in to see Tai-sun on board the vessel in the evenings, and through him I got to know Tien-fu who would become one of my lifelong mentors and friends.

Both Lins were from among the first batch of students at the Fisheries School. Tien-fu excelled academically and although he was a native Taiwanese, he got himself elected as a class monitor year after year. After his graduation, Tien-fu joined NYK as a third mate, serving on board the passenger-cum-cargo liner, *Fuji Maru*, which plied between Taiwan and Japan. He had worked as an instructor in the Seaman Training Centre of the Japan Maritime Affairs Association during the war and as a technician with the Japan Insurance Society.

Soon after Taiwan's retrocession, a relative of Lin Tien-fu, Chang Ming, got married to the daughter of a high-ranking government official, Ju Cheng. Tien-fu thus came to be a relative of Ju Cheng in the process. This kinship coupled with his remarkable track record in shipping soon lifted Tien-fu's fame to a new height, enabling him to befriend many government officials in high places.

In 1946, the second year of Taiwan's liberation, the government of the day began taking over the control of Japanese vessels operating in Taiwan, placing the majority of them under the management of two agencies – the China Merchant Steam Navigation Bureau and the Taiwan Navigation Company.

In those days, Ren Xian-Qun was the official the mainland government had despatched to oversee this particular operation in Taiwan, for which he was appointed president of the Taiwan Navigation Company. Ren had previously had dealings with the Taiwanese, whom he trusted and with whom he was also extremely friendly.

Before that, Ren and Lin Tien-fu had been friends for many years and he also held Lin in high regard. This friendship was deep enough for Ren to make Lin the captain of a 500-tonne cargo ship, *Fung Shan*, and to allow him a free rein to recruit his entire crew, an extremely rare privilege at the time.

It was through Lin Tien-fu's well-placed connections that Taiwan nationals had a chance to work as seafarers, a profession that was otherwise an exclusive preserve of mainland Chinese from Shanghai and Ningbo.

Following Lin Tien-fu's appointment as captain of *Fung Shan*, he promptly invited Lin Tai-san to join him as the ship's first mate. As I was still without a job then, I was keen to work on the vessel too. When Lin Tai-san inquired with Tien-fu on my behalf about the possibility of my joining *Fung Shan*, the latter agreed without any hesitation.

Much to my disappointment, however, although I was promised a clerical job, I found out when I got on board that I was actually going to be a hatch-keeper. The confusion arose, as I discovered later, apparently because job titles meant different things to different people. In my case, for example, what was supposed to be a "clerk" by Japanese definition for some reasons turned out to be a "hatch-keeper" in Chinese.

For someone like me who had studied arts and literature in school and was only used to doing sedentary work of an administrative nature, a physically demanding hatch-keeper's job was definitely out of the question. Worse, most of my shipmates were old acquaintances from my previous company, and they certainly could not resist having a dig at me, seeing that I had been reduced overnight from an officer hitherto responsible for the company's crew roster to a lowly hatch-keeper.

Although I very much resented the situation I found myself in, I knew I had to swallow my pride, as after all, the livelihood of an entire family depended on me. Lin Tai-san was rather taken aback by the modest assignment I was given, but he told me to stay on and to be patient nevertheless. He was indeed a constant source of much needed moral support.

Rather than wallow in self-pity, I told myself that probably the most senior position I could possibly climb to was that of a purser even if I was to start out as a clerk. So why not accept the job of a hatch-keeper for the time being and spend whatever spare time I had at sea to brush up on my studies? If I worked hard, I could one day become a skilled seaman too. In any case, I already had two ready tutors, Lin Tien-fu and Lin Tai-san, to provide guidance.

To those seamen who belittled me, I vowed to work hard so that the day would come when I would be captain of a vessel, while they would probably still be where they always were, as ordinary sailors.

It is perhaps in our human nature that we dig our heels deeper in whenever we are up against life's challenges. Likewise, in the situation that I found myself in, I was determined to put in extra effort to prepare myself for the all-important skilled seamen's certification test. My positive outlook at the time was to have a profound bearing on my career in the years to come.

It never occurred to me when I established Evergreen Marine Corporation some years later that these same people, who had made fun of me previously when I was a hatch-keeper, would flock to our company in search of employment as mere sailors. The reason I mentioned this was not because I was vindictive or I was intent on having the last laugh, but rather I wanted to highlight the point that we can never foretell how life's ups and downs will affect one's destiny.

I also believe, as long as we have the means, we should always try to help those who are less fortunate. Thus, in the same manner that my father recommended Lin Tai-san to work as a third mate on board the vessel *Kishu Maru*, the latter in turn helped me to secure a job with Lin Tien-fu's *Fung Shan*, so that I could earn a living to support my family. While at sea with the two gentlemen, not only did they constantly encourage me to upgrade my skills and knowledge, they also taught me many practical aspects of maritime navigation. In fact, they were largely instrumental in helping me switch over from a manual job to that of a skilled seaman successfully.

Studying on board ship

So anxious was I to pass the seamen's examinations that I seized whatever spare moments I had to pore over my books whilst working as a hatch-keeper. Very often I would study well into the night before retiring to bed, sometimes to the extent that I would mumble away in my sleep.

One night, overexerted, I fell fast asleep at my desk. I dreamt of my mother asking me whether I was actually preparing for my Imperial Examinations since I was pushing myself so hard. What a strange coincidence it was, as I had not told her or anybody else about my plans. I was simply too preoccupied with getting the certification test over and done with first.

On hindsight, my single-minded determination truly paid off as I went on to pass my exams without any difficulty, although my tasks were made much easier by the fact that any theoretical issues that I could not understand could easily be put to the test on board the vessel. The shipping fraternity in those days generally barred females and non-navigational crew from stepping into a vessel's wheelhouse, as it was considered a sacred place. I was, however, an exception to the rule as Captain Lin Tien-fu gave me free access to the bridge so that Lin Tai-san could teach me the practical aspects of maritime navigation.

Moreover, whenever I had doubts on any aspect of the ship's instrumentation or operations, I could always turn to the more experienced deck officers for guidance. There were even occasions when we would carry out practical exercises together. In this manner, not only was I able to master more effortlessly the theoretical issues found in the books, thus making learning all the more interesting, I was also able to establish new insights based on my own observations.

Because navigational gadgets were relatively backwards in those days, pinpointing the position of a ship in the high seas called for the use of a sextant. It measured the angles from the horizon up to the sun or moon or stars manually, based on which the reading was calculated within a matter of minutes. I found this method to be an excellent way to test an individual's powers of concentration.

This is one reason why Evergreen subjects job seekers to a numerical dexterity test to gauge their ability to concentrate on certain specific tasks, which would in turn determine their suitability for the positions they seek.

A dream fulfilled

My labour and sacrifices aboard *Fung Shan* were not in vain for I was finally rewarded with a third mate's licence. The two Lin's were delighted for me.

In retrospect, although what I had studied in school was not exactly useful to me in my job as a hatch-keeper, my resolve and commitment helped see me through the difficult months, enabling me to qualify as a skilled seaman. I also developed a voracious appetite for books at the same time, from which I derived tremendous joy and satisfaction.

But I did not rest on my laurels. Instead I worked even harder in the years that followed, which also saw my seafaring career span several shipping companies, including Taiwan Transport Company, Shanghai Shipping Company, Da Chen Shipping, and Taiwan Marine Company. I also went on to acquire further qualifications, thus enabling me to rise from the ranks of a second mate to that of a captain.

The shipping industry in Taiwan's post-liberation days was in a state of limbo, largely because the bulk of the merchant fleet had already been destroyed during the war. Shipping companies would consider themselves lucky if they happened to own vessels that were in the 200- to 300-tonne capacity range, and whoever had the good fortune to operate, say, a 500-tonne ship would surely be the envy of everyone else in the industry.

Looking back, my experience as a first mate on the banana-carrier run by Taiwan Marine Company was a happy and unforgettable one. On the one hand, it gave me a great sense of achievement to be a high-ranking officer on a 2,000-tonne giant of a ship by any standards, apart from the fact that the position also afforded our family a better standard of living. On the other hand, my love for reading, especially in my spare time on board the vessel, also added more zest and pleasure to my personal life.

As I recalled, whenever our vessel was berthed at a Japanese port, I would spend the bulk of my free time browsing through the local bookstores, scouring for professional maritime books. Should I come across any new publications on either technological advances of ships or those pertaining to shipping management, I would invariably snap them all up, as if I had stumbled upon a treasure-trove.

Containerisation was still very much unheard of in commercial shipping in those days, although the American military did use this mode of conveyance to replenish supplies to their troops. Nevertheless, I had had the opportunity to read up on a great deal of Japanese-language publications dealing with this subject, and had become quite knowledgeable about the various characteristics and applications of this mode of shipping.

I recalled one occasion on which Lin Tien-fu was returning to Taiwan from Japan on board the same vessel I was working, and I mentioned to him in passing that, in my view, the containerised mode of transportation would take the shipping world by storm someday.

Fortuitous or not, my prediction came true a decade or so later as containerisation gathered feverish pace and intensity across the globe. What I had not anticipated though was that Evergreen would find itself at the forefront of this revolution, thus paving the way for it to become the world's foremost container carrier within a relatively short period of time.

Lin Tien-fu still occasionally reminds me about this interesting incident on board the vessel. It had not occurred to us then that my reading of the situation would turn out to be so prophetically accurate.

Tying the nuptial knot

Having now settled nicely into my job, and as our family's financial situation gradually improved, my mother began to worry about one of the most important issues in life – my marriage. Although I had had two girlfriends previously, neither relationship worked out due to personal as well as family reasons.

I got to know my future wife through the introduction of a certain Captain Yang when I was 27 years old. My mother dutifully accompanied me to have a good look at her prospective daughter-in-law, as after all marriage is something that is not to be taken lightly. I very much respected the opinion of my mother, which was why she was the first person I turned to for counsel. Much as I had expected, my mother gave me her blessings to marry the girl, thus paving the way for us to tie the nuptial knot a short time later.

After the wedding, my wife and I continued to live in Keelung together with my mother and my younger siblings. I was by then a third mate and had some savings that I withdrew to pay for the construction of a new house, also in Keelung, for the whole family to live in.

I was practically going up and down the East China Sea continually in those days, on a banana-carrier that plied between Taiwan and Japan. As the ship's crew was entitled to very little shore leave, I recalled I had to report for duty exactly 15 days after our marriage, which took place at the beginning of the year. By year's end, I was already the proud father of a bouncy baby girl.

In retrospect, the only regret I have of my seafaring career was the very little time I had with my family, especially after my children were born. As I had to be away from home most days, the amount of time I spent with them during their crucial formative years was shame-fully limited. In those days, the crew of banana-carriers were only allowed to stay overnight at home before they had to report for duty again the very next day, which thus made it impossible for them to help look after their families. In the event, I had to leave the responsibility of bringing up our children completely in the hands of my wife.

But although I could not be with my family most of the time, they were never far off from my mind. I was also fortunate to have a capable wife who cared for my mother and the children in my absence, so that I could concentrate on my work without having to worry about things at home.

Becoming a small-time ship owner

I was able to acquire a great deal of practical experience and knowledge in my 15-year career as a sailor through a combination of hard work and a voracious appetite for professional maritime publications. One of my greatest desires at that time was to run my own business with just perhaps one small vessel for a start.

Indeed, it had long been my dream to own a smallish 400- to 500-tonne ship into which I could put all my energy, knowledge and experience to the test and to turn it into a big success one day.

But considering my personal circumstances at the time, I dared not put my head in the clouds or be overly ambitious. Nevertheless, the hope of becoming a ship owner some day never really deserted me, as I found greater enthusiasm in burying myself in piles upon piles of maritime books and publications.

You can say that shipping is in my blood, an unquenchable passion, the flame of which has not subsided with passing years. As a matter of fact, I have not stopped the pursuit of new frontiers. I also derive enormous pleasure from talking shop with my good friends about anything and everything pertaining to the shipping industry.

In the days I was a first mate on *Tai Yun*, a vessel belonging to Taiwan Marine Company, my colleague, Liao Wen-liang, then the company's vice-president and head of business development, and I often found time to meet whenever I was in Keelung. We would talk about shipping-related matters, including the current and future trends of the industry.

In the spring of 1961, following Liao's decision to leave Taiwan Marine, I invited him to join me in setting up a new shipping company called New Taiwan Marine Company. He in turn brought along one of his close friends, Chu Shiang-zong, as a third partner.

The new set-up was capitalised at NT$1.8 million, which meant each one of us had to come up with NT$600,000 in equity. But the problem was I only had a paltry NT$100,000 in my savings at the time. I thus had no choice but to turn to the bank for a loan. The manager at the Jen-Ai branch of Chang Hwa Bank in Keelung, Wu

Jia-zhen, and his assistant, Huang Ming-fa, were most helpful on account of our friendship, and with Chu Shiang-zong acting as my personal guarantor, the bank agreed to lend NT$500,000 to me.

New Taiwan Marine officially opened for business in June 1961. Chu was made the chairman of the company, while Liao and I were appointed its president and vice-president, respectively.

In terms of responsibilities, Chu was to oversee the financial affairs of the company, whilst Liao would take care of business development and planning, leaving me in charge of the shipping operations. Our office was located on the second floor of Liao Wen-liang's residence in Keelung in the early days.

But because Taiwan Marine had not been able to find a suitable replacement for me in the meantime, it was only three months later in end-September that I was able to leave the company to join New Taiwan Marine officially.

From the outset, the three of us set ourselves a common goal, which was to give our all to make the venture a resounding success. We set out to acquire our first vessel soon after the company was established. It was a 1,600-tonne second-hand ship, which a certain Mr Yashiki of Japan had brokered. Renamed *Shin Tai*, the vessel was deployed on the regional routes.

I remembered in July 1962, while I was in Japan to inspect the ship and to finalise the purchase formalities, a shot of adrenaline coursed through my veins as soon as I caught a glimpse of the vessel. After all, I had always wanted to run a 400- to 500-tonne ship some day, but that I would very soon become the proprietor of a vessel many times bigger, albeit with two other people, now seemed like a dream. That night, alone in the hotel room, I could not stop worrying about the future of the company. Considering the amount of effort and energy I had put into this venture, as well as the loan I had taken from the bank, which I was not so sure when it could be fully repaid, I was naturally concerned.

Fortunately, our operations went right on track from the word go. Hence, in 1963, we added a 4,220-tonne used vessel, which we renamed *Min Tai*, followed by a 4,410-tonne second-hand ship, *Fu Tai*, a year later. These two freighters were primarily deployed on the Taiwan/Japan sector, which, because of the boom in the exports of banana from Taiwan at the time, was regarded as the "Golden Route". At the same time that we acquired *Fu Tai*, we also bought the 8,640-tonne used ship, *Rong Tai*, which we deployed to carry timber.

New Taiwan Marine did reasonably well over the years, as a result of which we were able to build up our finances. However, I thought it important that we look beyond the present to the distant future in order to ensure the survival and progress of the company in the long run. In my view, it was absolutely essential that we continue to break new ground and to plan ahead, for there was a real chance that we would be eliminated from the marketplace if we failed to go forth with the times.

A case for new ships

It was a common practice in those days for most Taiwanese shipping companies to scour Europe and elsewhere for second-hand reefer vessels that they could use in ferrying bananas. Although these ships were relatively cheap, they were often old and in a state of disrepair, with their refrigeration facilities constantly breaking down. As a result, they often had to undergo extensive repairs, which were not only costly in the longer run, but which also caused enormous inconvenience to the customers. New ships, on the other hand, were reliable and operationally more efficient, and with proper care and maintenance, their useful life spans could be extended by many more years. Besides the reefers, shipping companies in Taiwan also went for 10,000-tonne "Liberty"-type wartime supply vessels, which were acquired largely for transporting timber.

Since these dames were not custom-built to carry lumber, their hatch openings and cargo holds did not, therefore, suit the very purpose for which they were acquired. Consequently, the speed of loading and discharging, as well as the storage capacity of these vessels were often unsatisfactory, thus resulting in highly uneconomical operations.

Newly-built and dedicated timber carriers, on the other hand, were highly efficient and cost-effective. They had larger hatch openings and wider holds, the floor of which was protected by steel plates to minimise damage to the ships. Equipped with powerful derricks on board, the loading and discharging operations of these vessels were very much faster compared to their 10,000-tonne derelict counterparts. Besides, they were also safer to operate, which best met the needs of both the customers and owners alike.

New Taiwan Marine was heavily reliant on the banana and timber trade in those days. With the financial situation of the company under control, I suggested to my partners that we could perhaps consider acquiring new ships to bolster our operations and ensure long-term growth.

The shipping fraternity soon got wind of our plans and reacted rather unkindly. People scoffed at me and criticised me behind my back as being self-opinionated. Their views were that no shipping companies in their right mind would want to custom-build a vessel for the specific purpose of transporting lumber. They also doubted our ability to finance such an undertaking. It was as though everyone was waiting to see me make a fool of myself.

The widely-held but mistaken perception of the shipping industry at the time was that there were cost savings to be reaped by using older vessels, and that there was no necessity at all to spend huge amounts of money on building new ships. The truth was, although new vessels entailed a heavier capital outlay up front, substantial savings, both in terms of time and money, could be found in such areas as repair and maintenance, fuel and operational efficiencies, crew requirements, as well as safety considerations. In the long run, they also offered greater economic returns compared to their dilapidated counterparts. Although I was a cost-conscious person myself, I nonetheless felt that we should not just look at the face value of everything, but what was also important was its intrinsic worth and quality.

Take, for example, the vessel's equipment and instruments. It definitely makes sense to pay slightly more for a quality and functional product rather than going for a cheaper or an outwardly appealing alternative. The rationale is simple: Without the support of hardware, even the most skilful and talented crew will be hard put to develop their potential to the fullest. More than anything else, therefore, my proposal to invest in purpose-built new vessels was borne out of long-term necessity.

Considering my many years of experience in the maritime industry, together with the knowledge I had gleaned from my incessant learning and observations, I believed my idea, though it might seem radical at the time, was not without any foundation.

So what if other people poured scorn on me, as long as I had absolute faith in myself? Besides, my partners had no problems at all in endorsing my views, which was most important as far as I was concerned.

Shortly afterwards, we commissioned Tsuneishi Shipyard in Japan to construct a 5,500-tonne banana carrier as well as a 6,200-tonne timber freighter. With that, I thus became the first person in Taiwan to champion the use of custom-designed, dedicated freighters, which some people thought was nothing more than just a fanciful concept.

Getting to know Marubeni

New vessels entail a heavy investment commitment in the best of times. For New Taiwan Marine, difficulties in getting banks to finance purchases only exacerbated the problems. Fortunately, Chu Shiang-zong, our chairman, who owned a bicycle factory, had quite extensive business dealings with Marubeni Corporation, one of the six largest trading houses in Japan. Through this connection, we sounded out Marubeni about the possibility of their financing our new acquisitions. Much to my relief, they agreed to extend a helping hand.

We soon found ourselves in Japan to discuss the matter further with Marubeni. Mr Isao Hashimoto was at Haneda Airport to meet us; he was a still relatively inexperienced person at the time as he had just joined Marubeni's Vessel Division. His superior was Mr

Kiyoshi Hosaka, who was a section head.

We settled down immediately to discuss the nitty-gritty details of the loan as soon as we arrived at Marubeni's office. Just when we thought we had covered all the ground, we discovered that we had an intractable problem in hand; Tsuneishi Shipyard was unable to provide Marubeni with any corporate guarantee.

Generally speaking, shipyards require from customers a certain amount of ready credit for the procurement of building materials before the commencement of any construction work. On their part, the builders are expected to furnish the bank or other lenders with some form of a corporate undertaking or collateral before the latter would disburse any money to the ship owner. In the case of Tsuneishi, however, it had pledged all its facilities with Itochu and other people. In the circumstance, although Marubeni genuinely wanted to help, its hands were tied.

Meanwhile, New Taiwan Marine had secured the relevant foreign exchange remittance approval from the government for the construction work to begin. Who could have imagined that such a situation would crop up at the eleventh hour. Luckily, we managed to convince Itochu into lending us a hand.

Our brief association with Marubeni thus came to an abrupt end at this point. But although our first deal did not work out as planned, it nevertheless sowed the seeds for my long-lasting collaboration with them in later years.

Flash fire delays launch

I enlisted the help of my good friend and schoolmate, Wu Pang-ji, to supervise the construction of the two vessels in Japan together with me. Wu was at the time working in Taiwan Shipbuilding Corporation and had ample experience in the area of vessel construction. He had told me earlier of his desire to join a private shipping company should a suitable opportunity arise. Hence his appointment as an engineer in New Taiwan Marine.

I also brought in my old acquaintance, Lonny Chiu, who used to be a harbour policeman at Keelung. He had earlier expressed his wish to join me if I had an opening, and since he was fairly conversant with the nature of seamen's duties, I asked him to take charge of crew management duties in New Taiwan Marine.

Major Japanese shipyards exacted a huge premium from their customers in those days, which made them beyond the reach of smaller shipping companies like New Taiwan Marine and others. By comparison, Tsuneishi was considered a medium-sized shipbuilder.

It was probably because of this that Tsuneishi's safety standard left very much to be desired. Over the one-year period that Wu Pang-ji and I were with them, we must have reminded their president umpteen times about the lack of proper safety measures in the shipyard. But nothing was done to improve the situation. In the circumstance, we could only exercise extra caution when we carried out our tasks on the premises.

As luck would have it, just five days before the banana-carrier was to be handed over to us, one of her cargo holds to the aft suddenly caught fire for no apparent reason. What stumped me was that although a pall of black smoke was seen billowing from the ship, no one had the initiative to deal with the emergency situation quickly. I was told they just stood idly by and watched.

True, under normal procedures, when a ship is on fire, its cabin or cargo-hold doors should not be opened immediately to prevent the flames from spreading. But in this case, from what I assessed of the situation when I rushed to the scene, the fire had already gone out. What was left was just heavy smoke coming out from inside the hold. Although I instructed the workers to prise open the doors immediately, nobody chose to listen, not before I had put my foot down anyway.

Sure enough, when the doors were forced open, what we saw was nothing more than thick dense smoke, which by then had already claimed the life of one person. As the reefer equipment contained sensitive and flammable parts, it was almost completely destroyed by the intense heat from the flash fire.

That Tsuneishi Shipyard should commit such a huge blunder at this critical juncture really enraged me. Mr Kamihara, the president of the company, who had also rushed to the site, admitted negligence on the part of his company, for which he apologised profusely. But what was the use of saying sorry now, when the damage had already been done? What infuriated me most was that no immediate action was taken to control the situation at the time of the incident.

Not only was the delivery of the vessel delayed, a life was also needlessly lost. Besides, our Taipei head-office had already sent out the invitation to all the guests in eager anticipation of the scheduled handing over of the vessel. What an embarrassment, and an inauspicious start it was. The much awaited reception had to be called off at the very last minute.

The vessel's entire refrigeration facility had to be replaced in the aftermath of the flash fire. Even though the shipyard was working round the clock with extra shifts added on, it was already more than 20 days behind the original delivery schedule when the banana-carrier was finally handed over to us.

As the vessel set sail for Taiwan, I started wondering if I would now become the butt of jokes, especially among all my erstwhile critics, given that I was the prime mover behind this ambitious project. What should have been a triumphant homecoming unfortunately turned out to be a decidedly muted and face-losing affair.

Fortunately, I was vindicated by the flourishing business that we experienced soon after the new vessel went into operation. In fact, New Taiwan Marine was doing so well with its latest acquisition that other shipping companies quickly followed in its steps in commissioning custom-built ships instead of going for used ones, which did not suit the purpose for which they were acquired.

Parting of ways

With the business and financial situation in New Taiwan Marine under control, I felt it was time to establish a proper organisational system to prepare the company for long-term growth. As most shippers had their main operations in Taipei at the time, I suggested that we relocate our office from Keelung to the capital city, where the majority of our own customers were also found.

To my surprise, my suggestion did not go down well with the staff, who claimed that the daily commuting to and from Taipei was too much of a hassle.

But I was living in Keelung too, and shuttling to and back from Taipei would have been just as much an inconvenience to me. But I felt very strongly that the overall interest of the company should precede individual considerations, which was why I persisted until I was finally able to convince the other shareholders that we would be better off if we relocated our office to Taipei.

It was then some ten years after Taiwan's liberation and the country was still in the grip of martial law, with shipping companies facing a really tough time. To make matters worse, the industry had to deal with a whole gamut of bureaucratic red tape. The industry came under the purview of some 10 regulatory agencies, which included the Transport Ministry, United Investigation Bureau, the Harbour Police, Central Intelligence Bureau, National Security Bureau, Police and Firearms Command Unit, Military Police, and the Port Authority. In this situation, it was not unusual for shipping companies to be constantly besieged by officials who abused their positions to secure jobs for their kith and kin, a case of emotional blackmail at its worst.

More often than not, people who found jobs through their connections seldom took their work seriously after they had joined us; some of them even had the audacity to knit woollens during office hours. Although it was a ludicrous state of affairs, we were also careful not to offend any of them. In my mind, I was wondering what would become of New Taiwan Marine if its entire workforce were to comprise loafers.

Which was exactly why I pushed so hard to have a proper personnel system instituted, under which we could adopt an open method of recruitment to ensure that only those qualified were selected to work for the company. But my colleagues thought otherwise; they felt we should continue to give face to these bureaucrats, lest they should deliberately find fault with us in the course of our normal operations.

Over time, because of differences of opinions, a chasm gradually emerged between the other shareholders and me.

In the meantime, our regional routes were doing remarkably well, and I thought it was an opportune juncture to explore the possibility of taking our business international. But again my idea was promptly shot down by the other shareholders who argued that we did not have suitably qualified seafarers with the requisite experience to man the intended operations. Despite my repeated assurance that we would have no problem at all in finding the right people to do the job, especially if a transparent recruitment method was used and through which we could minimise the element of favouritism, they simply would not listen.

This episode, over and above other disagreements in the past, caused the abyss between us to deepen further. As the time bomb continued to tick, I felt it was perhaps best that we go our separate ways. When Chu Shiang-zong learnt of my desire to leave, he tried his best to get me to stay on. He even threatened to quit too if I did not change my mind. That would not be a good idea, I told him, as it would result in New Taiwan Marine breaking up eventually. With my mind firmly made up, the shareholders convened a meeting to approve my resignation, during which Lonny Chiu and Wu Pang-ji elected to leave together with me.

In my four years with New Taiwan Marine, I had learnt several invaluable lessons. For one, an enterprise cannot do without a professional businessman at the helm, someone whose responsibility it is to manage the company with an autocratic touch so that all the policies can be vigorously and thoroughly implemented.

Furthermore, as I discovered belatedly to my cost, it only takes two people at the top echelon to bring the entire operations of a company to a standstill, especially if they cannot see eye to eye on how the business should be run.

A second try: Central Marine

After my departure from New Taiwan Marine, I had actually wanted to take a short break before considering my next move. But when Hsiao Ru-hsui and his brother, Yi-hsui, heard that I was available, they promptly asked Tien Jiu-jing, the husband of their maternal aunt, to come see me in the hope that I would be persuaded into starting a new shipping company with them.

Hsiao Ru-hsui was an apprentice-engineer aboard the same vessel I was serving during my seafaring days. We hardly knew each other then. Tien Jiu-jing, on the other hand, was head of Keelung Central Intelligence Office, with whom I had become acquainted when New Taiwan Marine still had its office in Keelung. Taiwan was under martial rule at the time and immigration controls were very strict, but Tien Jiu-jing was always there for me whenever I needed help.

Tien Jiu-jing was aware of my passion for the seas, and since I did not have any immediate plans, he duly invited me to set up a new shipping venture in collaboration with the two brothers. However, because of the painful experience I had with New Taiwan Marine, I was, in all honesty, not very keen. But owing to Tien Jiu-jing's persistence, apart from the fact that he was an elder whom I respected, I finally relented and agreed to have a go at it.

Thus was born Central Marine Corporation in 1965, which had its office along Nanking East Road in Taipei City. I was appointed the company's chairman, while Hsiao Yi-hsui was made its general manager. Lonny Chiu and Wu Pang-ji also joined me, with Chiu as business manager and Wu, operations manager.

As the company was financially weak in the early days, we could only afford to ply the coastal and regional routes using second-hand vessels, although I was already setting my sight on transoceanic services. We did reasonably well at the beginning. Unfortunately, the management style and arrogance of the Hsiao brothers soon became a potential stumbling block to the long-term growth of the company.

The high-handed Yi-hsui had installed his in-laws to look after the company's finances, despite the fact that they were completely unversed in these matters. Although I was not happy to see nepotism rear its ugly head in Central Marine, I tried my best not to offend the two brothers, primarily out of my respect for Tien Jiu-jing.

To my profound disgust, they took my reticence for submissiveness as they sought to discredit me in front of Tien Jiu-jing, who would then try his best to calm things down between us. I always listened to Tien's advice in deference to him, but the more forbearing I was, the increasingly more disdainful the two brothers would become.

On a separate front, simmering discord between some of the individuals in the company was slowly boiling over. While Hsiao Yi-hsui was bent on taking full reins of the company's financial and personnel matters, Lonny Chiu wanted his say too, as a result of which they could not see eye to eye on many issues.

On one occasion, Hsiao Yi-hsui and Lonny Chiu were in Singapore attending to some business when a bitter row erupted between them. Unlike Hsiao, Chiu was rather proficient in the English language, which enabled him to conduct all the meetings with their Singapore counterparts in this foreign tongue, as it were. But he made the mistake of not briefing Hsiao beforehand with the gist of the discussions. As general manager of the company, Hsiao naturally felt slighted as he reckoned he deserved better treatment from Chiu. The tiff, which began in Singapore, lasted all the way back to Taiwan.

Because I had recruited Chiu into Central Marine, Hsiao Yi-hsui felt he should reason things out with me when he got back from Singapore. He told me in no uncertain terms that since it was impossible for him to work with Chiu any longer, one of them would have to go.

Caught in a dilemma, I could only try my best to defuse the situation. I urged him to be more tolerant with colleagues and to value harmony, instead of hurting each other's feelings over some trivial matters. We could always work things out, I said. But he would not have any of it. From then on, the fissure between them widened and eventually reached a point where they refused to talk to each other.

Just because Chiu had followed me to Central Marine did not mean that I was biased towards him. But the two brothers thought otherwise and vented their displeasure on me, which in the event marked the beginning of the end of Central Marine Corporation.

Central Marine's first liner vessel

In the second half of 1967, Mr Itagaki, a section head in Marubeni's Vessel Division, whom I had known since my New Taiwan Marine days, dropped by to see me one day when he heard of my new entrepreneurial pursuit.

I explained to him the reasons behind my leaving New Taiwan Marine and the difficult situation I was facing in Central Marine. I said I could clearly foresee that if Central Marine did not pursue a growth strategy, it would definitely run into the same sort of bottlenecks that New Taiwan Marine encountered to its detriment.

In the midst of our chat, I asked Itagaki San half in jest if he was willing to do business with me in my new set-up. He said that should not be any problem.

"Then please help me find a suitable vessel when you get back to Japan, a vessel that I can deploy on long-haul routes, and which Marubeni can perhaps finance," I said, trying my luck.

To my pleasant surprise, Itagaki San told me straight away that there was indeed such a vessel available and that he would be in touch with me again once he had ascertained the status when he got back to Japan. We could always talk about the financing issues at a later stage, he assured me.

Shortly after his return to Japan, Mr Itagaki called me to say that Dowa Shipping Line had a general-cargo ship, *U Shin Maru*, for sale. I flew to Japan at once to discuss the deal with Marubeni's Vessel Division, where I still had many old friends; Kiyoshi Hosaka had meanwhile been promoted to head the division, while Isao Hashimoto was an experienced member of the team. We later acquired the vessel and renamed it *Central Trust*. Built after World War II by the Japanese, *Central Trust* had a capacity of 10,095 DWT.

The so-called liner vessels in the past were more like general-cargo ships, with the main hold sub-divided into several decks in order to stow different types of goods. They were for some reasons considered the forerunners of modern-day container ships. Bulk carriers, on the other hand, are essentially ocean tramps used in carrying commodities such as grains. They do not have the multi-decked cargo holds seen in general-cargo ships, and they run on no regular line.

Central Trust was already 15 years old when Marubeni recommended it to us. Due to the lack of proper maintenance by the previous Japanese owner, its performance was far from ideal when we acquired it, although it was still serviceable. But only just.

Wu Pang-ji and I were fully aware of the vessel's limitations when we inspected it in Japan. Nonetheless, we decided to buy it not only because of its low price tag, but more importantly, Marubeni was willing to finance the purchase. It was a once-in-a-life-time opportunity we could not afford to pass, especially if we wanted to extricate ourselves in the long run from the financial quagmire we were in at the time.

Moreover, the vessel would serve as a touchstone for future forays into the cutthroat business of transoceanic liner services. *Central Trust's* price tag was US$540,000, of which 60 per cent Marubeni had agreed to finance, while the balance 40 per cent would come from Central Marine itself. The loan had a three-year tenure, since we did not yet have any operational track record.

I duly signed the loan agreement with Marubeni on behalf of Central Marine in December 1967, and *Central Trust* was officially handed over to us in April of the following year.

Around May 1968, Central Marine applied for and secured a preferential loan to build a general-cargo vessel through the government's shipbuilding incentive programme. Under the scheme, beneficiaries only need to bear 20 per cent of the cost of the vessel, while the remaining 80 per cent would come from Japan's EXIM Bank, but which the Bank of Taiwan would guarantee. For Central Marine this was not much of a problem, as it had the financial backing of Marubeni.

My departure from Central Marine

Following her handing over, *Central Trust* set off from Japan on her journey to Taiwan, calling on the way at Yokohama, Osaka and Moji to pick up Keelung-bound general cargo. En route, we discovered to our dismay that her condition was far from satisfactory. As a result, we were compelled to withdraw the vessel from service soon after it arrived in Keelung so that it could undergo the necessary repairs, which in the event took almost a month.

After the ship had left the dock, I negotiated a one-year time-charter with Mr Igarashi, the section head of Showa Line's liner division. To my horror, *Central Trust* suffered a humiliating setback on her very first voyage under Showa.

The journey was to have taken *Central Trust* from the port of Yokohama on 14 August 1968 to Seattle on the US West Coast with a shipload of plywood and other general cargo. But as fate would have it, while the vessel was steaming along in the vicinity of the Aleutian Islands, its feed-water pump suddenly seized up, promptly incapacitating her, in the wake of which she was left adrift on the high seas for three days.

On the third day, the crew managed to have the problem rectified and *Central Trust* was on her way again, albeit at a much slower speed of five knots so as to get her safely to the ports of Seattle and Vancouver. Due to lost time, her expected arrival date had to be pushed back by more than two weeks. Because Christmas was fast approaching, there were aboard the vessel urgent cargo that had to be delivered quickly, especially to inland customers. In the event, Showa Line had no choice but to rush these consignments out by air as soon as the ship had come alongside.

As one of the most important criteria of a liner services provider is a reliable schedule, a delay of more than two weeks in the vessel's arrival date was a very serious matter indeed. In *Central Trust's* case, it resulted in an endless stream of customers seeking redress from Showa Line, which already had to bear the hefty costs of the air shipments. It thus did not come as a big surprise when Showa's management duly sought substantial damages from Central Marine, not long after which it decided to terminate the charter-party altogether when *Central Trust* was still steaming blissfully towards her destination in the USA.

Coincidentally in that same period, other problems began to emerge in Central Marine. Firstly, inadequate capitalisation in the early days had severely impeded the company's growth and cash flows; secondly, internal strife between employees was threatening to boil over, what with Hsiao Yi-hsui and Lonny Chiu constantly at odds with each other since their return from Singapore. Eventually, the Hsiao brothers' dislike for Chiu spilled over to me, to the extent that the normal operations of the company almost ground to a complete halt.

As a matter of fact, two to three months into the initial operations of Central Marine, I had already noticed the high-handed and self-centred manner in which the Hsiao brothers conducted themselves. A case in point was how they vested the financial matters of the company in the hands of family members, who blatantly disregarded the views of their colleagues. Their callous behaviour towards others brought about pervasive disunity and discord, which soon turned Central Marine into a fractious organisation with a rather bleak future.

As if these headaches were not enough, Showa Line had now revoked prematurely the charter-party. The Hsiao brothers capitalised on this incident to unleash a barrage of unfounded accusations against Chiu and me, and held us responsible for *Central Trust*'s below-par performance, both technically and financially. They even had the audacity to make an abrupt U-turn by claiming that they had absolutely nothing to do with the company's initial decision to go into long-haul services, thus effectively laying the blame for the series of events squarely on my shoulders.

In the same breath, the brothers told me that since the financial situation of the company was tight and getting worse by the day, and because *Central Trust* was my brain-child, I had better assume all its liabilities in order to forestall any further drain on the company's cash flows.

Round about the end of August 1968, while I was in Japan on

official business, Hsiao Yi-hsui promptly orchestrated my ouster from the company's board of directors in an emergency meeting that he had hastily convened, in which he also demanded that I take over the ownership of *Central Trust*.

Lonny Chiu was at the meeting and he called me immediately afterwards to tell me all that had transpired. Having now been stripped of my directorship, I was expected to relinquish my position as chairman of the company too. The only option after that, I reckoned, was to quit Central Marine altogether.

Had I instituted legal proceedings against Hsiao Yi-hsui at the time, I was confident I would have won hands down. After all, he and his people had blatantly abused their rights as directors in convening a meeting that was by all accounts unconstitutional. But I did not want to make matters worse. Besides, it was never in my nature to be unforgiving towards other people, even if they had committed wrongs against me. Hence, instead of kicking up a storm, I accepted the board's decision graciously.

Frankly, it was because I cherished Tien Jiu-jing's friendship, over and above his persuasiveness, that I had agreed to collaborate with the Hsiao brothers in the first place. I would have left the company much earlier had it not been for my respect for him. As it happened, the situation had deteriorated to such an irretrievable extent that there was really no reason for me not to leave, even if I had to accept the ludicrous demand of the Hsiao brothers that I take possession of *Central Trust*.

As soon as I heard the shocking news from Lonny Chiu, I went to see Mr Hosaka and told him the entire sequence of events leading up to my eventual expulsion from the board of Central Marine.

It was very gracious of Mr Hosaka to inquire about my future plans. I expressed my gratitude to him for all the help he had given me in the past and that I really should not bother him anymore. As for *Central Trust*, I said I would take over her ownership as well as her operations, including all her outstanding liabilities. But I begged him not to cut off the shipbuilding loan that Marubeni had earlier agreed to extend to Central Marine.

"But how are you going to survive with just one vessel?" asked Hosaka, looking somewhat incredulous.

"You're right," I replied, sensing hope in the tone of his voice. "It would be very difficult, if not impossible! But I could perhaps count on your help, again?"

I told Mr Hosaka I would let him know my detailed plans later, but right now, I had better rush back to Taiwan to sort out the mess. Central Marine's loan agreement with Marubeni was to all intents and purposes negotiated and signed by me alone. From this perspective, its validity could well be called into question if I left Central Marine. Indeed, Marubeni had every right to alter the terms of the contract or even terminate it altogether.

I was mindful of the great lengths Central Marine had gone to in getting itself qualified under the government's shipbuilding incentive programme. If anything should happen to the loan agreement with Marubeni at this critical juncture, I believed it would end Central Marine's hopes of ever owning a newly constructed vessel.

For this reason, I literally pleaded with Mr Hosaka not to alter the original terms of the contract, although I could see that the abrupt and dramatic turn of events in Central Marine had certainly diminished Marubeni's desire to work with the Hsiao brothers. But following my repeated appeals, Mr Hosaka said he would reconsider the matter justly.

Once back in Taiwan, I promptly got down to tying up all the loose ends with Central Marine. In a way, I was sad, though not resentful, that I did not get a penny back from all the effort and money I had put into a company I had worked so hard for. Worse, I was made to carry the can as a result of somebody else's incompetence.

Finally, with everything settled, I looked up Tien Jiu-jing and explained to him the reasons behind my departure, so that he could see the entire picture in its proper perspective. With that, my association with Central Marine thus came to a bitter conclusion as Lonny Chiu and I made our exit.

My ancestral home in Penghu.

My mother taught me the virtues of moral excellence and uprightness from young.

When I was a youth.

Sextants were commonly used on board vessels in the early days to determine their exact positions. Despite modern-day technological advances, it is a useful skill that sailors must still possess.

With my mother (sixth from right), wife (sixth from left) and other family members.

Belting out a popular song during one of the regular reunions with my primary schoolmates.
Such gatherings are still held these days.

A voracious appetite for reading, a habit I cultivated in my seafaring days.

New Taiwan Marine days, on one of those frequent business trips.

In Japan where construction work on New Taiwan Marine's 5,500-tonne banana carrier
was about to begin.

At Tsuneishi Shipyard, Japan in 1965, supervising work in progress on New Taiwan Marine's newbuilding.

Central Marine days, after leaving New Taiwan Marine.

2

A New Era

*Even a down-to-earth mariner with all his earnestness, hard
work and devotion is not spared life's trying moments. It is
perhaps God's will that I go through all these trials and
tribulations so as to mould me into a better person.*

My departure from Central Marine was as abrupt as it was hasty. Central Trust was still at sea when I took possession of her. I later renamed the vessel [长信轮] in Chinese.

In a move to allay the anxiety and fear that might have already crept into the minds of the ship's crew, I wasted little time in establishing a new shipping company, Evergreen Marine Corporation, which came into being on 1 September 1968.

Considerable thought went into giving the company an appropriate Chinese name. I had originally wanted to call it Yung Fa Marine Corporation, Yung Fa [荣发] being my given name. Later, I thought of using [张荣], the first two characters of my Chinese name, but it sounded rather odd. In the end, I settled for [长荣], which is an adaptation of my surname and middle name.

However, my friends told me that [长荣] might easily be confused with the name of another company called [李长荣]. But to me there was quite a clear distinction between them as the latter stressed its surname [李] whilst our emphasis was on the two Chinese characters

[长荣]. So eventually it was [长荣] that I chose to call my company.

As for the English version of the Chinese name, I had initially wanted to call it Chang Yung, which was a transliteration of the Chinese words [长荣]. I also dabbled with other possible permutations such as Ever Lasting and Ever Glory, but they were all not appropriate.

Finally, we settled for Lonny Chiu's suggestion of the word Evergreen. It symbolises everlasting vigour and prosperity, and at the same time aptly depicts the company as a beautiful island much like Taiwan, imbued with a perennial verdant green teeming with life and activity, as if it is spring in perpetuity. This is why the Evergreen Group has consistently adopted brilliant green as the corporate colour since its inception.

Prior to my departure from New Taiwan Marine, I had bought a four-storey building along Chang An East Road. The third and fourth floors served as my residence while the second level was tenanted out to the Japan Banana Association. Evergreen started its corporate life on the first floor.

As soon as the new company was formed, I despatched a cable to Central Trust's crew informing them of her change of ownership and that Evergreen Marine Corporation would henceforth be responsible for their payroll and other operating expenses. In which case, I told them, they should go about their usual tasks and not worry about anything.

By then Marubeni's Hosaka had learnt of the reasons behind my leaving Central Marine. Nevertheless, he wanted to have a complete grasp of the situation before deciding whether to lend any money to the Hsiao brothers. He was also keen to know if I needed help. Hence, after my return to Taiwan, he discreetly sent his subordinate, Hashimoto, over on an investigative trip. I was in the dark all this while as Mr Hosaka did not think it necessary to divulge anything to me beforehand. It was only some years later that I came to know about this clandestine mission.

The first stop for Hashimoto was Marubeni's branch office in Taipei, where he was able to gather the bulk of the information he had set out to collect. He also sought the views of other people in the shipping fraternity in order to understand better the modus operandi of the Taiwanese maritime industry.

It was not at all surprising that Hashimoto's report was highly critical of the Hsiao brothers, whose management style, it pointed out, left much to be desired. It also revealed that the majority of people Hashimoto spoke to had serious doubts about the future prospects of Central Marine, now that I had left the company.

In contrast, Hashimoto noted that I was "a conscientious and true-blue mariner". He pointed out in his report: "From the very day he stepped into his first job until the present moment, Chang Yung-fa has not wandered beyond the outer limits of the shipping industry. He is a unique example of an individual who has successfully switched from doing mundane clerical tasks to becoming a skilled seafaring professional through tireless self-education. Whether on shore or out at sea, he is equally adept at his jobs. Not only is he highly experienced, he also shows an unparalleled vision and entrepreneurial streak, particularly in the area of shipping and operational management, besides being a hardworking and responsible person, all of which make him a rare talent in the industry indeed."

He went on to strongly recommend that Marubeni render me its utmost support. "Chang Yung-fa is a truly accomplished and consummate mariner," he said. Moreover, this was also in line with Marubeni's objective of pursuing a long-term collaboration with a promising Taiwanese shipping company. Isao Hashimoto's boss, Kiyoshi Hosaka, readily shared his views. The latter had known me for quite some time.

With regard to the shipbuilding loan that Marubeni had originally agreed to extend to Central Marine, Hashimoto was of the opinion that since a memorandum of understanding had already been signed, any sudden change on its part would give rise to unnecessary problems. Besides, the Hsiao brothers might misconstrue that I had personally instigated Marubeni into changing its position.

Moreover, Central Marine had already qualified for the much

sought after government shipbuilding incentive programme, and even if it should one day fall on hard times and could not repay the loan, *Central Trust* could always be disposed of to recover the debt. On balance, therefore, Marubeni's 20 per cent portion of the loan was a calculated risk that it should feel comfortable with.

For the sake of consummating the deal, Marubeni should honour the terms of the agreement and extend the loan to Central Marine accordingly, Hashimoto recommended. But the scope of the assistance would be restricted to just the one vessel, as it would not render any further financial support to Central Marine in the future.

Money problems at Evergreen

Evergreen was established in a hurry and with a very tight budget. In order to pay the crew and other employees their wages, as well as take care of other operating expenses, I often had to resort to banks for financial help, a seemingly intractable problem from which I was unable to extricate myself.

I was the company's sole proprietor at the time. One way to put our finances on a stronger footing, I thought, was to invite my friends to invest in the business and let them run the operations together with me. But none of them were interested. There was nothing much I could do in the event, except be philosophical about it. Was it because I was predestined to go through all these trials and tribulations alone, I asked myself?

Frankly speaking, were it not for the immense financial pressure I was under, I would not have contemplated going into a partnership with anybody in the first place. After all, the experiences I had had with New Taiwan Marine and Central Marine had taught me painful and unforgettable lessons.

For a company to grow, I believe management must be seen to be sharing a common destiny, without which even the most promising operations will lapse into a state of paralysis in no time. What is particularly critical, especially when the company is still at the early phases of its development cycle, is that it has a professional manager at the helm, who understands the business and who has the capacity to lay a firm foundation for steady growth.

But the irony of it all is that partners do not necessarily share the same management philosophy, no matter how hard they try. In our case, for example, although there was no denying that an amateurish approach to managing the business was bad for the company, my partners were, however, not quite ready to listen to, much less embrace, the constructive views and ideas other people had to offer either.

This dilemma only served to heighten my anguish, much like a situation in which a person intent on pursuing life's ideals has his progress constantly blocked by endless obstacles, yet in the face of all the setbacks, he is not prepared to give up.

My stance was that since I had come this far, I had better carry on with it, even if I had to do it all alone. If all should fail, which was not implausible, as the income generated by the lone vessel in our entire operation could barely cover mounting expenses, I could always return to seafaring. The financial millstone, heavy and asphyxiating that it was, really cast an ominous shadow over the future of Evergreen.

In the end, I had no choice but to turn to Marubeni for help once again. I explained to them the predicament I was in at the time, and after patiently hearing me out, they agreed to defer by six months the principal and interest I had to pay for the loan Central Marine had earlier taken for the purchase of *Central Trust*. This welcomed breather enabled Evergreen to make use of the freight income in the interim to ease its cash-flows, without which I would be hard pressed to cope with the monthly debt burden, let alone get the business going.

Steeped in a financial quagmire we were desperately trying to free ourselves from, I was acutely aware that the only viable solution was to work towards acquiring a reasonable number of vessels for the fleet. There was no way we could rely on just one rickety ship for our livelihood or survival. All things considered, I decided to take the bull by the horns and came up with a fleet development plan that aimed to procure several more "medieval" vessels to add to our existing operations.

I was relieved that Marubeni was most supportive of my game plan. They promised to look out for any such vessels that might suit our intended operations.

In this respect, Mr Hosaka wasted little time in tapping the wisdom of his father-in-law, Mr Ito, who once served as the president of Showa Line. With his help, we were able to purchase one of Showa Line's bulk carriers, *Nishiryu Maru*, which we later renamed *Ever Glory*. The vessel was sold to us on a charter back basis, which allowed Showa Line to time-charter it back from us after the completion of the transaction, but with Evergreen responsible for running its entire operations.

Marubeni agreed to finance 95 per cent towards the purchase price, with the remaining 5 per cent to be borne by Evergreen. But as I was going through a most difficult patch then, I did not even think I could afford the vessel's fuel or other expenses, let alone bear the remaining 5 per cent of the purchase price.

In the end it was through the good offices of Marubeni in Japan that I was able to secure the necessary financing from Shanghai Bank and Chang Hwa Bank, without which I honestly would have been at a complete loss. In this instance, Marubeni's branch office in Taipei acted as my guarantors for these loans.

Under the terms of the time-charter, Showa Line was to pay to Marubeni *Ever Glory*'s charter fee, from which the latter would deduct the monthly amount that we owed them before returning the balance to us. But, because of the trust Marubeni had in me, it later asked Showa Line to pay the money to Evergreen directly instead. In the meantime, we were able to service our loans punctually, thus paving the way for a mutually trustworthy and beneficial relationship to be established between Evergreen and Marubeni.

Fortunately for us, as *Ever Glory* was still in relatively good condition, it did not give us any operational problems, which enabled us to have a regular rental income. Although we now had two vessels, we were not about to slow down on our expansion plan. On the contrary, we had every reason to be even more aggressive about acquisitions.

I recalled those days I had to shuttle back and forth Japan once every two to three days to attend to the company's financial and business matters. The punishing schedule coupled with my pre-occupation with every aspect of our operations, especially while I was away from the office, often left me without enough sleep. As a result, I often appeared haggard and uptight.

On one occasion, when Mr Hosaka saw the exhausted look I was wearing, he tried his best to comfort me. "Take it easy, we're behind you all the way. Just carry on with what you do best and leave the rest to us," he said patting me on my shoulders. Although these were simple words of encouragement, I was nevertheless deeply touched; it was a spontaneous gesture on the part of Mr Hosaka and I never forgot it.

Crossing oceans

Because Evergreen was something of an unknown quantity in the shipping industry in the early days, its ability to solicit sizeable volumes of cargo was very limited in almost every market around the world. It was for this reason that we consciously centred our operations around the acquisition of second-hand vessels and then time-chartering them out to other shipping companies to earn a rental income.

But such an approach called for a thorough negotiation with interested parties on the terms and conditions of the charter well before a final decision to purchase a suitable vessel was made. The cumbersome nature of such a mode of operation notwithstanding, for someone like me who had not known any other professional skills all his life, running my own shipping company one day was a natural progression, and a long-cherished goal. Ultimately, my dream, if not my passionate desire, was to embark on long-haul, transoceanic liner services.

Although I was also involved in the liner trade during my time in New Taiwan Marine and Central Marine, it was primarily regional in nature, lacking in scope and challenge. While I very much wanted to go into transoceanic scheduled services, my partners were resolutely against the idea.

But liner operations were anything but easy to manage in the difficult environment that prevailed at the time. A business of a rather complex nature, a liner services operator generally has to canvass a lot more customers in a bid to secure a sufficient base load of cargo for every sailing that it mounts. More critically, however, he must be able to provide a consistently reliable service with his vessels calling at scheduled ports at regular intervals. Given this formidable challenge, a company must have in place the necessary infrastructure, in terms of a sizeable organisational set-up and operational scope, before it can really provide this highly demanding service with competence.

At the other end of the shipping spectrum are the bulk carriers which neither offer any regular schedules nor ply any fixed routes. Wherever the place, as long as the cargo is there, arrangements can be made to have the goods, which are usually bulk commodities such as salt, steel scrap, coal and grains, picked up.

Bulk carriers often rely on chartering brokers to solicit and secure cargo. Such an arrangement takes a heavy workload off the ship owners, and obviates the need for them to have a complicated organisational structure for their business to function normally. But, to me, an operation of this nature lacked challenge and would certainly not help my aim to be at the forefront of the shipping industry.

Other activities such as tanker shipping, which usually involves long-term charters of 15 to 20 years, are rather straightforward. Once an agreement on freightage had been reached between the client and the shipping company, the latter can proceed to acquire a suitable carrier to fulfil the terms of the contract.

The problem with an oil tanker is that, after discharging its liquefied cargo of, say, crude, it has to de-sludge, usually in the open seas, thus causing serious environmental pollution. Never mind that the operations of some of the major carriers like NYK encompass liner, tramp and tanker shipping all under one roof, the tanker trade never interested me the slightest even though the market for such services was extremely buoyant at one stage.

As far as I was concerned, the future of the global shipping industry rested with liner services. Hence, the so-called "flower" of the maritime trade, a term popularly used at the time to describe the dazzling prospects of liner services as being the most promising mode of marine transportation in the world.

Indeed, it had always been my firm belief that shipping companies gear themselves towards the provision of transoceanic liner services, especially if they were to break new grounds and position themselves for uninterrupted growth. In any case, the coastal and regional shipping market was already approaching saturation point, with practically every carrier represented in the action. Given this scenario, I felt we should gradually shift the focus of our operations towards the global stage, as that was where I believed the future of Evergreen lay.

With little more than just the broad concept in hand, I approached Marubeni to explore my transoceanic ambition further and to seek their usual backing in the event that my game plan should come to pass one day. Not long after that meeting during which I also requested their help in looking out for any vessels that could be suitably deployed in transoceanic operations, word came that K Line had a number of old ships for sale.

We did not waste any time in cutting a deal with K Line to acquire two of their vessels, *Aoshima Maru* and *Eiho Maru*, which we later rechristened *Ever Island* and *Ever State*, respectively. *Ever Island*, a general-cargo ship, would be deployed on our long-haul transoceanic liner services whilst *Ever State*, a bulk carrier, was to be time-chartered to Showa Line. The transaction was 90 per cent financed by Marubeni while the remaining 10 per cent had to be borne by Evergreen itself.

At the same time that we decided on the purchase of *Ever Island*, we also announced the impending launch of our maiden liner operations, the Far East-Arabian/Persian Gulf services, taking the industry and business community by complete surprise. None of the shipping lines in Taiwan was plying this route until then, with the majority of them involved in regional trade only.

The Taiwan-Middle East market had long been a monopoly of the powerful freight conference, whose members comprised major shipping lines like NYK, OSK, and Maersk, among others. Traditionally, these carriers were laden with Japanese cargo with very limited space allocated to Taiwan shippers, who were also made to pay exorbitant rates.

The freight cartel did not necessarily admit new members automatically, even if they were keen to join. But, on the other hand, any independent operator seeking to grab a piece of the action from the conference in its stoutly defended market would be forced in most cases to beat a hasty retreat. Those bold enough to take the formidable challenge head-on would at best be able to last two to three months before coming to grief. Others were less fortunate, as they found themselves unceremoniously bundled out of the market after just one or two voyages, unable to secure any cargo from shippers who had long been at the mercy of the cartel. As a result, not many private carriers were brave enough to risk their fortune taking on the might of the freight conference without careful consideration.

This was largely why the much-anticipated export boom for Taiwan-made products never really took off, even though they were cheap and good and attracted the interest of many customers in the Middle East countries. It was a well-known fact that Taiwan manufacturers had a great deal of difficulty in securing sufficient cargo space from conference lines, as a result of which they were often unable to provide their customers with a firm and reliable delivery schedule.

Having observed this phenomenon for some time, as well as pinpointed the industry bottlenecks, I came to the conclusion that the Middle East route presented Evergreen with the best bet to embark on its maiden liner operations with a reasonable chance of success. On the one hand, we could help alleviate the recurrent shortage of vessel space Taiwan shippers faced. On the other hand, working in concert with Taiwan manufacturers, our proposed services would go a long way towards boosting the country's trade with the Middle East countries. An added spin-off from Evergreen's standpoint would be an exclusive clientele in the making, which would hopefully underpin future growth.

The freight conference did not take much notice of our intended operations when we first made our plan public. Nevertheless, I was acutely aware of its unbridled determination to make life unbearable for whoever dared to encroach into a market that it considered sacrosanct. In this respect, I was mentally well prepared in the event that Evergreen would one day meet with the same fate as numerous others who had the audacity to challenge the insolent freight cartel on their turf, and lost.

Crossing swords with the freight conference

I recalled the occasion I had to be in Japan to finalise the handing-over formalities of *Ever Island*, and Marubeni's Hashimoto saw me off at Haneda Airport on the day of my departure. Just as we were alighting from our car, I noticed from afar that Showa Line's Igarashi San was already there, apparently waiting for me. He hurried towards me as soon as he saw me.

"Are you here to see me off or are you expecting guests, Igarashi San?" I asked, half in jest.

"I'm here to see you off, Mr Chang," he replied matter-of-factly, which surprised me somewhat.

"Oh yes? Looks like the sun is going to rise from the West!" I said, in mock disbelief, although I could sense from his grim expression that he had something really important that he wanted to discuss with me. Since it was still early, I invited the two gentlemen to join me for a drink at the airport terminal's cafeteria. Once comfortably seated, I asked Mr Igarashi what was it that he wanted so urgently to talk to me about.

"You see, the freight conference had just convened an emergency meeting to discuss the potential threat posed by your widely-publicised move to enter the Middle East trade. It was agreed during the meeting that I should represent the conference to try to talk you out of your intention," he explained.

This less than subtle message that the freight conference had asked Mr Igarashi to convey did not surprise me at all, as I had seen it coming.

What I did not know until then was that Showa Line was also a member of this infamous grouping. It was probably because Showa Line, but Mr Igarashi in particular, and Evergreen had known each other for some time that they had been asked by their fellow members to make a last-ditch effort in trying to get me change my mind.

"What if I choose to ignore your advice?" I asked, taking a swig of my coffee at the same time.

"In that case, I believe the freight conference will use all the means it has at its disposal to prevent Evergreen from securing any cargo from anybody. One of the things it can do is to reschedule member-carriers' services to deliberately coincide with your intended departure. For example, if your vessel's departure date is, say, 16th of the month, the conference will ensure that its carriers set sail on the 15th and 17th, thus effectively shutting you out from the market completely. Furthermore, we'll slash our freight tariffs dramatically to entice shippers to come to us," Mr Igarashi warned, adding that I stood to lose my fortune if I did not listen.

"Tell me, as a friend, what do you think I should do?" I ventured.

"You tell me what you want to do first and I'll tell what my personal views are," he offered, with a glint in his eyes.

"Okay, I'm going ahead, come what may! I won't give up without a fight!"

As a friend, he said, he supported my decision.

As far as I was concerned, the freight conference's threats did not make any difference, coming as they did at this late hour. In any case, I had already anticipated their moves some time back. Besides, this was not the first time that the cartel had adopted such a high-handed approach towards non-member carriers. Instead of back-pedalling, I had every reason to pick up the gauntlet and give the Taiwan shippers a good run for their money.

Since Mr Igarashi was an emissary of the cartel, I thought it was only proper that he should also convey my decision to his fellow members. Personally, I knew that if I did not find the courage to get our maiden liner operations off the ground quickly enough, I would probably not have another chance in the future. Hence, I thought it was best that I faced the challenge head-on, no matter how daunting the task, so as to fulfil the dream I had cherished for so long.

Looking back, I did not expect then that our modest forays into the Middle East market would actually herald in a new era for Evergreen. It also marked the beginning of the presence of Taiwanese carriers in a market that had long been an exclusive preserve of foreign shipping companies.

Following the hand-over of *Ever Island* to Evergreen in Japan in mid-August 1969, the vessel was ready to load cargo for the journey to Taiwan. It was a dismal start to our maiden Far East/Arabian-Persian Gulf liner services, for we were unable to collect any general cargo, let alone talk about high-yield shipments. All we could manage was a consignment of steel and cement, which we were able to secure only through the indulgence of Mr Toriumi, who was then head of Marubeni's Cement Section, and presently the company's president.

But worse was yet to come. As fate would have it, *Ever Island* caught fire as she was coming alongside Pier No 18 in Keelung Port on 7 September 1969. One of the two boilers in the engine room suddenly burst into flames just as the workers were in the midst of unloading the steel coils.

The cause of the fire, as we discovered later, was due to overheating. Because of the antiquated condition of the instruments on board, the crew was totally unaware that one of the boilers had been left high and dry without water for a considerable length of time. We only realised that a fire had broken out when we saw smoke spewing out from the engine compartment.

Amid the rush to have the flames put out before the fire engines could arrive on the scene, we inadvertently drenched the entire engine room, turning it into a mess. It was tough luck really, as I watched the ordeal unfold in horror.

That this unfortunate incident should occur while the goods at Keelung port were in the process of being loaded onto the ship caused a great deal of anxiety among the shippers. Thankfully though, not a single consignment of goods was damaged, as the cargo holds were unscathed. I thus instructed the crew to continue with the loading as soon as the situation on board was under control.

But getting the damaged boiler pipe replaced was easier said than done, as it was a very time-consuming affair. Worse, although we practically scoured the length and breadth of Keelung, we could not find a suitable replacement part.

In the end, it was in a factory in Kaohsiung that we found the pipe that we wanted, and the people there had the expertise to do a good job. The only snag was that they could only carry out the repair work in Kaohsiung, where they had all the necessary equipment and facilities. In other words, if we wanted to have the pipe fixed, we had to move the vessel to Kaohsiung. But the problem was that we had to have prior clearance of an approved ship classification society before the vessel could leave Keelung.

Ever Island was at the time in possession of two classification certificates issued by the China Corporation Register of Shipping (CR) and Nippon Kaiji Kyokai (NK) respectively. The reason why it was also certified by NK was because CR was not an internationally accredited classification agency.

NK did not have a resident surveyor in Taiwan at the time. Its responsibilities were handled by the office of the American Bureau of Shipping (ABS), which was manned by an American called Philip.

Philip made things very difficult for Evergreen right from the beginning. He flatly refused our repeated requests for permission to move the vessel. It did not matter how hard we tried to explain to him that since Kaohsiung was only a stone's throw away, the vessel could easily make her way there safely on just one boiler, he simply would not listen.

Perhaps if *Ever Island* had been classed under the ABS standards, Philip would probably have been less sticky about the whole thing. But since the vessel bore a CR and NK classification, he was in no mood to make any concession no matter how frantically we pleaded with him.

While all this fuss was going on, Evergreen sought, and was given, CR's green light for the stricken vessel to leave port; *Ever Island* was after all registered in the nationality of Taiwan, as CR put it succinctly, and as such it had the jurisdiction over the matter. Other government departments including the port authority had no objections either. But most importantly, Evergreen's insurer, Yasuda Insurance, whose opinions we also sought, argued that since all the relevant authorities in Taiwan had given their consent, there was no basis for them to go against that decision.

Of all the people, I really regretted that it had to be the arrogant Philip who repeatedly stood in our way. In frustration, I was driven to call NK's head office in Japan, hoping to get a favourable hearing. Instead, all I received was a curt response.

"If our representative in Taiwan said no, there was nothing much we at the HQ can do to change his mind," NK told me brusquely on the phone, devoid of any grace and basic courtesy.

I was by then at the end of my tether; if a solution could not be found very soon, the inconvenience and delays our customers had had to put up with thus far could only get worse. After due consideration, I instructed our crew to get the ship ready to leave for Kaohsiung. When Philip got wind of the news, he promptly tried to stop me. But I was not in any mood to listen to him.

"Please leave me alone, Philip!" I bellowed. "I'd had enough of your nonsense. What matters most to me is that Yasuda, my insurance company, and CR, as well as the port authority, have all given us their unconditional go-ahead!"

We were already into the third week of September when we set sail for Kaohsiung.

The technician at the shipyard started work on the boiler as soon as the vessel arrived in Kaohsiung the next day. They laboured round the clock to have the damaged pipe replaced as fast as possible. I also decided to give the machinery and equipment on board a thorough overhaul.

With the repairs completed, CR and the port authority duly certified that the newly installed boiler pipe fully satisfied international safety standards and that it was unlikely to pose any problems in the foreseeable future. Not so, in the opinion of ABS's Philip, who insisted adamantly that it was only good for temporary use.

By then *Ever Island* had already been laid up for some forty days, which seriously disrupted our schedules. Shippers were understandably agitated and getting increasingly impatient by the day, although we did try to placate them as best as we could.

Frankly, who could have been more anxious to get *Ever Island* back in service as quickly as possible? Indeed, I could not remember how many sleepless nights I went through worrying over the desperate situation we were in.

Ever Island set off for the Middle East as soon as she had been given a clean bill of health. On the return journey back to the Far East, when the vessel called at Osaka, I made it a point to have NK inspect the piping works again.

I was not the least surprised when NK confirmed that the boiler pipe was fit for permanent use under the international code of practice. *Ever Island* went on to ply the Middle East route year after year without any serious trouble at all.

But ABS's high-handedness and inflexibility certainly left a bitter aftertaste in me. I was actually more frustrated than angry that Philip should make life so difficult for us when we were already facing an uphill task in our everyday operations.

This unsavoury incident prompted us to give wide berth to the ABS standards of ship classification since then. It was not until many years later when some of their people in America came to know about the matter that its chairman personally apologised to me in the hope that I would put this episode behind me.

Arduous first steps

When Evergreen first started out on its Middle East liner operations, it was hard put to collect any high-yield general cargo. This was mainly because trade between Taiwan and the Middle East had not really taken off in a big way as earlier anticipated. Moreover, we were still a relatively unknown quantity without an established customer base. In the circumstance, all that we could solicit was low-yield cargo such a steel bars, cement, and other types of steel products.

We also did not have to wait very long for the freight conference to fire the first salvo. True to its promises, the cartel did not spare any effort in trying to shut Evergreen out of the market. It deliberately rescheduled member lines' departures to coincide with that of *Ever Island*'s, besides slashing their rates across the board to discourage shippers from coming to us. Furthermore, cargo owners were systematically told not to engage the services of Evergreen, unless they were prepared to face the consequences.

But I was not about to give up so easily without a fight. I knew for sure that the cartel's acts of commercial sabotage was not without any adverse impact on the business of the member lines themselves, what with their otherwise regular schedules now badly disrupted and their freight revenue drastically reduced. Ultimately, it would have to be the individual members themselves who had to bear any losses or costs incurred as a result of their collective action. A protracted and concerted campaign against Evergreen was thus as much a detriment to the cartel itself as it would be to Evergreen in the long run.

I had worked so hard to get this far and it would be such a shame if I were to give it all up now. Thus, no matter how daunting the task, I vowed to plod on, not only to break new ground, but also to garner the support of shippers.

Amid the uncertainty though, I reminded our staff to be united in mind and courage, so that we could summon up all our strength and defeat the freight conference at its own game. Also, I believed, by offering a superior service at reasonable cost, shippers would in return be inclined to back us more readily.

In the meantime, we were helping Taiwan manufacturers make inroads into the Middle East market by vigorously promoting their products wherever we went. We even took on the role of an unofficial trade development agency by freely disseminating information about

Taiwan's manufacturing industry, especially to those who wanted to source their requirements from the Far East. A noted beneficiary of our effort was a company called Tatung, which made electrical appliances and other consumer products. Our matchmaking activities did not go unnoticed either, as manufacturers happy with our assistance invariably entrusted the delivery of their export cargo to us.

Overall, we were able to build up Evergreen's business gradually, one step at a time. Looking back, I really had nothing but praises for the unity and indefatigable spirit that our staff unyieldingly displayed in the face of adversity. I also recalled, with just about forty odd people in the company, I had a hand in almost everything, from running around all day long attending to the routine business and financial matters, to being preoccupied with its long-term growth prospects.

But alas, the passage ahead was not exactly as plain sailing as we had hoped for, what with our handful of vessels running into one problem after another, leaving the future of the company hanging in the balance at times.

3

The Fury of
an Untamed Sea

*Successive setbacks coupled with growing pains often left
me exhausted but not crushed as I persevered and gave
my all in pursuit of a little kingdom in the turbulent
world of shipping.*

What was supposed to be a happy occasion on 7 September 1969 turned
out to be a decidedly anticlimax when *Ever Island* caught fire in Keelung
Port, which resulted in a repair bill of US$100,000. Yasuda Insurance
contributed 65 per cent towards the costs, with the balance borne by
Evergreen.

Over the period that *Ever Island* was out of action, Evergreen
suffered further losses. Whilst the revenue had all but ceased to flow,
crew's wages and other expenses still had to be paid for in the meantime. All in, when the final figures were totted up, they came to some
US$250,000 in lost earnings and operating costs.

Misfortunes, as they say, often strike when we least expect them.
Barely a month later in early October 1969 when *Ever State* was on
her way from Japan to the USA, she suddenly developed engine
trouble, forcing her to turn back immediately for repairs. The ship
was in docks for one month, during which we were literally left high
and dry. On the one hand, we had no income from the vessel, while

on the other, we had to worry about mounting expenses. To make matters worse, the ship had to be given a thorough overhaul to prepare her for the mandatory annual inspection. In all, the damage done amounted to some US$150,000, no small change by any means.

Round about the same time, the decrepit *Central Trust* had to be docked again in Keelung for a major maintenance job, following a circuitous journey from the USA to Japan and India, and back to Japan. The vessel had been time-chartered to a foreign shipping company in April of 1969. Called Worldwide Carriers Ltd., the charterer was a Liberian-incorporated company owned by a Jewish American who had set up shop in New York.

Central Trust had picked up a shipload of cargo in the Far East, and after refuelling at Yokohama on 12 September 1969, she left for the USA. En route, the vessel called at Los Angeles, Panama, port of New London in the State of Connecticut before arriving in New York on 14 November.

After discharging her load of cargo in New York, the empty ship was on her way down south when on the night of 17 November she rammed into a Swedish container vessel near the port of Norfolk. The force of the impact caused *Central Trust*'s bow to almost completely cave in, and although it did not spring a leak, the section had to be totally replaced later.

As *Central Trust* could still move under her own power, she left the scene of the collision and headed for Bethlehem, Pennsylvania, in search of a ship-repair yard. But the shipyards there had never heard of the name "Evergreen Marine", and unless we could get an insurance company to furnish them with some form of a bank guarantee, they would simply not have anything to do with us.

It was estimated that the cost of the repair alone would come up to more than US$200,000. I had contemplated scrapping the vessel, but a valuation showed that it was still worthwhile to get it restored and going.

I thus got in touch with Japan's Yasuda Insurance and requested them to provide the Americans with an undertaking to pay on our behalf all the expenses that would be incurred in connection with the repair job. Only with this assurance in hand did the shipyard allow us to dock our vessel, where she remained for two months from 18 November 1969 to 14 January 1970.

No sooner had *Central Trust* docked in Bethlehem than a flurry of compensation claims arrived at our doorsteps from the Swedish shipping company. Judging from the situation at the time, I was inclined to believe that it was our fault that brought about the accident. We thus asked Yasuda to look into the matter urgently, who in turn promptly cabled the claimant and assured them that it would settle everything once the insurers of both parties had completed the investigation into the mishap.

The gentleman in charge of this case in Yasuda at the time was a managing director whose name I cannot recall, but who was certainly most helpful to me, and to him, I am eternally grateful.

In fact, Evergreen had not been a customer of Yasuda's for very long when the collision, which was not a minor accident by any account, occurred. If it were not for the Japanese insurer's readiness to provide the Americans with an undertaking to foot the hefty repair bill, so that *Central Trust* could have its damage fixed, over and above their willingness to process the claims promptly, Evergreen would have faced a crisis of immense proportions.

Because of this matter, I personally offered my profound apologies to Yasuda for making them pay such a heavy price and for putting them to so much trouble. But the managing director's remarks touched me no end.

"Not to worry, Mr Chairman," he said, "this is what insurance is all about, and you needn't be apologetic or feel sorry about anything."

Of course it is true that insurance companies have an obligation to accept responsibility for any genuine claims that may arise, but not all of them treat their clients with the same attitude and manner that Yasuda approached the problem. That this gentleman from Yasuda did not shirk his duty at a most crucial juncture when *Central Trust* was in such a tight spot, but that he should evince so much sympathy and understanding, literally moved me to tears. It was a compassionate gesture on his part that I cherished forever, and which also paved the way for a long-lasting relationship between Evergreen and Yasuda.

Marubeni throws a lifeline

Although Yasuda came to our immediate aid and agreed to pick up the tabs for the repair of both *Central Trust* and the Swedish vessel, our problems were not over yet. For the two months that the ship was out of action, not only were we not generating any income, we actually had to deal with a whole host of daily expenses and overheads. As a result, we incurred a total consequential loss of about US$140,000, excluding the huge compensation Yasuda had to pay out separately.

I was at a loss to explain why, within a matter of months, *Ever Island*, *Ever State* and *Central Trust* had run into problems one after the other. Moreover, that all these setbacks should come hard at the heels of an already difficult situation we were in almost drove us to the point of despair.

The company was literally on the brink of ruin at the time. On the one hand, we were devoid of any income, but on the other, we had to face higher insurance premiums and increasingly bigger repair bills and other expenses, which were really beyond our means. Our survival was in question unless we could quickly secure enough financing to turn the grave situation around.

My original intention was to borrow NT$500,000 from Chang Hwa Bank as a temporary solution. But hopes of getting any money all but evaporated when the bank made things so difficult for me. Apart from the mountain of forms and supporting documents I was asked to fill up, the bank also required me to produce three guarantors, when normally two would have sufficed. I was virtually at a dead end; even friends and acquaintances seemed to have deserted me when I needed them most.

With all the possibilities I could think of practically exhausted, I had no choice but to turn to Marubeni again. In my estimate, I had to have US$300,000 to tide over the difficult period. But how could I open my mouth and ask Marubeni to lend me such a huge sum of money? Besides, it is not in my nature to seek financial assistance from other people if I can help it.

I was wrestling with myself as to what I should do, although I also realised that Marubeni was probably the only way out. So I plucked up my courage and went to see them in Tokyo. Arriving at their office early the next morning, I explained to Mr Hashimoto the purpose of my visit. But because he was still a relatively junior staff in the section at the time, he suggested that I brief his superiors, Mr Hosaka and Mr Nagasawa, on the matter in detail.

The four of us were seated in a conference room as I began to present my case in a rather doleful tone.

"I'm truly grateful for your unstinting support in the past. I thought with your assistance I could give my entrepreneurial dreams a real good shot. But, unfortunately, it was not to be, as our company experienced a run of bad luck. I'm afraid we're now teetering on the verge of collapse and unless we can get some immediate relief somewhere, our days are numbered. I know it won't be easy, but I would really appreciate it if you could lend us a helping hand one more time," I pleaded, half-expecting the worst.

When I had finished, Mr Hosaka asked me how much money I needed to stave off the crisis and how soon I reckoned I could pay back the whole amount. I said I was looking at US$300,000, which was equivalent to NT$12 million in those days, and that I should be able to settle the loan in full within a year. To my surprise, after a brief deliberation among the three of them, Mr Hosaka offered to help me find an even better solution.

"The US$300,000 you've in mind is perhaps sufficient to see you through your present crisis. But don't forget you still need working capital. What if you run into more problems again in the future, and you've no money left in the kitty? How about the old debts you've run up? I think you ought to work out a contingency plan, because it won't be easy for Marubeni's top management to lend you any more money in the future," he advised.

After a brief silence, Mr Hosaka continued: "I'll see if I can get you a bigger loan, just in case. We also have to think of how quickly you can draw down the US$300,000, which you need most urgently, as it takes at least 20 days for the loan to be processed."

His thoughtfulness really left me speechless.

At this juncture, Mr Nagasawa interceded: "Our management has just appropriated a sum of US$1 million in loan for another company. But since the borrower is not expected to make use of the money just yet, we can always lend the money to you first."

Mr Hosaka agreed and further suggested that I borrow US$600,000 instead. Even if the extra US$300,000 was not spent at the end of the day, all that I stood to lose was the interest charges, not a heavy price to pay for peace of mind, he explained. Also, with the reserve, I could concentrate on my business without having to run around everyday looking for capital. Moreover, the money was there for my immediate use, as I did not have to wait for the loan to be processed, which would take quite awhile.

I am truly indebted to the three gentlemen for their invaluable help. I will never forget their generosity and thoughtfulness.

We finally agreed on a US$600,000 loan with a five-year tenure. Marubeni would disburse the money to Evergreen in two tranches, with the first to be released immediately. I remembered I was still in Japan when they wired the US$300,000 to our bank account in Taiwan. News of the remittance instantly boosted the morale of our employees who had not known the outcome of my negotiation with the Japanese.

That night, Mr Hosaka invited me for a drink. Because I still had not got over the loan issue just yet, I supposed I looked rather glum.

"Don't worry, we're behind you all the way," he said, trying to cheer me up as he patted me on the shoulders.

Next morning, I took the first available flight out of Tokyo, anxious to get back to Taipei as quickly as possible. No sooner had I stepped into the office than the accountant told me that Marubeni had already transferred the money to our bank. I heaved a big sigh of relief; it was as if a dense cover of overhanging dark clouds had just been swept away, thus freeing me from the gloom and doom.

The loan was by no means an insignificant sum of money we were talking about in those days, but the steadfast and efficient manner in which Marubeni dealt with the matter was admirable. Its attitude and that of our local banks in Taiwan were indeed poles apart.

With the money in hand, we were able to pay our employees their wages on time, as well as take care of other expenses. The company's operations were soon back on track again. Resuscitated and given a new lease of life, everybody buckled down with a new-found zeal to fight for a bigger slice of the Middle East market.

Through collective effort and an unyielding sense of mission, our business in Taiwan began to show a marked improvement. Not only were we able to achieve better loads, the yield was also better. In the meantime, our operations in Japan, Singapore and other Southeast Asian regions also showed signs of a pick-up.

In less than a year, six months to be exact, I was able to repay Marubeni US$300,000, followed by the other US$300,000 subsequent to the disposal of the vessel *Ever State*.

What was meant to be a five-year loan was actually redeemed within a matter of one year, a remarkable achievement by all accounts. It also marked the beginning of a steady ascent in the trust and reputation of Evergreen in the shipping community.

Back into the storm

Just as we were working doubly hard to recover lost ground, we ran smack into a totally unexpected situation, plunging the company into yet another crisis.

After two months of repair at the yard in Bethlehem, *Central Trust* was back in action again. The journey took her from Houston, through Port Arthur (Texas), to Veracruz (Veracruz State, southeast of Mexico), New Orleans (Louisiana), Norfolk, and finally to Canada's Digby Port in the State of Nova Scotia, where it arrived on 21 March 1970.

There, the vessel picked up a full load of wood pulp before

Worldwide Carriers notified the captain that Yugoslavia was where the shipment was destined.

Although *Central Trust* was Panamanian-flagged, its crew was entirely made up of Taiwan nationals. Under the terms of the government's prohibition order, which was categorically spelt out in the charter-party, the vessel was not supposed to call at any communist countries or their vassal states. Evergreen's agreement with Worldwide Carriers also stated this condition clearly. As Yugoslavia was a socialist state, it was by definition a communist country as far as Taiwan was concerned.

Worldwide Carriers' notification sent the skipper of *Central Trust* into a panic. He quickly sought the advice and instructions of Evergreen's head office in Taipei.

It was no trivial matter, this. Taiwan was still in the grip of martial law at the time, and if any member of the crew should defy the standing order and set foot on communist soil, the consequences would be unthinkable. We immediately instructed the captain of *Central Trust* to stay put in Digby until further notice.

In retaliation, Worldwide Carriers demanded US$250,000 in compensation. But to me, the fault clearly did not lie with us. Unable to overcome the stalemate, both sides resorted to legal action to settle the issue. In the meantime, *Central Trust* was arrested in Digby under a court order.

I promptly despatched Lonny Chiu, Evergreen's president, to the USA, and later to Canada, to sort out the legal wrangle. But just before he left, he asked me what would happen if we should lose the court case. Sensing doubts in his mind, I told him not to worry; if worse should come to the worst, I said, we could always let Worldwide Carriers keep *Central Trust*. With my assurance, Chiu set off at once for the USA, promising to do his best, although at the back of my mind I was wondering how we could repay Marubeni the few hundred thousand dollars we still owed.

To prove our case, Chiu brought with him supporting documents issued by both the Taiwan Foreign Office and the Panamanian Consulate in Hong Kong. But the Americans would not budge.

Worldwide Carriers contended that the term "communist" was only a nominal definition, and that in its opinion Yugoslavia was a Socialist Federal Republic, not a communist state. It put forth three reasons to back its claim:

- Yugoslavia was not a member of the Eastern Bloc's Warsaw Pact.
- Yugoslavia received US aid-in-kind not granted to communist countries.
- Citizens of Western democracies could travel freely in and out of Yugoslavia, and none of these countries imposed any trade sanctions on Yugoslavia.

With no hope of an amicable settlement in sight, much as we tried, we decided to engage a prominent New York attorney, Mr Byron K. Kallan, to handle the case for us. Together with Lonny Chiu, they flew to Managua in Nicaragua where Chiu obtained his Canadian entry visa before moving on to Halifax, Nova Scotia. There, in the local maritime court, Evergreen counter-sued Worldwide Carriers for US$400,000.

The main bone of contention in the suits was Yugoslavia's form of government. The court held several open hearings during which the top brains in constitutional law and jurisprudence from the University of Halifax were invited to present their expert opinions. Legal arguments pertaining to the structure of Yugoslavia's government and its society, the electoral system and party politics, as well as the rights and obligations of the ordinary citizens were advanced and analysed. Lawyers representing the government of Panama were also present at the hearings. All the representations were consistent in the belief that Yugoslavia was indeed a communist country.

The legal proceedings dragged on for three months, during which Lonny Chiu appeared in court several times in his dual role as both plaintiff and defendant. The protracted hearings also took a heavy toll on *Central Trust* as she languished in Digby Port, without fuel and electricity. Deprived of freedom and work, the crew could only sit it out and hope for the best. It was, to put it mildly, a pathetic and heart-rending state of affairs.

Their plight attracted the sympathy of residents living in the vicinity of the port, who provided them with food and other daily necessities to help them get by. The compassion and care of the locals towards a bunch of stranded foreigners, who were but unwitting victims of circumstances, really touched the hearts of everyone.

When the verdict finally came, the court absolved Evergreen from blame, but found Worldwide Carriers guilty of breach of contract. Although it was adjudged that Worldwide Carriers pay Evergreen US$240,000 in compensation, we did not receive a penny in the end when the company promptly declared itself insolvent. There was really nothing valuable in its New York office that we could seize to recover some of the money. Worse, the owner of the company had meanwhile vanished without a trace.

All in all, *Central Trust* was stranded in Digby for just under four gruelling months, at huge costs to Evergreen in terms of both financial and manpower resources, not forgetting the intense emotional stress we had been subjected to.

But although we had won the battle, the war was not exactly over yet, as another high drama was just about to unfold, adding new twists to an already complex situation. What was at issue was the cargo of wood pulp that was aboard *Central Trust*, for which a bill of lading had been issued. Furthermore, Worldwide Carriers had already been paid two thirds of the ocean freight by the consignee.

With the court case all wrapped up, *Central Trust* was supposed to be free to leave Digby. But just as we were contemplating whether to off-load the wood pulp before we set sail, a Yugoslavian state-owned enterprise surfaced to claim ownership of the cargo, and insisted that it be delivered in accordance with the terms of the bill of lading.

As Worldwide Carriers had supposedly gone bust, I was afraid that we might run into more legal problems again unless we sorted out the mess quickly. Considering that Evergreen and the Yugoslavian customer were both innocent victims of Worldwide Carriers' unscrupulous act, another round in protracted and costly legal battle would not serve anyone's interests. Besides, there was no guarantee this time that Evergreen would win the case. In the interest of a fair settlement, a compromise was reached between the two parties, the gist of which was:

- That the consignee settled the outstanding one-third in ocean freight directly with Evergreen.
- That the cargo be shipped to Trieste, an Italian port situated near the border of Yugoslavia, where it would be discharged into the custody of the owner.

Thus, after refuelling, *Central Trust* left the Canadian port of Digby on 14 July 1970 and headed for Trieste. But the problem was far from over yet.

Just as *Central Trust* was about to discharge the cargo, which was estimated to take nine days from 28 July to 5 August 1970, the proprietor of Worldwide Carriers appeared out of the blue in Trieste. He had purposely flown in from New York, in the vain hope that he would secure a favourable hearing in Italy compared to the judgement passed down by the Canadian court. He sought US$100,000 in compensation from Evergreen this time round, failing which, he threatened, he would sue. But I flatly refuted his dubious claim, in the wake of which he successfully applied to the court in Trieste to have the vessel arrested, pending the outcome of the court decision. That was on 5 August 1970.

This sudden turn of events plunged the crew of the vessel into a tailspin once again. Our Taipei office promptly despatched the Canadian Court's written judgement to our attorney in Trieste, who in turn spent a week translating the documents into the Italian language. Based on the evidence we tendered, the court in Trieste was able to establish the facts of the case and eventually cleared Evergreen from any wrongdoing, thus freeing *Central Trust* from her unwarranted detention.

From the time the vessel was detained to the day the court exonerated Evergreen from blame on 31 August 1970, one whole month had elapsed, a situation we could well have done without.

After her release from Italy, *Central Trust* immediately set sail for France where she docked in Sete before heading via the Strait of

Gibraltar for the Indian port of Daman to pick up a cargo of Bombay-bound fertilisers. From Bombay (now Mumbai) the vessel headed south towards Goa, where she uplifted a shipload of mineral ore before making her way back to Kaohsiung where she finally arrived on 4 December 1970.

That Central Trust should run into so many problems plunged what was then a somewhat financially wobbly Evergreen into a seemingly bottomless abyss. Fun though it now appears to jog down the memory lane and reminisce about those eventful days, the experience undoubtedly left in me a bitter aftertaste; I could in fact liken it to a thorough baptism in the choppy world of shipping.

Looking back, within the two years after Evergreen was formed in1968, we were confronted with so many unexpected problems that we found ourselves teetering on the brink of ruin on several occasions.

On the one hand, the financial situation of the company was so tight that I literally had to knock on the doors of banks every other day. On the other hand, we were struggling to make headway with our nascent transoceanic liner operations, which we had launched without the benefit of an existing customer base. As if these were not enough, we had to put up with the antics of the formidable freight conference.

We were literally struggling to make ends meet in those days. While we could not afford to buy any new vessels to add to our existing operations, the second-hand ones we had posed one problem after another in rapid succession. The three most serious incidents involving Ever Island, Ever State and Central Trust, for instance, all happened within a short space of three months.

Because of my hectic schedule and the enormous stress I was under at that time, I lost a lot of weight within a short period. In bed at night, I often found myself tossing and turning, racking my brains and constantly worrying about the future of the company. Overwhelmed by a succession of setbacks, and with nobody to turn to, I could only console myself and suffer in silence. It was a feeling of hopelessness and of torment that was beyond the comprehension of anyone else.

Honestly, had my will not be strong enough then, I would certainly have yielded to the unremitting pressure. But thankfully, I had the courage of my conviction to see the troubled days through and to establish a kingdom of my own in the turbulent world of shipping.

From steam to diesel

The three old vessels that Evergreen deployed on its Middle East route – *Ever Island*, *Ever Light* and *Ever Spring* – all had steam-turbine engines with very high fuel consumption. They were not particularly suitable for long-range operations. Moreover, the emerging trend across the shipping industry at the time was towards the adoption of diesel-engine vessels. In view of the long-term development potential of Evergreen and to bolster our competitive position in the market, I felt we should also go for the more efficient diesel-powered engines in the future.

In the meantime, our Middle East liner services were beginning to show a steady growth in the volume of freight carried, as well as a gradual improvement in yield and profits. We also consolidated our fleet along the way with the acquisition in 1971 of two diesel-engine ships, *Ever Fortune* and *Ever Lasting*.

With the Middle East operations firmly on track, I switched my attention to other possibilities in a bid to widen the scope of our services. But because it was a fleet of old and rickety vessels that we operated, I did not think we could compete with other carriers, especially when it came to lucrative routes. All things considered, the Central and South American market, I reckoned, presented the best bet for us to embark on our second liner operations with more than an even chance of success.

There were no direct shipping links between Taiwan and Central and South Americas (the Caribbean) in those days, and most of the cargo had to be transhipped via Japan, which invariably gave rise to a high incidence of damage to the shipments. Moreover, the vessels often made unscheduled stops at other ports in the USA and Canada in order to pick up more cargo, with the result that the voyages were unusually long and the frequency erratic.

Furthermore, members of the freight cartel, particularly the Japanese carriers, had long had a stranglehold on this route, exacting a high price from shippers in the form of exorbitant freight charges. The prohibitive costs of shipping gradually eroded the competitive edge of Taiwan's manufactured goods in the Caribbean market.

It was thus not surprising that Taiwan shippers greeted with enthusiasm Evergreen's bid to launch a Central/South America liner service in the shape of an independent carrier, although at the back of their minds they were also wondering if we had the staying power. The last thing shippers wanted to happen was a situation in which we were driven out of the market by the powerful freight conference and they then had to go back to the cartel members to beg for space again.

Evergreen had by then established quite a formidable customer base, as well as a good reputation in the Middle East trade. But we were far from complacent despite our early success. On the contrary, everybody, from the top down to the peon in the office, was all the more determined to carve out an equally impressive victory in our second foray into liner operations. As one would expect, the freight conference was not about to accord us an easy passage into the market.

To allay their doubts and misgivings, and to drum up long-term support at the same time, we intensified our efforts in reassuring customers of our absolute commitment in this undertaking. We also tried our utmost to convince them of the benefit of a direct and more economical service, which would go a long way towards helping them penetrate the Central/South American market.

Evergreen was able to secure a government shipbuilding loan in September 1971, which enabled it to commission Japan's Hayashikane Shipyard to build a 15,000-tonne vessel, *Ever Safety*, in preparation for the launch of our Caribbean services. My plan was to deploy a total of four ships on this route, with the acquisition of three second-hand diesel-engine vessels to complement *Ever Safety*.

Ever Safety heads for the Americas

Following the handing over of *Ever Safety* to Evergreen in early 1972, the vessel left Japan for Taiwan where she was to pick up a load of cargo before setting off for Central/South Americas on her maiden voyage. In commemoration of *Ever Safety's* first appearance in Keelung Port on 13 February 1972, a grand reception was held at the passenger ferry terminal, during which guests were taken on a tour of the vessel.

The Caribbean is a collection of mostly island nations. When we first started out on this sector, the ports that we took in en route included Cristobal (Panama), Curacao (Dutch Antilles), La Guaira (Venezuela), Port of Spain (Trinidad & Tobago), San Juan (Puerto Rico), Santo Domingo (Dominica), and Kingston (Jamaica). We also accepted transhipment cargo that was destined for other ports in the area.

To maximise capacity utilisation, we collected as much general cargo as possible in Taiwan, Hong Kong, Japan and Korea on our outbound journeys, while on the return leg, we carried mostly phosphor ore and fertilisers. Because we were the first native Taiwan carrier to offer a direct liner service to the Caribbean region, defeating the foreign players at their own game, our operations quickly gained the widespread recognition of many a shipper in Taiwan.

In a further bid to strengthen our sales effort, I personally led the then vice-president of Evergreen, Yeh Fu-hsing, and our shipping agent on a comprehensive tour of the countries in this far-flung territory. Places included on our itinerary were Panama, Dominica, Puerto Rico, Jamaica, Dutch Antilles, and Venezuela, among others. Everywhere we went, we called on the offices of all the major local shippers.

While we were in Colon, Panama, we went to see an important shipper, Mr Abraham Kardonski. A businessman of Jewish extraction, he imported mainly partially knocked-down electrical goods from Taiwan and Japan, which he then assembled in Colon's FTZ (Free Trade Zone). We tried to promote Evergreen's liner services, particularly our Central/South American sailing, to him as it dovetailed with his shipping needs.

We had arranged to meet in a hotel and although the ensuing discussion went on for hours on end, in fact well past midnight on that particular occasion, we could not agree on a freight rate that was mutually acceptable. Finally, Mr Kardonski went for broke and told me rather straightforwardly that another shipping company had offered him a much more attractive deal, and if I really could not reduce my rate any further, he would give his business to the other guy.

I could not but feel disappointed even if I did not show it. Nevertheless, I told Mr Kardonski that if he really felt our rates were so high that he could not make any profit out of his shipments, he should by all means take his custom to the other carrier. It was not possible for us to match his freight idea, I said.

Still, I was not about to give up trying just yet. I asked Mr Kardonski to reconsider his position, given the unparalleled convenience that Evergreen's services offered, which would translate into considerable savings for him in terms of both time and money. I also assured him that our rates were fair, as I would never enrich myself at the expense of other people. My personal philosophy in business, I explained to him, was to always work towards a sustainable and mutually beneficial relationship in the long run.

To my relief, Kardonski relented. But the catch was, he would let Evergreen handle his Taiwan-origin shipments only, nothing more. I responded by telling him that as a major shipper, he would enjoy lower freight rates and better quality of services all round if he were to deal exclusively with Evergreen.

"Why don't you give it a try and leave everything, including your cargo ex Japan and other countries, to us to handle?" I ventured.

Our conversation dragged on for a lot longer before Mr Kardonski finally bought my ideas. I am glad to say that he has since remained a loyal customer of Evergreen and we also became good friends along the way. Looking back, the unstinting support of shippers like Mr Kardonski and numerous others over the years certainly contributed immeasurably towards the growth and success of Evergreen today.

A growing Evergreen

The load factor on our Caribbean services continued to show an upward trend from day one, culminating in a situation in which almost every single voyage was laden to the brim. We were also able to solicit more of the high-yield general cargo. At the same time, our Middle East services were not doing too badly either. Overall thus, it was a satisfactory state of affairs, as business continued to grow unabated. Worth mentioning here is that, compared to now, the average freight rate in those days was very much higher, with each ton of cargo fetching as much as US$60 to US$70, thus enabling shipping companies to reap a handsome return on each round trip.

With the labour pains and teething problems behind us, Evergreen's operations moved ahead on an even keel. Although our age-old vessels tended to break down frequently in the early days, they were relatively trouble-free in later years, especially following a thorough revamp of the fleet.

Generally speaking, compared to nowadays, the environment in which shipping companies operated was vastly different in the past, what with practically all the lucrative routes firmly in the grip of one freight conference or the other. Given the situation, the eventual outcome of Evergreen's bid to carve out the Middle East and Caribbean markets was bound to impinge heavily on the future prospects of the company. In retrospect, I am truly gratified to note that in the midst of adversities, Evergreen showed unparalleled courage and resolve in overcoming the might of the freight cartel, and emerged in triumph to lay an even firmer foundation for growth and prosperity in the long run.

A good friend found

Frankly speaking, had it not been for Mr Pei Tsun-fan, a member of Taiwan's legislature who has since passed on, *Ever Safety*, the first new vessel in Evergreen's fleet, would at best have remained a pipe dream.

The government implemented several rounds of the shipbuilding programme in the early years with a view to developing a sizeable merchant fleet quickly. The scheme called for a certain quota of vessels to be built in each round.

By virtue of a mainland Chinese-dominated Transport Ministry in those days, indigenous Taiwanese carriers seldom, if ever, benefited from the scheme. Priorities were invariably accorded to provincial shipping companies from the mainland or to those who had the all-important connections or "guanxi". As a matter of fact, ministry officials often colluded with well-connected shipping companies to decide in advance the requirements of the latter before the authority ostensibly announced the plan publicly. This probably explained Evergreen's apparent lack of success in this area in the earlier days.

But I was fortunate enough to bump into Pei Tsun-fan at the right time. Friends had introduced me to him while we were having dinner one evening in a restaurant that he also patronised.

Pei had been a mayor of Kunming in Yunnan before he moved to Taiwan where he became a member of the Transport Commission in the Legislative Yuan. Told by mutual friends that I was very much involved in shipping, he casually asked me if I needed his help in any way.

"Most certainly there is," I blurted out, half in jest. "We have always wanted to build a vessel or two with financial assistance from the government, but no matter how hard we tried, we never succeeded."

After a brief pause, Pei said he would see how he could assist and that he would be in touch with me again very soon to find out more about the nature of my problems.

Frankly, Pei's promise of help did not register in my mind at all; I did not think he was being serious. But to my pleasant surprise, he kept his word and looked me up at my office a few days later to have a better understanding of the problems I was up against.

I later came to know that when Pei was still mayor of Kunming, he and the then secretary-general of the Kuomintang, Zhang Qun, were forced to flee the Chinese mainland together after the KMT troops were overrun by the communist forces at the end of the civil war in 1949. Zhang Qun's son, Ji-zheng, was now Taiwan's Minister of Transport.

Immediately after our meeting, Pei went straight to see Zhang Ji-zheng who promised to look into the matter urgently. True to their words, Evergreen did not have to wait very long before it was given a loan which it promptly employed to build *Ever Safety*.

I honestly did not expect a high-ranking bureaucrat like Pei to show any concern for the plight of Taiwan's private shipping companies. Come to think of it, he was a tailor-made gift, a blessing to Evergreen, for without him things would probably have been very different for us today. He actually did not have to go to such great lengths to ensure that we got what we wanted. I still recalled all the envy and jealousies that our loan award stirred up among both friends and foes alike.

Going by the social norms in those days, we were obliged to give Pei a "hongbao", a gratuity of sorts, in return for his invaluable help. But to my astonishment, he flatly refused to accept a penny, saying that he had not done anything worthwhile to deserve such a reward. Considering the prevalence of corruption and cronyism in Taiwan at the time, Pei's honesty and uprightness really stood out in the crowd.

The next best thing we could do was to invite him and his wife to grace the occasion of the launch of *Ever Safety* in Japan. There was no denying that Pei was largely instrumental in bringing about the fruition of Evergreen's dream to acquire a new vessel, and his presence would add a special meaning to the celebration. Following his retirement from the civil service some time later, I made him an advisor to Evergreen Line, a position he held until the time of his death.

Flag of convenience

Taiwan was under martial law in those early days and the government imposed many restrictions on businesses, among which the control of foreign exchange transactions was the most stringent. As a result, shipping companies faced numerous constraints in their operations, and Evergreen was no exception. This was why we deliberately started out in overseas markets, where the overall environment was more conducive to operate in, before making an appearance on home ground.

A large part of Evergreen's fleet, for example, had been flying the Panamanian flag of convenience from the outset. This was not because I am a lesser patriot than my fellow countrymen but, more pragmatically, Panama happens to be a nation that offers an open ship's registry, which is one of most critical preconditions in determining the ultimate success or otherwise of any shipping operations.

The term "flag of convenience" primarily refers to merchant ships that are registered in the nationality other than that of their country of origin. The biggest advantage of such a practice is that, apart from the nominal registration fees and some taxes that are payable, owners are not liable for any other forms of dues or levies, nor are they bound by international crewing standards. The net result is that the running costs of these carriers, whose day-to-day operations are not necessarily constrained in any way, are drastically reduced.

Indeed, more than anything, it is for the specific purpose of keeping crew-related expenses low that Japanese and American carriers also choose to fly the ubiquitous flag of convenience. As for countries like Liberia and Panama, which offer open registries, they also benefit from this modus operandi in that their treasuries derive substantial revenue annually from these activities, over and above the investments carriers usually pump into the local economy.

Taiwan was comparatively undeveloped in the early days, as a result of which it was totally devoid of any international recognition. Foreign financial institutions were reluctant to lend to Taiwan-flagged carriers due primarily to the misguided perception that Taiwanese-owned companies were prone to defaulting on their loans. Domestic banks were not of much help to private enterprises either; their conservative management style together with cumbersome internal red tapes only served to worsen the financial woes of businessmen. It was for these very reasons that a large part of Evergreen's fleet elected to fly the international flag of convenience, while the company sought to establish a firm foundation for long-term growth and prosperity.

As a major Panamanian-flagged carrier, Evergreen contributes significantly to the state coffers of this Central American nation. In fact, our association with the government of Panama dated all the way back to our formative years. Panama appreciate, indeed value deeply, Evergreen's active participation in its economy, which goes a long way towards promoting the well-being of everyone in the country.

[4]

The Container Revolution

Evergreen Line capitalised on the dramatic transformation of marine transportation to consolidate its emerging position in the world of liner shipping. Yet, while its remarkable success was quickly extolled, the amount of perseverance and courage, which underpinned it, had gone largely unrecognised.

Prior to 1971, the entire Evergreen fleet comprised mostly second-hand turbine-engine vessels such as *Central Trust*, *Ever Glory*, *Ever Island*, *Ever State* (disposed of in 1970), *Ever Light*, *Ever Ocean* and *Ever Spring*. They were dubbed Evergreen's "first-generation" fleet.

But in July and September of 1971 respectively, two relatively old diesel-engine ships, *Ever Fortune* and *Ever Lasting*, were acquired. Their debut heralded the beginning of Evergreen's shift to diesel-fuel technology. Evergreen's armada was further enhanced by the purchase of additional second-hand diesel-powered general-cargo ships – *Ever Lucky*, *Ever Nobility*, *Ever Welfare*, *Ever Beauty* and *Ever Bright* – between 1972 and 1973. They were the "second-generation" fleet.

Generally speaking, older vessels are more prone to breakdowns, which usually entail costly repairs and maintenance at frequent intervals. As a result, it is difficult, if not impossible, to control overall operational efficiency.

Good tools, as they say, are a prerequisite for the successful execution of a job. Similarly, a well-planned service has to be complemented by appropriate hardware if its intended mission were to be realised.

In the earlier years, every time just as Evergreen was about to embark on a new venture, fortuitous breakdowns of its vessels would invariably occur, thus disrupting operations and causing the company to fall short of success for lack of proper hardware. From a long-term perspective, therefore, building new ships was a fundamental requirement towards attaining a smooth and efficient operation.

Lack of financial resources, however, was not the only constraint stifling our ambition at the time. We were also not sufficiently acquainted with Marubeni to ask them for a shipbuilding loan. Equally bleak were our prospects for obtaining government shipbuilding incentives. Given the situation, our operations continued to be stagnated.

Although the government's shipbuilding incentive programme was already several phases into its implementation, we only managed to get one of our many applications approved, which was for the construction of a multi-purpose general-cargo ship. Evergreen took delivery of the vessel, *Ever Safety*, on 31 January 1972. In the ensuing years, as Evergreen grew from strength to strength, it embarked on a programme of self-financed newbuildings, which enabled the ageing first-generation turbine-powered vessels to be gradually retired.

Originally, my plan had called for the successive construction of five P-class general-cargo ships, which were to be deployed in the liner trades. However, just after contracts for the building of *Ever Pioneer* and *Ever Promoter* were inked in September 1972, I had had the uncanny feeling that something was amiss. I was awakened to the realisation that the global shipping industry was trending towards large-scale containerisation. Considering the 20-year useful life span of a general-cargo vessel, Evergreen would invariably lag behind competitors should it continue to build such kinds of ships. Containerisation, I thus reckoned, was the viable option I had to aim for.

A paradigm shift in transportation

The evolution from general-cargo vessels to full-container ships could well be hailed as a rebirth of sorts in shipping terms. It was a window of opportunity that I fully capitalised on, a move that was to have a profound impact on the later developments of Evergreen.

I have always been a habitual reader of all kinds of professional maritime books since the early stage of my seafaring career. But I had a particularly ravenous appetite for the latest news and development on container shipping as I could foresee then that this mode of transportation was to be the trend of the future.

The post-World War II era saw a boom in international commerce and industry. Increased trade flows in raw materials and other types of goods resulted in an unprecedented demand for shipping and logistics services. The main beneficiary in this turn of events was the shipping companies, prompting them to move towards the development of dedicated as well as bulk carriers.

The ensuing rise in shipping tonnage was, however, not met with a corresponding improvement in port facilities around the world to cater to the growing demand. As a result, severe port congestion became a ubiquitous phenomenon in those days.

On the other hand, shippers were clamouring for better handling and greater security for their consignments, especially those high-value items, to prevent theft and pilferage. In general, the extent of damage and loss sustained by cargo on liner vessels ranged from five to ten per cent, although in some cases, it could reach as high as 30 per cent. Even though insurance did provide some degree of protection, it did not come cheap to cargo owners. It was against this background that container ships, which offered both security and convenience, emerged as a major force to be reckoned with.

But the concept of container shipping was not widely embraced in the earlier years, due as much to the conservative approach of many carriers as to the lack of proper port and related facilities. Personally, however, having followed the trend for some time, I was inclined to believe that containerisation, with its greater efficiency and productivity, would one day revolutionise the entire shipping industry, in the wake of which many countries around the world would be compelled to establish dedicated container ports and terminals to keep up with demand.

While on the one hand I was working on further expanding Evergreen's liner services, I also kept a watchful eye on the pace of containerisation in the shipping fraternity of the more advanced countries. As development in container transportation facilities gained momentum, goods of every conceivable kind, including general cargo of all shapes and sizes, machinery, steel products, perishable items, even liquid, gaseous and bulk commodities were increasingly moved in purpose-built containers. An added advantage with containers was that, come rain or shine, work could be carried out uninterrupted.

Through containerisation, not only were packing and handling of goods made simpler, and delivery time shortened, the incidents of damage to cargo and pilferage were also virtually eradicated completely. Moreover, shippers and consignees could enjoy the convenience of door-to-door services.

From what I had observed of the emerging trends, I strongly sensed that containerisation was beginning to draw the attention of the international shipping community. Predictably, the bulk of the goods resulting from growing world trade would be transported on container ships, gradually replacing the general-cargo liners.

The shipping community in Taiwan, however, remained undecided. The general perception at the time was that since the country's exports consisted primarily of low-value, labour-intensive goods, it seemed inappropriate to have them transported on container ships, which cost tens of millions of greenbacks each to build. Furthermore, it would take at least four vessels to mount a new container service, not considering the equally massive investments in boxes per vessel, as well as in truck chassis and related facilities. Compared to a general-cargo vessel, which had a price tag of around three to four million US dollars, the cost of container shipping was thus vastly out of proportion.

Nevertheless, Taiwan's robust economic growth and ballooning external trade seemed to bode well for the future of shipping. But should Evergreen continue to cling steadfastly to its old ways, instead of accelerating innovation by building up a fleet of container ships to meet changing market needs, it would eventually perish, I thought.

Timing was central to our future success or failure; missing one step would set us back a long way behind competitors. Likewise, if we allowed competition a head start, the hope of overtaking them later would be out of the question. It was thus against this backdrop that I decided to embark on the containerisation of Evergreen's fleet of vessels.

Winning Marubeni's support

To embark on a full-scale containerisation programme, foremost on my agenda was to discuss the matter with Japan's Marubeni, in the hope that they would share my bold vision and render the much needed support.

Evergreen Line was by then a sizeable company, and banks and trading houses jostled to offer their loan facilities. Nevertheless, I felt I should accord Marubeni the right of first refusal to arrange the financing in view of our long association and mutual understanding, as well as its thorough knowledge of our corporate history and culture. I would invite other financial institutions to participate in the loan syndication only if Marubeni had no objection.

But first, I needed to explain to Marubeni that I wanted to proceed with the building of only two of the five P-class general-cargo vessels originally on order, and which they were to finance. I told them that I wanted to switch the rest to container ships instead.

My proposal took Marubeni's executives by surprise.

"Container operation is not as easy as one might think." They told me, with a smile on their face. "Even here in Japan," they continued in the same breath, "the six shipping giants – MOSK, NYK, K Line, Showa Line, Japan Line and Y S Line – had to join forces to get the operations going, and you want to go it alone straightaway? Are you serious?"

I told them that I was dead serious; I did not want to miss out on this window of opportunity in anticipation of the global trend towards containerisation. It was, therefore, imperative that I grasped this chance of a lifetime.

After getting an earful from me, the executives hurried back to report the matter to their department heads, Mr Hosaka and Mr Nagasawa.

Mr Hosaka was shocked by what he had heard. "You can't be serious, can you?" he blurted out at me. But after much explanation and persuasion, the two gentlemen finally saw my point.

I gave them my observation and analysis of developments in the global shipping industry. Containerisation was an idea that had occurred to me a long time ago, but due to lack of capital during our start-up years, I was unable to pursue my ambition until after the company's operations had gone on track, and its financial position strengthened.

Container ships had already been around for some five years then. Further procrastination on my part would lead to increased difficulty in rallying the support of shippers, let alone compete with incumbent operators. Were I to miss the boat this time, I was certain there would not be a second chance.

My proposal eventually found its way into the office of Marubeni's managing director, Mr Fukumoto. Although his initial reaction was also one of surprise, I soon won him over. He nevertheless remained circumspect and proceeded to seek the counsel of the company's Transport Insurance Department.

Mr Sato and Mr Suda of the Transport Insurance Department were at the time responsible for farming out Marubeni's cargoes to various liner shipping companies for conveyance. Evergreen Line had not been able to secure any business from Marubeni for quite some time, mainly because Mr Hosaka (from the Marine Department) was not on good terms with both Mr Sato and Mr Suda.

Mr Fukumoto had deemed it necessary then to consult Mr Sato on Evergreen's containerisation plans. Owing to the relative ignorance of the Transport Insurance Department in shipping matters, it was not surprising that Mr Sato had nothing but contempt for Evergreen when Mr Fukumoto told him of our decision.

"Evergreen wants to follow in the steps of others to build container ships? Who do they think they are?" he sneered. "Even the world's major carriers, including Japan's, have not had it easy. Evergreen is a nondescript entity, what sort of container vessels do they want to build?"

Mr Sato's caustic remarks rendered Mr Fukumoto momentarily speechless. He felt I should discuss the matter with Mr Sato personally.

I recalled the powder-keg atmosphere that hung over our discussion, which quickly degenerated into a heated exchange between us. Mr Sato was vehemently against my views; he uttered some profanities and told me off straight in my face.

"You're dreaming!" he bellowed.

"You know next to nothing about shipping!" I shot back. "Tell me, how much do you understand about the future trend of the industry?"

"Help me, if you wish," I continued, firmly, "it's also fine with me if you don't. But I'll bet my bottom dollar with you that container shipping will be the in thing, and it'll be too little too late if I don't do something about it now!"

Mr Sato felt strongly that small-time Evergreen was ill-equipped to undertake container shipping; only the big shipping companies, in his opinion, had the resources to do so. Much as we tried, we failed to reach a mutual understanding, eventually forcing Mr Fukumoto to intercede and tell us to call it a day.

A meeting was held the next day between Mr Hosaka and the heads of the company's other relevant departments to discuss the Evergreen issue. Mr Hosaka explained that I was a strong-willed person who had accomplished much in the past, and that by virtue of my professionalism and uncanny foresight, it was unlikely that I would err in my judgement.

After much pondering and deliberation, it was finally agreed that Marubeni would endorse Evergreen's plans to construct container ships.

I was still in Japan when news of Marubeni's endorsement reached me, cheering me up no end.

"Heaven does not forsake those who persevere!" I murmured to myself.

That night, together with a few friends, we celebrated the outcome over a good many drinks, during which I also vowed to myself not to let any obstacles stand in the way of success.

Market survey begins in earnest

In the face of such a momentous strategic decision, I was deeply aware that our action plan had to be prudently and soundly thought out in order to assure our future success. To this end, it was of paramount importance that we undertake a diligent and comprehensive market survey without delay.

I established a container development task force in October 1972 to start gathering information and lay the groundwork. At the same time, I mobilised my shipping agents in Hong Kong, Singapore, Korea, Japan, and other places, to collect market intelligence.

In February 1973, a team of Evergreen's executives was despatched to the USA, and together with our sole agent in New York, they studied in detail the state of the container shipping industry, as well as current developments among leading shipping companies in the country. They visited the major ports of New York, Baltimore, Charleston, San Francisco, and Los Angeles to have a firsthand understanding of the berthing operations of container ships, as well as the availability of container terminal facilities, and the cost of doing business.

Information and data collected by the task force was promptly analysed and evaluated before a comprehensive business plan was produced.

As far as the choice of shipping route was concerned, we took the cue from the then prevailing market trends. The US trade, buoyed by exports of general cargo from the Far East to the Eastern and Western seaboards of America, was dubbed the world's most lucrative "Golden Route". Besides the usual general-cargo vessels that plied the route, the major carriers were literally falling over each other to also deploy their container ships on this trade.

Our feasibility study had revealed the still immense growth potential this particular route offered, based on which I decided to make the Far East-US East Coast sailing the first fully containerised liner service to be launched by Evergreen.

The US West Coast trade had to be relegated to second position in the meantime as it was already saturated with container services of the world's various mega-carriers. The situation would, however, be reviewed later depending on the outcome of our East Coast service.

With regard to the type of vessels to be deployed on the route, we planned to have four 600-TEU full-container ships built based on our considerations of such factors as market response, fuel efficiency and crewing requirements, among others. Other complementary facilities like containers and truck chassis had to be acquired too.

For the purpose of differentiating the various types of vessels that would be deployed in the fleet in the future, the English name of each of these first four ships was to begin with the alphabet "S", with a view to classifying them as the "S-type" vessel. This standard of naming the ships was to be strictly adhered to thereafter for all newbuildings.

In addition, in order to dovetail with the impending launch of the US East Coast service, I had the company's existing fleet of general-cargo vessels streamlined to pave the way for us to embark on the arduous task of developing new liner services.

The entire market survey was conducted in several stages over a period of two years, and at a staggering cost of US$1 million. Because Evergreen had no prior experience in container shipping, it was not a well-known name in this market then. As such, developing the business was anything but easy. We had to start virtually everything from scratch, paying undivided attention to every minute detail.

In August 1973, I personally led a study mission to the USA and the Caribbean region for a period of 40 days, where I tirelessly visited all the local shippers. Mr Hashimoto came along on this trip, and having seen how I conducted my business over the many days we were together, he was visibly impressed and felt very much assured by my commitment.

The dawn of the containerisation era saw an unparalleled sea change in the modus operandi of the entire marine transportation industry; whether it was conveyance by sea or by land, or port operations, dramatic transformations were vividly evident.

The inland haulage sector boomed with the times due to the pivotal role it played in complementing the demands of container shipping. The fusion of these two modes of delivery produced several notable advantages – simpler packing requirements, negligible theft and pilferage to cargo, shorter delivery time, and ease of customs inspection – thus further enhancing the flexibility of containerised transport operations.

In a move to ensure the quality and efficiency of both our sea and land conveyances, the company set up Evergreen Transport Corporation in September 1973. This brought the last of our preparations for the inland-leg in Taiwan to a close, setting the stage for the ushering in of our first container service. An electronic data-processing centre was also established with a view to fully computerise all aspects of the container operations.

Complex and capital-intensive, container shipping not only posed an immense challenge for Evergreen, it also had profound implications for the future well-being of the company. Thus, besides vigorously laying the groundwork in preparation for the launch, the company also specially trained up its sales personnel to educate Taiwanese shippers on the advantages and benefits of container shipping. Efforts were also stepped up to solicit both the outbound as well as inbound cargo of shippers, and to encourage them to containerise more of their shipments, thus boosting our customer base in the process.

As regards our overseas business development, marketing efforts in the Far East were far less onerous, due largely to the many years of cooperation between our branch offices and the local agents. Nevertheless, we still had to strengthen our capability in canvassing cargo more effectively, and to vigorously promote to the local shippers

Evergreen's maiden container service.

In the USA, on the other hand, besides appointing Hansen and Tidemann Incorporated as the sole agent, we also set up a representative office in New York, followed by the incorporation of a full-fledged company sometime later. The company was managed by high-calibre executives seconded from Evergreen's headquarters in Taiwan, whose responsibilities it was to oversee the container operations and to develop the local market.

Winning over foreign shippers

With the preparation for the launch of the full-container liner service almost complete, our people at Evergreen's headquarters in Taiwan were all raring to go, anticipating an easy victory in the US market. But alas, progress was not as smooth as we had expected.

In those days, foreign businessman made their annual pilgrimage to Taiwan during the peak buying season between the months of March and September; they descended on the country in droves to procure, or place orders for, manufactured goods.

In our bid to prospect for customers, Evergreen Line's business executives literally had their ears to the ground, eagerly trying to find out which hotels these foreigners were putting up in so that they could introduce Evergreen's shipping services, especially its soon-to-be-launched container sailing, to these potential customers.

Prior to this, our commercial representatives had already done the rounds of Taiwanese shippers who, because of our excellent relationships with them in the past, strongly endorsed Evergreen's effort to start the container service. As decisions relating to the choice of carriers for the shipment of goods from the Far East to the USA rested with the American buyers, our Taiwanese customers would kindly tip us off as to where their American clients were staying so that we could get in touch with them.

There were but few hotels of international standards in Taiwan in those days, and most of the overseas buyers chose to put up at the President Hotel whenever they were in town. Armed with nothing more than a good dose of zeal, our representatives would station themselves at the hotel lobby, eager to peddle Evergreen's shipping services to whoever looked like a prospective customer. Those executives who happened to have a prior list of the guests' names would call them up to try to get an appointment to see them.

Much to our surprise, however, most of these businessmen did not even want to take the phone calls of our staff, presumably because they had not met each other before, let alone accept any appointment for a meeting. No matter how hard our people tried, they were unable to get their foot in the door. Frankly, we did not expect such a poor response, and we naturally felt rather uneasy about it.

After all, since these buyers had come all the way to Taiwan, Evergreen's home turf, to source their annual requirements for manufactured products, there could not be a better opportunity for us to plug Evergreen's services to them. If we could not get to see them while they were in town, hopes of carrying their cargo would all but evaporate once they had gone home.

After much agonising, we finally came up with an innovative idea to see if we could break down this subtle wall of resistance. We would present to targeted customers, via the hotel staff, gift hampers or bouquets bearing the business cards of our sales people. Our efforts proved fruitful; these businessmen were pleasantly surprised by our gesture and called the office to express their appreciation.

Seizing this not-to-be-missed opportunity, our sales people promptly asked to meet up with them, which they readily agreed to this time round. The idea had worked, and beautifully too.

Evergreen's front-liners at the time comprised sales personnel like Frank Hsu, George Hsu, Thomas Chen, Richard Huang, Marcel Chang, Owen Wu and Bronson Hsieh, among others, all of whom are currently senior executives with the ranks of vice-president and above in the Evergreen group of companies.

While most of our executives were all geared up to take on the challenge, a minority, however, remained sceptical. Among this small bunch of cynics was the then president, Lonny Chiu, who had in fact opposed the containerisation plan all along.

His feeble excuse was that the project was fraught with too many risks and uncertainties. Needless to say, Chiu's non-committal attitude upset me no end. He had learnt so much about shipping from me over the years, and yet he could not understand my grand design for Evergreen.

Chiu had personally seen me painstakingly overcome successive setbacks to build up Evergreen from scratch. He was thus perhaps of the opinion that, with what we had already accomplished, we should just add a few more new vessels to the existing fleet and maintain a satisfactory performance; why go into container shipping at all?

But I had loftier aspirations. I was determined to seize this opportunity and scale new peaks. Otherwise, the day would come when we could only stand helplessly by and let competitors annihilate us.

Fearing that Evergreen's attempt to proceed with the containerisation programme would come to grief, and would thus swallow up its accumulated earnings, these gentlemen asked to withdraw their shares in the company.

This handful of cadres had been with me since Central Marine days, and had followed me to Evergreen. I had, out of my own initiative, given them free shares in the company in recognition of their service. Since they did not share my long-term vision, I thought it best that they leave. I thus paid them off in cash based on the amount of shares they had originally received. With this unsavoury episode behind us, we could now concentrate our efforts on getting the launch ready.

I was fully aware of the effects of shippers' first impression of Evergreen's service on long-term cooperation possibilities. Hence, I urged our executives to make sure that they were sincere and earnest towards customers, and to provide a consistent level of service, even to shippers with only one or two tonnes of cargo. We should never forget the unequivocal support of cargo owners even before our container service had taken off. Such was the service ethos that Evergreen had always emphasised.

Prior to the launch, I despatched Kuo Shiuan-yu (he is currently the chairman of Evergreen Sky Catering Corporation) off to the USA to oversee the preparatory work there. I reiterated to him not to overlook even the smallest detail so that customers were able to receive their cargo without any delay.

I felt that since this was Evergreen's first full-container scheduled sailing, it would be sensible to establish our own unique brand of practical and quality service. As the shipments cargo-owners had entrusted to us on this maiden voyage were in a way meant to test our standard of service, we could not afford to commit any blunder, resulting in inconvenience or dissatisfaction among customers.

In addition, I specifically instructed our people in the US office to prime their American colleagues in such areas as telephone etiquette, conversational skills, documentation, vessel space allocation, and general logistics, among other things, to ensure that they discharged their responsibilities with sincerity and dedication.

The christening ceremony for Evergreen's first full-container ship, *Ever Spring*, was due to be held in Japan on 26 April 1975. Although my wife and I were scheduled to attend the function, we had to cancel the trip at the eleventh hour due to the unexpected death of my mother.

On 17 July 1975, *Ever Spring* set sail on its maiden journey from the Far East to the East Coast of the USA, marking the official launch of Evergreen's first dedicated container liner service. It also made Evergreen the first carrier in Taiwan to offer such a service.

Ever Spring was delivered at a time when the market was still in the throes of the global oil crisis. The shipyard seized the opportunity to unilaterally jack up the construction cost of the vessel by one-third, citing price hikes of building materials as the reason behind their demand.

I strongly objected to the shipyard's request, as I was certain that the construction materials had been procured before the onset of inflation. Moreover, we had already agreed on the vessel's price, which was clearly stipulated in the contract. It was thus most unreasonable of the shipbuilder to ask for such a huge increase at this juncture. It would perhaps have been a different matter if we were talking about a vessel that had yet to be built. It took several rounds of negotiation before we compromised on a smaller increase, thereby bringing the matter to an amicable settlement.

Riding out the oil crisis

The maiden voyage had a dismal performance; almost every shipper had only a meagre one or two containers of cargo to offer. The oil crisis had at the time precipitated a global economic recession that drastically shrank the supply of cargo. We incurred a colossal loss of US$500,00 on this inaugural sailing alone.

This poor performance notwithstanding, we were fortunate that preparations were exceptionally well coordinated at both our American and Taiwan ends. *Ever Spring* set sail on schedule, calling punctually at various US ports, and all the critical services supported and complemented each other seamlessly. We counted our blessings. Overall, despite the financial losses, we did well, winning customers' trust in the quality of our services.

The economic turmoil brought about by the energy crisis had caused an otherwise thriving international trade to falter. For the first time, foreign trade in Taiwan and other Asian countries posted negative growth. Businesses of shipping companies went into a tailspin, triggering a huge surplus in shipping tonnage around the world.

Faced with a cargo crunch and a sluggish global shipping market, many freight conference lines operating on the Far East-US trade broke ranks and deserted the alliance; they engaged in vicious price wars in a bid to survive.

When Evergreen first started out on this route, there were merely three to four non-conference operators plying the trade, with the freight rate remaining at a relatively stable level. In a little less than a month, however, the scene changed considerably as more than twenty erstwhile conference carriers joined the fray. One could thus easily imagine the extent and ferocity of the competition that ensued.

Fortunately for Evergreen, we had, during the preliminary planning stages, taken into account a myriad of crucial factors such as the nascent state of containerisation in the industry, untapped sources of cargo, as well as potential competition posed by other major carriers in the world. The main considerations in the design of our container ships then were market demand and return on investments. These full-container vessels incorporated features like fuel efficiency, optimal cargo-carrying capacity and economy of speed, but at costs, which were comparatively lower than their larger and more powerful counterparts in the industry.

Because these vessels were diesel-powered, we reaped significant savings in fuel costs. This factor not only gave us a competitive edge over rival carriers, it also abated the impact of the oil crisis on Evergreen Line.

In the past, shipping companies tended to favour faster and more powerful vessels, which were costly and uneconomical. Although Evergreen ran right smack into the oil crisis in the midst of its containerisation programme, it emerged from it unscathed, proof that it had done its homework thoroughly.

The shipping industry, as I recalled, had scoffed at our move into full-container service. They reckoned that we grossly lacked the requisite operational capability and a proper concept. In truth, Evergreen had carried out a comprehensive and detailed feasibility study, even to the extent of designing our S-type container ships with a built-in flexibility to deal with fluctuating demands.

In other words, if, due to fierce competition between various carriers in the major markets, Evergreen was unable to mount the US service, these 646-TEU vessels could be redeployed on either the coastal or regional container routes, or they could serve as feeder vessels for other container lines.

If, however, the freight market stayed buoyant and the prospects were good, the capacity of each of these vessels could be enlarged, as had been provided for during the construction stage, by means of a "jumbo" process to cater to rising demand. It was a practice that enabled shipping companies to react swiftly to changing market conditions, besides reducing the start-up costs of a newly launched container service.

Through experience and an unending search for new and

innovative ideas, I was able to contribute meaningfully to the ingenious designs of Evergreen's new series of vessels in the ensuing years, thereby enabling our fleet to always maintain a high level of competitiveness in the global shipping market.

US West Coast service takes off

Although the maiden voyage from the Far East to the US East Coast did not enjoy a full shipload, winning shippers' trust and confidence in our service more than made up for our initial disappointment. The second sailing fared better and by the third, the vessel was filled to capacity. The performance has since remained consistent.

In the wake of Evergreen's creditable achievement in the newly launched container liner operations, shippers began to clamour for a similar service to the US West Coast.

As a matter of fact, I had, in March 1976, not long after the Far East-US East Coast trade was launched, set up shop in the US West Coast region of California to start gathering data for a market research.

Following umpteen rounds of deliberations, I felt that the time was ripe for us to mount a service to the US West Coast. Hence, in October of the same year, I deployed *Ever Spring* on this route, marking the start of a regular full-container service from the Far East to the West Coast of the USA.

Within a matter of months of its launch, this service attracted a dedicated following, drawing an endless supply of freight from shippers. Its success, in my mind, was solely attributable to the solid foundation we had laid down earlier in our US East Coast trade.

As our business continued to grow unabated, cargo-space constraints began to surface on our S-type vessels. Although construction of our newbuildings was progressing according to schedule, the existing ships were barely able to accommodate the incessant stream of cargo coming our way.

To alleviate the problem, I decided to have the hull of our S-type vessels lengthened in a bid to boost the capacity of each ship from the original 646 boxes to 866 TEUs. In addition, as our crew members were by then already well trained and adept in their jobs, their numbers were reduced from 30 to 24 on each vessel. Meanwhile, construction of a new series of full-container ships proceeded non-stop.

In retrospect, the first year of our US East Coast operations was by far the most nerve-racking period in the history of Evergreen Line. This was not exactly surprising considering that the company had pinned its hopes for the future on the eventual outcome of its containerisation programme. Worse, the global energy crisis with its far-reaching repercussions had struck unexpectedly at a most inopportune time, when we had just invested so much of our financial and manpower resources in the project. Faced with the situation then, it was imperative that everybody in the company, from the top management downward, pulled in the same direction and resolved strongly to overcome the adversities together.

Fortunately, in little more than over a year, we saw a rebound in sea-borne commerce. The fact that Evergreen's container service had been able to weather the storm only served to consolidate its position as a reliable operator.

With the US West Coast trade firmly established, Evergreen Line's container services entered into a period of consistent growth. In the meantime though, break-bulk and general-cargo carriers were experiencing a rapid decline in business as a result of shifting market trends, and they had no choice but to containerise their services. But Evergreen's business was already miles ahead by then.

Evergreen Line's unparalleled feat in carving out two full-container liner services within a short span of one to two years not only earned the company the recognition of shippers in the Far East and America, its reputation also spread quickly further afield to the shipping community in Europe.

New directions for container services

Following the launch of our Central/South America liner services, my original plan was to embark on a regular sailing on the Far East/ Red Sea/Mediterranean Sea route. The idea, however, had to be shelved when war broke out unexpectedly in Egypt in 1973, which led to the closure of the Suez Canal. The plans were revived in 1976 with the reopening of the Suez Canal, and in the June 1977, the general-cargo ship, *Ever Promoter*, was deployed on its inaugural voyage on this new route. In the meantime, preparations were underway to turn the trade into a containerised service.

I despatched a task force to Italy, France, Spain and other countries in the Mediterranean region to carry out an in-depth study of the facilities present in the various container ports there, as well as to evaluate the related costs of operations in these places. Ports in this region at the time were already moving slowly towards the container age, amid fierce competition between conference carriers scrambling to offer their containerised services on this trade.

Sensing that the market was ripe for picking, Evergreen decided to replace its general-cargo vessels plying this route with full-container ships, with a view to giving conference carriers a good fight. On 25 May 1978, the retrofitted container vessel, *Ever Humanity*, made her debut on the Far East/Red Sea/Mediterranean Sea route.

Prior to this, we had made several trips to the Caribbean and US Gulf region to evaluate the economic returns of operating a containerised liner service to Central and South America. We studied the sources of cargo in this market, as well as the availability of logistics support in the various container ports.

Evergreen built four 16,850-tonne M-type high-capability full-container ships in 1976. Each vessel was equipped with four container lift-on/lift-off cranes, which were designed to overcome the lack of quay-side gantry cranes in the container ports of Central and Latin Americas.

On 24 March 1977, *Ever Mercy*, the first of the four M-type vessels to be commissioned, set sail on its maiden journey on the Far East/ Caribbean Sea sector, marking the start of containerised services from the Far East to Central and South Americas.

The Far East/Arabian-Persian Gulf service was the first liner operations launched by Evergreen. In little more that a decade, the region's once moribund freight market was transformed into a bustling mecca in which a hundred odd carriers competed intensely for custom. This situation, coupled with the antiquated port infrastructure in the area, soon gave rise to severe congestion at these harbours; vessels often had to wait twenty or more days before loading and/or unloading could take place, making it virtually impossible to maintain their regular schedules. As a result, many general-cargo operators plying this trade were unable to provide a good service to their customers due to the long turnaround time of each trip. Against this background, I thus decided to temporarily suspend this service from March 1978 onwards, while we revamped our fleet of vessels.

Evergreen re-entered this service on 23 January 1979. *Ever Pioneer*, which had been retrofitted into a new-look containerised vessel, was deployed on the route, giving shippers in the Far East and Middle Eastern regions a good run for their money.

With it, Evergreen Line had accomplished its mission as it launched itself into a new era of fully containerised liner services. The rest, as they say, is history.

Total dedication to container shipping

As Evergreen's container-shipping services gathered momentum, and with the company's financial position firmly on track, general-cargo vessels, which were built earlier, were either phased out or converted into container ships. Fleet expansion policy henceforth was centred on building new-generation full-container vessels. As for those break-bulk carriers on lease to Showa Line, they were also disposed of later.

Between 1974 and 1976, Evergreen had five H-type break-bulkers constructed which were then leased out to the Japanese shipping line, NYK, on a time-charter basis.

Later, however, as a result of the slowdown in the bulk trade, these five vessels operated by NYK fared very poorly, prompting the Japanese carrier to seek an annulment of the charter contract with Evergreen. NYK's action was most unreasonable, considering that both parties had mutually agreed on the terms and conditions of the charter before the vessels were built. Now, out of the blue, NYK wanted to have the contract terminated prematurely.

Going by the terms of the agreement, Evergreen's position was legally tenable. I, nevertheless, consented to NYK's request. I recognised that the bulk market was actually going through a bad patch then, and NYK must have encountered some genuine problems if they had to ask me for help. Besides, it was never in my nature to make life difficult for other people. Thus, instead of carrying on with the time-charters, I decided to repossess the five vessels from NYK.

But because we were by then already moving in the direction of wholesale containerisation, we subsequently opted to convert these bulk vessels into full-container ships from September 1977 onwards.

Logically, Evergreen should thereafter have dedicated itself fully to operating container liner services. Yet in 1981, we commissioned Hakodate Shipyard in Hokkaido to construct six O-type break-bulk vessels.

Mr Hosaka, formerly with Marubeni, was then the president of Hakodate Shipyard, at a time when the global shipbuilding industry was in the doldrums. He approached me and expressed his desire to have an opportunity to construct Evergreen's vessels. Coincidentally, it was generally expected at the time that the bulk market was beginning to see an upturn and, as a gesture of goodwill to Mr Hosaka, I took the decision to have Hakodate build six bulk carriers for us.

These O-type vessels were later deployed on Evergreen Line's tramp services. But because the company's emphasis still revolved around its core full-container liner operations, and since the much anticipated boom in the bulk market turned out to be rather short-lived, I decided to mothball the tramps and had them converted into full-container ships.

I recalled the time when Evergreen's first vessel was being constructed, we were virtually a nondescript shipping company that did not warrant the attention of the big shipyards. However, as soon as we had attained prominence, these large shipbuilders began to beat a path to our doorsteps. How times had changed, I told myself.

Evergreen Line had never commissioned Mitsubishi Heavy Industries (MHI) to build any of its vessels in the past. Quite unexpectedly, they approached us of their own accord expressing their wish to be given a share of Evergreen's newbuilding contracts. Since Evergreen was (and still is) one of the world's largest container shipping companies, MHI reckoned it would be a slap in their face if they did not build any of our vessels.

"We weren't gutsy enough to approach such a huge shipyard like MHI to help build our vessels in the past as we were a virtual non-entity then." I rejoined, tongue-in-cheek. "Anyway, we don't usually go to a big hospital if we've got a minor ailment, do we?"

Nevertheless, I did not turn away MHI. On the contrary, we subsequently entrusted them to build many of our jumbo-sized vessels. Other than MHI, Evergreen also maintained long-standing collaborations with shipbuilders like Onomichi Shipyard, Hayashikane Shipyard and China Shipbuilding Corporation.

Hayashikane was considered the larger of the medium-sized shipbuilders in Japan in those days. But the recession in the global shipbuilding industry had taken a heavy toll on the company and its business saw a gradual decline. It even contemplated selling out at one point.

As soon as news of Hayashikane's intention began to make its rounds, a wave of panic swept through the company's employees, who feared for their jobs. The situation was not helped by the fact that Hayashikane was trying to negotiate a deal with a builder of fishing boats, which, if it should be consummated, would sound a death knell for the workers, whose skills lay in merchant shipbuilding.

The then president of Hayashikane, who was also the ex-section chief of the company's Ship Design Department, and a close acquaintance of mine, specially came to see me, in the hope that I would agree to acquire the shipyard and have it merged into Evergreen's organisation.

"There're so many big financial consortia in Japan which can easily take over your shipyard, why me?" I asked him, perplexed.

"Because Evergreen is trustworthy and reliable, that's why," came the reply, without any hint of insincerity, "and we've absolute confidence in you."

He went on to explain to me the plight facing the shipyard's workers. After due consideration, I accepted Hayashikane's proposition and acquired the shipyard in early 1992. Renamed Evergreen Shipyard Corporation, we began to revamp and rebuild the facility into a force to be reckoned with.

The Marubeni connection

Evergreen grew by leaps and bounds following the wholesale contain-erisation of its fleet. Catapulted to the forefront of the world's con-tainer shipping industry in so short a time, its remarkable achieve-ment was an obvious threat to other carriers. On this account, the president of NYK, Mr Kikuchi, deemed it useful to enlist the help of Mr Matsuo, Marubeni's president, urging him not to support Ever-green any further, lest the business of Japanese shipping lines should be adversely affected.

Mr Matsuo, nonetheless, felt that the ties between Marubeni and Evergreen were purely commercial in nature, not a patronising act on the part of his company, as some people had alleged. Besides, both parties had always enjoyed close collaboration.

"Kikuchi San, our relationship with Evergreen is not about giving them financial assistance or support or anything of that sort," he told Mr Kikuchi bluntly, unconvinced by his unreasonable demand.

"As a customer of Marubeni's, Evergreen has to pay interest on all the shipbuilding loans it took from us, just like the rest of our clients." Mr Matsuo continued. "Whether or not we want to do this business with Evergreen is our sole prerogative based on our own evaluation; it has absolutely nothing to do with NYK."

The truth was, Evergreen's spectacular transformation had taken Marubeni by surprise. Although they knew with certainty that I was a seasoned professional in the shipping industry, little did they envisage that we would one day rise to become the world's foremost container shipping company. In a way, Evergreen's phenomenal success gave Marubeni a deep sense of honour and satisfaction.

Mr Matsuo told me later that he was actually somewhat doubtful of my ability to see the overly ambitious containerisation plans through when I first mooted the subject to him. However, he had nothing but admiration and praises for us when he saw Evergreen's unremitting growth, which even surpassed the initial target I had set.

Mr Sato, formerly with Marubeni's Marine Insurance Department and an erstwhile detractor of our containerisation bid, had since risen to become head of the company's shipping department, at a time when Evergreen's achievement had started to attract global attention. Thus, when I bumped into him later, he kept saying to me that it was beyond his wildest imagination that our bold plans actually came to pass.

"It would have been too little too late by the time you come to your realisation!" I told him.

The hand-in-glove collaboration between Evergreen and Marubeni had long been a subject of great interest and speculation to the outside world. Rumour had it that Evergreen was bankrolled by the Japanese, and that I had married the daughter of Marubeni's president, which had accounted for the meteoric rise of our business.

Evergreen was but a virtual nonentity during its formative years at a time when Marubeni was already one of Japan's trading juggernauts. Considering the lofty position of a company's president, there was no way that I would have met Mr Matsuo, what with my modest status then, let alone talk about marrying his daughter.

Moreover, Marubeni was a highly reputable "sogoshosha", and a public-listed company to boot, with more than a million shareholders, many of whom were financial institutions. Being a prestigious, blue chip company, it bore a heavy fiduciary responsibility towards all its shareholders. From this wider perspective thus, even if I had a relationship with a president's daughter, Evergreen need not necessarily have received any special treatment from Marubeni.

Furthermore, the presidents of Japanese corporations were normally appointed for a fixed and relatively short tenure, and Marubeni had had six of them since the time Evergreen first started doing business with the company. It thus defied simple logic that every single one of these chief executives would unfailingly lend a helping hand to

Evergreen for the sake of a president's daughter.

If it were true that Evergreen had special connections with Marubeni, it should not have had any problems in securing loans at all during its start-up years. Moreover, of the huge quantity of cargo Marubeni moved regularly, Evergreen could not have been allocated such a paltry volume, or even nothing at all sometimes.

What existed between Evergreen and Marubeni had always been a purely commercial relationship. They were not a shareholder of any of the Evergreen Group's companies nor did I have any special ties with any of the company's top executives.

What Marubeni did acknowledge at the outset though was that Y.F. Chang was a very capable man, a true-blue seafaring professional. Moreover, since it had hitherto not had any cooperation with Taiwan's shipping industry, it was keen to forge a long-term relationship with one of the country's carriers that showed good potential. For this reason, Marubeni had on a number of occasions rendered much needed support and assistance to Evergreen during the early years.

According to the Marubeni staff in charge of Evergreen, my style of dealing with people and business impressed them tremendously. Their faith in my vision and capability in the field of shipping, having worked with me for sometime, helped pave the way for mutual co-operation in the long run.

Shipping is a labour of love for me. All these years, my pace has not slackened, as I am a person who cannot live without work. Even during those difficult periods, I constantly egged myself on in getting the company's operations back on track quickly, not only to prove to cynics that we were dead serious in our pursuits, but so as not to disap-point our friends who had put their faith and high expectations in me.

Professionalism and credibility – keys to fruitful cooperation

Trust and integrity have long been my guiding principles in business. When I first sought Marubeni's help at the beginning, I gave them a truthful and detailed account of Evergreen's operations, as well as my conceptual ideals and approach, in addition to my erstwhile roles in

123

the New Taiwan Marine and Central Marine ventures. I wanted Marubeni to judge me objectively, free from any prejudice.

Our relationship at the time was still in the embryonic stage where I had yet to establish my credibility. As the loan we were trying to secure was not an insignificant figure, Marubeni found it necessary to have a full and clear picture of Evergreen's financial and business status. For this reason, they proposed that they send auditors to examine our books at fixed intervals.

I welcomed Marubeni's request without any reservation whatsoever; as I had always advocated honest bookkeeping, I had nothing to hide. Moreover, these loans would be used strictly for their intended purposes; diverting the funds for private or other illegitimate uses was something I would not even dare dream of. I was thus not surprised that the auditors' due diligence did not throw up any irregularities in our financial records.

Over time, Marubeni came to understand intimately Evergreen's financial position and accounting practices. With their faith in us strengthened, coupled with a marked improvement in our business, they stopped sending people to vet our books from 1975 onwards, just before we embarked on our containerisation programme.

Evergreen began to build up its trust and reputation in the industry gradually when its business started to generate profits and its loans were all repaid on time. As a result, the company also found it much less of a hassle to secure bigger financing from Marubeni.

Having won Marubeni's trust with our credibility and professionalism, they took their relationship with Evergreen one step further by offering us their financing facility of their own accord.

Many Taiwanese enterprises, which only saw the superficial aspects of my enduring relationship with Marubeni without knowing the underlying reasons, also tried to court them and other Japanese companies.

It is the norm, however, for most Japanese trading houses to evaluate thoroughly their prospective customers by scrutinising not only their professional experience, but also their potential and creditworthiness, as well as their management style, attitude and credibility, among other things. At times, they even seek the views of other people in the industry before coming to a final decision. As such, there is no way that personal connection or friendship will help people secure loans from the Japanese companies.

As far as the Japanese are concerned, even if borrowers had a good financial standing at one time or other or are reputable companies in their own right, they will not simply hand out the loans on a platter so long as they have the slightest doubt.

Worth noting here though is that whether or not the executives of a Japanese trading house have a keen eye and a good sense of judgement has a profound impact on the company's growth potential. If their assessments are spot on, which in turn enable them to bring in customers with bright prospects, their company will reap handsome returns down the road. On the other hand, it is obvious that these same executives also bear a heavy responsibility in their tasks. In a sense, therefore, it is as though the company's staff and the borrowers share a common destiny.

The fact that Mr Hosaka and his colleagues stood unwaveringly by me from the outset and urged Marubeni to support Evergreen, however, also put me in an unenviable position with immense pressure; if I had failed, they would have been compelled to resign to take responsibility for the fiasco.

The bottom line is, if you are able to convince the Japanese trading companies that you are a capable and trustworthy professional, they will go all out to render full support, especially when you are in dire straits. They are never fair-weather friends.

As an illustration, if they see that you are sliding into imminent helplessness as disaster looms, they will not hesitate to throw you a lifeline, encouraging you to persevere. Their rationale is that if they do not act promptly enough, they stand to lose the loans they had given you earlier. But if you survive the crisis with their help, and your business is rehabilitated, they will eventually be able to recoup both the principal and interest.

Mutual benefit in business

It was in the course of my dealing with Marubeni that I came to have a profound appreciation of the meaning of mutual benefits in business.

For example, whenever I wanted to buy a vessel, I would invariably analyse our potential operating costs based on the price quoted by the seller. I would never squeeze the seller unfairly just for the sake of paying a little less. After all, he deserves his profits. It also makes poor business sense to quibble over how much the seller makes in the transaction. Rather, we should base our decision objectively on whether the purchase meets with our own cost expectations.

Only if, for example, evaluations reveal that the price quoted by the seller is too high for us to be able to make any profit would I then ask, within reasons, for a reduction. But on the flip side, I also would not want the seller to incur any loss as a result of the price cut.

If people want to succeed in business, there must, I strongly believe, exist mutual benefits. After all, who wants to do business with you if there is no profit to be had? Moreover, making money at the expense of others does not exactly constitute good business sense.

We should not be tempted by greed, but be contented with our fair share of profits. Let us not envy, or be jealous of others just because they have made more money than we have.

Those who have associated with me long enough know that I will never enrich myself through ill-gotten gains.

Some proprietors of shipping companies seize the opportunity to feather their nests when buying vessels. They inflate the quoted price of a vessel costing, say, US$1 million by, for example, US$200,000. Although the value of the ship is reflected in the books as US$1.2 million, in reality, the proprietors for their own benefit have siphoned off the US$200,000.

Such malpractice has never occurred in Evergreen Line. Some people might say that this is because the company, and the money it makes, belong to me anyway. So what difference does it make? The truth is, although I am the majority shareholder of Evergreen, I will never seek to enrich myself through unconscionable means.

Others may erroneously entertain the notion that since the company is only a corporate entity, the interests of the individuals should come first. Not surprisingly, therefore, their priority is to line their own pockets whenever opportunity arises, so that if the company should go bust someday, they will not be unduly affected.

To me, such practices are immoral and contrary to God's ways. In business, we should first make use of our own financial resources to strike out; only if we run out of capital do we then resort to taking loans from others, and these loans must be repaid promptly as a top priority as soon as we are able to. Marubeni knows very well that the last thing on my mind is to seek to enrich myself in any transaction by deliberately inflating the quoted price of a vessel. My adherence to this basic principle all along only serves to reinforce the Japanese's trust in my selfless dedication to safeguarding the interests of Evergreen at large.

In short, I feel that my observance of moral scruples has been an important ingredient of the lasting and happy relationship between Evergreen and Marubeni over the decades.

Cherishing friendship

In spite of Evergreen's undisputed success today, I am eternally grateful to the three people in Marubeni who gave me their unstinting support in the early days; they are Mr Hosaka, Mr Nagasawa, and Mr Hashimoto. I later invited them to join Evergreen's affiliated companies in Japan.

When Mr Hosaka retired from Marubeni, I relinquished my chairmanship in Evergreen Japan Corporation and offered the position to him. It was a lifetime employment with a generous remuneration package. Sadly, we lost Mr Hosaka in early 1995. In memory of his past devotion, and to mourn his death, I specially held a grand funeral to which people from the shipping fraternity, as well as the top executives of Marubeni all came to pay their last respects.

I later presented a substantial gratuity to Mr Hosaka's family so that their livelihood would be taken care of, following his death.

Because of this, Mrs Hosaka specially called on me to express her deep gratitude.

The one-time president of Marubeni's branch office in Taipei, Mr Nagato, also wrote to me regarding this matter, in which he mentioned how touched he was by the funeral I had arranged for the late Mr Hosaka in Tokyo.

He told me in his letter how everyone from Marubeni was visibly moved by the grand but sombre ceremony at the funeral, which also prompted the Japanese business community to echo unanimously that "it's inconceivable that there still exist people in this world who cherish friendships so dearly".

I was touched by Mr Nagato's comments. Not that I like people to sing praises of me, but rather it was the honour of knowing that there are others out there who genuinely appreciate the importance I attach to friendship.

At least the outside world now has a better understanding of me as a person who truly values comradeship. There were perhaps those who felt that I need not have been so emotionally worked up about the whole thing as after all Mr Hosaka and I had nothing more than a purely business relationship. But I begged to differ; had it not been for Mr Hosaka's wholehearted endorsement and effort in mustering his company's support for me during my difficult start-up years, not only would I have failed to secure any loans, I would probably have had to pull the plug on my ambitions too.

In other words, it was not the company in the abstract which endorsed me, rather a person did. Therefore, it was only natural that I had to thank the person because what was crucial at the end of the day was whether he believed in me or not.

Mr Hosaka knew from the outset that I was an accomplished professional with a lot of potential; what I lacked then was capital. He firmly believed that I could achieve a great deal if only I had the seed money. Looking back thus, I cannot but still feel deeply indebted to his belief in me all these years.

Apart from Mr Hosaka, the other two gentlemen were also

appointed to senior positions within the Evergreen Group. Mr Nagasawa was made Chairman of Evergreen Shipyard Corporation (formerly known as Hayashikane Shipyard); he passed away in March 1997. Mr Hashimoto is the incumbent Chairman of Evergreen Japan Corporation.

I did not forget Marubeni's help either, as I still maintain an excellent business relationship with the company. Although many people have urged me to network with more Japanese companies, now that we have such an impeccable reputation in the market, I choose not to. The reason is very simple; had Marubeni withheld the much needed financial support from me initially, and if I had not cherished their friendship quite so much, Evergreen's fortunes could have taken on a drastically different dimension altogether.

Suppose I work with one trading house today and another the next, very soon no one will really value my business. On the other hand, if I maintain a regular and consistent relationship with Marubeni, they would in turn look upon us as a worthy customer.

Viewed from the perspective of my long-standing association with Marubeni, therefore, you can perhaps attribute part of the success to my unyielding emphasis on mutual trust and comradeship in business.

The shape of things to come: Evergreen Marine Corporation first started out with this dilapidated used vessel, *Central Trust*.

With Marubeni Corporation's Isao Hashimoto (second from left) and Lonny Chiu (far right).

Despite the financial strains, a second vessel *Ever Glory* was acquired with the help of
Marubeni Corporation's Kiyoshi Hosaka.

Opening up the Middle East trade: with my Arabic clients.

Fire broke out on board *Ever Island* while discharging steel coils in Keelung Port on 7 September 1969.

En route from Japan to the USA in October 1969, *Ever State* encountered engine problems unexpectedly.

Plying the Middle East route in the early days, *Ever Light* was one of three general-cargo vessels that had steam-turbine engines.

The more efficient diesel-powered *Ever Fortune* was acquired in 1971 to boost Evergreen's competitiveness.

The newly constructed *Ever Safety* was ready to set sail on her maiden voyage marking the inauguration of Evergreen's Central/South America services.

Making the rounds of shippers in the Caribbean: with Mr Abraham Kardonski (centre) in Colon, Panama.

In the Caribbean in 1973 to get a better feel of the market and agents' operations.

In a celebratory mood: Evergreen secured a preferential loan to construct *Ever Safety* under the government's national shipbuilding programme.

Mr and Mrs Pei Tsun-fan (front row, third and second from right) were invited to the launch of *Ever Safety*.

A fully laden Evergreen container ship making her way through the Panama Canal.

A S-type container ship under construction, in preparation for the launch of the Far East-US East Coast all-container liner services.

Inland road haulage played a pivotal role in the overall container shipping revolution.

Ever Spring, Evergreen's first full-container vessel.

"Jumboisation" increases the capacity of a S-type all-container vessel from the original 646 to 866 TEUs.

M-type container ships with four onboard derricks to facilitate loading and unloading operations, particularly in Central/South American ports.

On a visit to Hayashikane Shipyard in Nagasaki, Japan.

With Mr Hosaka, whose unwavering support I am eternally grateful for.

Old time's sake: Mr Nagasawa was appointed Chairman of Evergreen Shipyard Corporation, Japan.

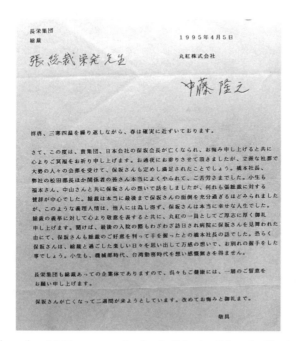

A moving letter from Mr Nagato, one-time head of Marubeni's branch office in Taipei, who described how the people in Marubeni and the Japanese business community were deeply touched by the extent to which I cherished Mr Hosaka's friendship.

[5]

Evergreen Rules
the Waves

Evergreen Line became the world's foremost container shipping company following its pioneering launch of a twin service that circumnavigated the globe and despite concerted opposition from the world's most powerful freight conference.

With Evergreen Line's network spanning the Americas, the Middle East and the Mediterranean countries, the company embarked on a programme of wholesale containerisation of its fleet of vessels. By this time, Evergreen had already established a sound reputation for its high quality of services in the industry.

Underpinned by a firm foundation, my next goal was to start a fully containerised liner service plying the Far East-Europe trade. This marked the beginning of another protracted battle that was to be fought with unprecedented ferocity. After all, our opponent was no less than the impenetrable and belligerent Far Eastern Freight Conference or FEFC in short.

The Far East-Europe shipping route, sustained by an abundance of cargo and high freight rates, was commonly known in the industry as the "Golden Route". And, traditionally, the FEFC had a stranglehold on this lucrative trade.

The FEFC, with its headquarters in London, had by then been around for 100 years. Its members comprised the major European shipping companies such as Ace Group, Trio Group, Scan Dutch Group and Maersk Line. Several Japanese shipping lines, which provided mostly scheduled container services, also joined the FEFC subsequently.

The FEFC had a huge fleet of state-of-the-art vessels under its wings. But its members had grown overly complacent, buoyed by years of unbridled monopoly. Its arrogance and high-handedness soon led to a deterioration of quality of service. In buoyant times, member-companies would pick and choose to carry only cargoes with high yield, ignoring the plight of other shippers whose low-value cargoes might be liable to be shut out without notice. With the FEFC in absolute control of freight rates, which it could adjust at its whim and fancy, shippers who did not comply with the wishes of FEFC ran the risks of not having their cargoes uplifted.

Over the years, cargo owners and shippers in the Far Eastern countries like Taiwan, Hong Kong, Singapore and Malaysia had little choice but to endure the ludicrous behaviour of the FEFC.

Plans mooted by an informal alliance of Taiwan shipping lines to operate a joint-service on this route were thwarted by the FEFC. They were subsequently compelled to withdraw from the market as their vessels were not able to secure any cargoes on their return journeys.

Several major European shipping companies that joined in the fray all met with a similar fate. Their vessels were only able to procure some ten to thirty 20-foot containers on their maiden voyages. Overall, it was a forlorn state of affairs.

Despite the powerful grip of the FEFC, the winds of change were nevertheless blowing as an increasing number of non-member lines entered the market from 1978 onwards. The resulting competition prompted a gradual improvement in the attitude of FEFC towards cargo owners.

Shippers had long endured the arrogance of the FEFC and were thus more than eager to support non-FEFC lines. These shipping companies valued their customers and were keen to cultivate their long-term support. Besides, freight rates of non-members were also far more competitive.

Previously, trade flow between Taiwan and Europe was insignificant due to the exorbitant freight rates that made Taiwan goods less competitive. The advent of non-FEFC lines altered the scenario and contributed enormously to the growth of trade between the two regions.

With the availability of non-FEFC services, shippers now had the freedom of choice and were able to save 15 per cent on freight costs. Furthermore, with a better feel of the vessels' schedules, shippers could load their cargoes in a more timely manner without the fear of having their goods shut out.

But although the situation had improved, there still existed a sense of insecurity among shippers. They were not sure whether non-FEFC lines would survive the FEFC's onslaught. On the one hand, they were pleased to see more shipping companies joining the non-FEFC services, but on the other hand, they were worried that these independent operators would one day be similarly driven out of the market by the cartel.

But since I had firmly made up my mind, I was psychologically well prepared to face all the impending obstacles and difficulties. During an internal meeting which we convened to announce our decision, I reiterated that: "we are all aware of the formidable reputation of the world's most powerful freight conference. We must therefore unite in our efforts and not be complacent."

I told my staff: "This is going to be a long and arduous battle. But since we have made up our mind, we should now go all out and not give up halfway through so that we can be accountable to our customers. We must all be thoroughly prepared to win this war with our courage and determination."

Surveying the market and rallying shippers

Against a freight conference that boasted a membership of a great multitude of shipping companies, I was deeply aware that were Evergreen Line to go it alone, not only would it face enormous risks, it would at the same time lack the requisite bargaining power. But if we were to bring in another shipping line as partner, it would be easier to ascertain our chances.

It was through the introduction of Marubeni Corporation that South Korea's Cho Yang Line, who was a customer of Marubeni at the time, became our partner in the proposed venture.

Originally, Cho Yang Line had requested to join the FEFC but was rejected because another of Korea's major shipping company, KSC, was already a member. Nevertheless, the Korean government was supportive of Cho Yang Line joining the European trade and it thus granted approval for Cho Yang to collaborate with Evergreen Line.

To allow us a better understanding of the market situation, I despatched a few study groups to Europe to conduct field surveys over a period of one year. The marketing team went to Germany, England, France, Holland, Belgium, Spain, and Italy and studied extensively the availability of cargoes emanating from these sources as well as their port facilities. They also explored potential ports of call and worked out operating costs and the need for vessel newbuildings, among other things.

The Europe route lacked the operating freedom that existed in the US market. This was because the shipping/maritime laws in the USA prohibited its freight conference members to employ unfair tactics to squeeze out non-members. Freight-conference members and outsiders were allowed to coexist quite openly. But the European shipping market could not be more different. Not only was the FEFC reluctant to accept new members, it was bent on destroying the business of non-member companies through a variety of underhand tactics.

All things considered, it was by no means easy to take on the powerful FEFC. The key to our success or failure would thus very much depend upon the show of support by shippers. When we were on our rounds in Europe, many shippers there told us that they had heard of Evergreen Line's plan to ply the European route, having successfully established the US trade. They welcomed Evergreen's participation as an independent operator. But they had one nagging concern: "Can

Evergreen win the battle against the world's most powerful conference?"

Other shippers expressed similar reservations: "How long can Evergreen carry on for? In the past, non-member lines had either been clobbered or simply driven out of business by the FEFC. None had been able to escape this fateful destiny."

We reassured the shippers: "If you entrust us to carry your goods, why shouldn't Evergreen survive? Haven't you seen the reality of our success in the US market?"

At the time, it was a common incentive for shippers who committed up-front a pre-set volume of cargoes annually to receive rebates from the FEFC. Shippers who had elected to use non-member operators stood to lose these rebates. Furthermore, they were also blacklisted by FEFC members who would then refuse to carry their cargoes. As a result, shippers were reluctant to have any open contacts with non-member carriers.

Many shippers discreetly promised to support us but were reticent in public for fear of attracting reprisals from the FEFC. Others had wanted to collect the rebates from FEFC before committing their cargoes to Evergreen.

When the FEFC got wind of Evergreen's plan to mount the European service, its initial reaction was at best ambivalent. Although it viewed Evergreen's move as some kind of a threat, it was not unduly perturbed. An insignificant outfit like Evergreen was never in any position to pose a threat to the FEFC, it reckoned.

We stuck to our original plan and proceeded with our relentless efforts to rally the support of potential shippers across the length and breadth of Taiwan.

I reiterated to our people: "Shippers you have visited verbally promise to back you. But won't we be in such a terrible bind if at the crucial moment they do not have any cargoes for us? We must therefore be absolutely sure of shippers' sincerity in their professed support of Evergreen. If they really want to help us, they must at the end of the day ensure they entrust their cargoes to us. Otherwise, our mission will fail."

On the part of Evergreen, although shippers had verbally pledged their unstinting support, we were frankly not entirely optimistic about our chances.

Only after repeated calls on the shippers were we able to coax them to admit: "If Evergreen is sincere, it can undoubtedly count on our support, provided it does not abandon the service even if it incurs losses. But if you are not committed, we will be in dire straits the very day you decide to pull out your service. We will then have to suffer more than ever before under the FEFC! You must, therefore, guarantee us that you are in it for the long haul."

As soon as I had learnt of the reaction and concerns of the shippers, I immediately called a meeting and instructed the staff: "Get back to the shippers immediately and give them our irrevocable undertaking that they are in good hands with Evergreen and that we are determined to be in it for the long-term."

We wanted to reassure the shippers that even if Evergreen were to lose money in this service, it would not back-pedal but would instead strive to provide a consistent level of service. As long as we had their support, we were confident that we would succeed and could then work with them to expand Taiwan's bilateral trade with Europe.

Plot to scupper Evergreen Line

With the exhaustive market surveys and a thorough review of our requirements over, Evergreen decided to commission the building of two modern, fully containerised vessels – *Ever Vital* and *Ever Vigor* – in Taiwan. Cho Yang Line opted to have its contribution of two vessels built in Japan. Our initial plan was to collectively deploy four 20,000-tonne vessels, each with a capacity of 1,214 TEUs. The service, with one sailing every 15 days, was to commence in April 1979.

To comply with the requirements of the Ministry of Transportation and Communications (MOTC), we submitted our detailed joint-venture proposal and applied for permits for the newbuildings. As soon as the Department had granted official approval, we set out to make all the necessary preparations both in Taiwan and overseas for the impending launch. Contracts for newbuildings were signed with the shipbuilders. At this juncture, however, a major shipping group in Hong Kong unexpectedly voiced its vehement objection with the MOTC. It wanted Evergreen's plan abandoned.

The Hong Kong company's rationale was that it was a member of the FEFC by virtue of an agreement it had earlier with the organisation and that according to admission criteria, only one shipping company from any one country could be admitted as a member. This shipping group thus laid claim to its right as the sole representative of the Republic of China in the FEFC and therefore had the prerogative to prevent other Taiwan shipping companies from plying this trade.

In reality, however, although this group did at that time own a shipping operation in Taiwan, the FEFC's membership rolls showed its parent company in Hong Kong to be a member. Not a single true-blue Taiwan shipping company had ever joined the FEFC. At any rate, according to its official registry, there were numerous glaring examples of a single country being represented by several of its shipping companies in the FEFC. For instance, England had eight; Japan, three; France, four; and Sweden, three.

The Hong Kong group nonetheless tried vigorously to pressure the MOTC to urge Evergreen to abort its plan. The Vice-Minister of Transportation at the time, Mr Chu Deng-kao, was more than an acquaintance of the boss of this Hong Kong company. But he handled this issue professionally.

In Minister Chu's opinion, the Hong Kong company had joined the freight conference strictly as a Hong Kong entity and was therefore not a representative of Taiwan. It thus had no reason to oppose the entry of Evergreen into the European market. Besides, Taiwan had never stipulated that only one of its shipping companies was entitled to operate this service.

As soon as the unreasonable request of the Hong Kong group was rejected by the MOTC, malicious rumours claiming that Evergreen was in financial difficulty began to surface in the market. It was insinuated that Evergreen was unable to pay wages to its employees and had to resort to price undercutting. Word even had it that the company was about to close down.

But as shippers slowly disentangled themselves from the grip of the FEFC and as their support for independent shipping companies gathered momentum, it responded by adopting a two-pronged approach to try to recoup lost ground. Apart from sending out warning letters to shippers not to engage the services of non-members, it also promised reductions in freight rates.

It was obvious that the FEFC's strategy was to stifle competition. It reckoned that its low freight rates would make it tough for non-members to procure cargoes, thus threatening their survival and that once competition had been driven out of business, its members could hike rates again.

Cho Yang breaks with Evergreen

Evergreen wanted to forge ties with Cho Yang Line. We invited 12 of their high-ranking employees to come to Evergreen for familiarisation. They received training in various aspects of container shipping operations as well as in computer applications and shipping documentation.

Prior to the commencement of our proposed joint operations in July 1978, I personally led a study team to England, Holland, Germany, Belgium and France for a period of two months. I wanted to find out more about the situation in each of these markets and at the same time to finalise ports of call and to recruit shipping agents. The team also included heads of departments from Cho Yang Line. Based on the results of this field study, I was confident that we were able to provide shippers with a scheduled Far East-Europe service with reasonable freight rates.

Unexpectedly, however, just prior to the launch of this scheduled service, news emerged from London that should Cho Yang decide to cooperate with Evergreen, KSC would be expelled from the FEFC.

The FEFC divulged that it would be compelled to seriously consider the tenability of KSC as a member should the Korean government allow Cho Yang Line to proceed with its plan. To forestall KSC's expulsion, the Korean government lobbied the FEFC to also admit Cho Yang as a member and pledged that it would henceforth wholeheartedly support all the commercial activities of the FEFC in Korea.

With pressure from the FEFC mounting and its promise to admit Cho Yang Line, the Korean government relented and did an abrupt 180-degree turn. The FEFC had successfully lobbied the Korean government through KSC. It stated in no uncertain terms that member lines would not tolerate competition, otherwise they would boycott Korean cargoes.

The maiden voyage was by then barely two months away when Cho Yang unexpectedly notified us of its decision to withdraw from the alliance.

This sudden turn of events resulted in immediate problems concerning the newbuildings and disrupted shipping schedules. Originally, the plan was for Evergreen and Cho Yang to each build two vessels. As fate would have it, the two ships commissioned by Cho Yang were first to be completed.

Since Marubeni had arranged the financing for all the four vessels, it sought Evergreen's assistance to acquire the two vessels from Cho Yang. I agreed. I decided to take the plunge ourselves without Cho Yang in order to fulfil our earlier pledge with the shippers.

At that time, the Japanese yen was fast appreciating which meant Cho Yang's two vessels would cost much more than were originally budgeted for. But things had moved so fast up to the point I was in no mood to bicker. My top priority was the launch itself.

As for Cho Yang Line, it went on to acquire new ships and joined the freight conference in which it has stayed as a member till this day.

A victorious maiden voyage

Just prior to the inaugural sailing when we were canvassing for cargoes, the FEFC chose to engage in a campaign of misinformation. Words were bandied about that non-member shipping lines were un-

149

reliable and financially weak and their services lacking. It even publicly declared that Evergreen would be forced out of the service within three months. The FEFC's intention was clearly to weaken our resolve and shake shippers' confidence in Evergreen.

But Evergreen had already built up a trustworthy name over the years, particularly from its successful service to the USA. Coupled with reassurances of our unwavering resolve to carry on come what may and to provide a high standard of service, the majority of cargo owners opted to support us.

We were on tenterhooks as the launch date drew closer. I was mentally prepared to forgo profits in our first year of operations.

On 10 April 1979, the newly commissioned *Ever Vital* set sail on its inaugural voyage. It was the beginning of a full-container liner service from the Far East to Europe. The vessel did not have a full load. But considering it was about 70 per cent laden with almost 1,000 units of 20-ft containers, it had already broken the dismal records set earlier by inaugural voyages of other non-conference carriers.

This commendable achievement showed that Evergreen had the trust and loyalty of shippers. Still, I believed that results could only get better. Indeed, after four or five voyages, we managed to achieve full loads followed by a consistent rate of growth in the ensuing years.

The FEFC's prediction that Evergreen would come to grief within three months of its launch did not come to pass. On the contrary, not only did Evergreen survive, its performance far surpassed everyone's expectations.

The success of the inaugural sailing was somewhat of a shock to many in the industry as it had been widely rumoured both in and outside Taiwan that Evergreen was beset by many problems prior to the launch.

To commemorate this inaugural sailing, I personally presided over lavish cocktail receptions and dinners in all the major European ports that *Ever Vital* had called at. Invited to these celebrations were local political dignitaries, shippers and other VIPs.

The accomplishment of Evergreen on its Far East-Europe service instantly propelled the company into the league of the world's seven largest container lines. Competitors viewed Evergreen's new status as a major threat. Once again, they connived to spread unfounded lies to disparage Evergreen.

Amongst the widely circulated stories at that time: Evergreen was bankrolled by a major Japanese trading house, Marubeni Corporation; Evergreen would not be able to wage its price war indefinitely, and Evergreen had to dispose of its vessels to ease financial strains.

Gossip would invariably hit Evergreen every time it launched a new service. Previously, Evergreen thought it unnecessary to respond to such innuendoes in the hope that our track record would speak for itself. But as rumour mills went into overdrive, we decided that we should no longer maintain our silence but to go on the offensive instead.

As I particularly pointed out in my press release: "People who think it fit to protect their vested interests by spreading lies and using unethical tactics to discredit competitors will certainly fail in their pursuits."

Between September 1978 and July 1979, the FEFC initiated several rounds of rate reductions for Taiwan export cargoes bound for European markets. Nevertheless, Evergreen continued to consistently achieve full shiploads, largely because the majority of shippers still supported us. They were fully aware that if Evergreen were to be forced out of the market, the FEFC would introduce rate hikes.

The cargo-owners' philosophical argument was: "The fact that Evergreen has survived for several years as an independent operator amply proves that it has inherent strength and capability. We must therefore continue to render our support and not let it founder. We do not wish to be at the mercy of the FEFC again."

Some cargo owners told us bluntly: "We will back Evergreen. You mustn't fail. Failure means having to endure terrible suffering under the FEFC."

Previously, when independent operators still lacked clout, shippers had to literally beg conference carriers for cargo space. They were not accorded any respect at all by the FEFC lines. Evergreen's approach was, however, radically different. Not only did it take the initiative to meet up with shippers, it also emphasised the importance of customer service.

Shippers were impressed by the high standards of our service, but we told them this was expected of us. Indeed, the fact that the FEFC subsequently adopted a more conciliatory stance could largely be attributed to competition from Evergreen.

Evergreen's accomplishments paved the way for other independent shipping companies to enter this market subsequently without their having to grapple with the complex feasibility studies.

As I later recalled, although every stage of our battle with the FEFC was fraught with suspense and risks, it was also extremely challenging. At the same time, the entire episode revealed in me a notable aspect of my personality: the more overbearing the opposition, the more unyielding I was. We were overwhelmed with joy as we looked back at our resounding victory against all the odds. It marked yet another new chapter in the annals of marine transportation.

Blockade by Japanese carriers

In line with the rapid growth in our European services, we commissioned Japan's Onomichi Shipyard to build four new L-type full container ships at the end of 1979. Japanese shipping companies that felt threatened by the phenomenal growth of Evergreen contrived to have work on the vessels delayed with the help of Japan's Department of Transport.

Although the shipyard had at the time all the construction materials on standby, we were puzzled as to why they would still not start work. When asked, their curt reply was: "Sorry, we have not received the construction permit yet."

Because of this matter, my good friend Mr Hamane, Chairman of Onomichi Shipyard, and I arranged to meet the former Vice-Minister of Transport, Mr Wakasa (he was to become the Honorary Chairman of All Nippon Airways).

We understood from Mr Wakasa that many Japanese shipping companies were under enormous pressure due to the formidable strength of Evergreen on the European route. The Japanese were worried that if Evergreen were to enlarge its fleet, they would be adversely affected to an even greater extent. Hence, their decision to impede Evergreen's plan to build new vessels by lobbying the office of the Transport Department.

The fact of the matter was that we had obtained the construction licences of these four vessels some time back. But the Japanese shipyard was unwittingly caught in an embarrassing and difficult position because of the Transport Department's abrupt refusal to issue a construction permit. I contemplated, and would indeed have instituted, legal action had the Transport Department not issued the permit in the end.

I felt strongly that shipping companies whose performance fell below their own expectations should improve their marketing strategies and operations and not resort to unethical practices to stifle the growth of others. Besides, the Freedom of Marine Transportation had always been a globally recognised convention and only through free and fair competition would one be able to prove one's mettle.

A gentlemen's agreement

The opening up of the European shipping market intensified competition between the FEFC and other shipping companies. Not only were the FEFC compelled to reduce their rates, some of their members even resorted to underpricing tacitly amongst themselves, with their rates some 20 per cent to 25 per cent below official tariffs. It was thus obvious that the FEFC's tariff structures existed only in name.

The FEFC's Maersk Line took the opportunity to threaten the organisation that if its allotted annual cargo-carrying capacity was not increased from 300,000 to 800,000 tonnes, and if it was not granted berthing rights to ports in England, it would withdraw from the FEFC with effect from June 1982.

Maersk's action compounded the existing problems of the FEFC.

If Maersk Line, with its large fleet of container vessels, were to quit and free itself from the restrictions of the FEFC, competition in the European shipping market was bound to worsen. The alternative was to give in to Maersk's demands, not a palatable solution either!

Mr Tung Chee Hwa, Chairman of Hong Kong's OOCL, a member of the FEFC then, was gravely concerned by this development. He thus thought it useful to seek the cooperation of Evergreen to resolve the problem. Shortly later, in end-November 1981, Mr Tung came to see me in his private capacity. The deputy chairman of NYK Line, Mr Yamada, a member of the FEFC also tried to mediate.

Evergreen Line and the FEFC held a formal discussion in London at the beginning of 1982 followed by another round in Singapore. Both sides were working hard to restore some semblance of order in an otherwise fractious market.

The upshot was that on May 21 of the same year, Evergreen Line and the FEFC signed a historic Gentlemen's Agreement in Hong Kong. The key points of the agreement were:

- Evergreen must not be coerced to join the FEFC.
- Evergreen agrees to reduce her cargo-carrying capacity from the Far East to Europe from an annual 1.5 million tonnes to 1.2 million tonnes. Its capacity from Europe to the Far East shall also not exceed 720,000 tonnes annually.
- Evergreen's vessels deployed on the Far East-Europe service are not allowed to load and unload cargoes in Jeddah port (Saudi Arabia) as well as ports in southern parts of Europe. These restrictions do not, however, apply to vessels deployed on its Far East-Middle East and Far East-Mediterranean routes.
- Evergreen's vessels deployed on the Far East-Europe services agree to carry Europe-bound cargoes contracted by the FEFC.
- Both parties shall not undercut each other so as to maintain order in the market.
- Both parties shall simplify their tariff structures; however, where Evergreen's rates are already lower than those set by the FEFC, Evergreen can maintain the competitive advantage.

This Gentlemen's Agreement was to remain in effect from July 1982 to end-1985.

The FEFC's objective in seeking Evergreen's agreement on peaceful coexistence was plain and simple. It merely wanted to capitalise on Evergreen's strength to quickly restore market stability.

Besides, the agreement also served to satisfy Maersk Line's demands and rid it of any desire to pull out of the FEFC, thus minimising any potential loss to the FEFC. Evergreen's magnanimous gesture in the broader interests of the entire industry drew a lot of admiration and respect from the market.

FEFC reneges on agreement

In view of Japan's unique nationalistic and market characteristics, Evergreen had in the course of the negotiation requested that the agreement categorically spell out the condition that Evergreen be allowed to carry Japanese cargoes which came under the purview of the FEFC. Otherwise, Japanese cargo owners would be reluctant to engage the services of non-member carriers. The FEFC, however, indicated that if the agreement were to contain this stipulation in black and white, it would probably contravene Japan's Anti-Trust Laws. To circumvent this potential problem, the FEFC therefore proposed that both parties agree on this condition verbally but the FEFC would inform the Japanese cargo owners that it would not stop them from engaging Evergreen's services. As it turned out, the FEFC never kept its promise.

I went to see the vice-chairman of NYK Line, Mr Yamada, regarding this matter on two separate occasions in Tokyo. On the first visit, he promised me that the FEFC would definitely inform the Japanese about its stance on this issue. But when I raised it again the second time round, he replied curtly: "It's very tricky! If we do so, we would run foul of the country's Anti-Trust Laws."

I could sense that Mr Yamada was making excuses. The FEFC was obviously not sincere right from the outset. Having bound Evergreen to the agreement, it then deemed it fit to blatantly renege on its earlier undertaking. This, I strongly felt, was most unfair to Evergreen which stuck faithfully to the agreement.

Relations between the two sides gradually deteriorated. In July 1984, the FEFC announced that it would prematurely terminate the Gentlemen's Agreement.

We deeply resented the FEFC's conduct. In response, Evergreen swiftly announced its decision to end the pact with FEFC.

With the unravelling of the Gentlemen's Agreement, the FEFC leaked information that it was contemplating legal action against Evergreen Line for violating the agreement and that it was demanding US$8 million in compensation. Evergreen was undaunted by FEFC's threats as it could easily have countersued FEFC for breach of contract. As it turned out, FEFC's feeble attempts fizzled out quickly and the matter eventually came to an ignominious conclusion.

The transatlantic crossing

Evergreen continued to containerise its shipping services, which had by then spanned Europe, the Americas and Asia. All that remained to turn it into a comprehensive round-the-world network was to add in the transatlantic trade.

In the Americas, Evergreen's services covered the Eastern and Western seaboards of the USA and various ports of Central and South Americas. In Europe, they served Holland, Belgium, Germany, England as well as various Mediterranean countries.

From a broader perspective, against a further week of sailing time that the transatlantic route would call for, a round-the-world service would lead to an improvement in overall operational efficiency (a more streamlined shipping schedule, shorter transit times for both vessels and containers, and better delivery) and cost-effectiveness.

From the customers' standpoint, this service would offer them even more flexibility in terms of logistics planning and delivery schedules, particularly for shipments between Europe and the Americas.

Historically, American and European carriers had a stranglehold on the transatlantic trade. It was difficult for any Far Eastern or Asian shipping line to get a foothold in this fiercely competitive market.

But my thinking was that if Western shipping companies could freely operate in Asia, why couldn't we Asian shipping lines do likewise in their backyard? For me personally, therefore, securing a slice of the transatlantic market was a challenge I could not resist.

I recalled one occasion in England just after the inception of Evergreen's European service, a knowledgeable shipping journalist, Mr Kenneth Brown (I knew him quite well; he has since passed away), from the Journal of Commerce came to see me.

He remarked: "You're indeed very brave to have taken on what has been the world's most invincible freight conference for the past 100 years. You're on record the only independent carrier to have successfully entered this fiercely protected market thus far."

Indeed Evergreen Line was instrumental in breaking down the entry barriers of the world's various freight conferences such as those governing the Middle Eastern, Central & South American and European trades. Its accomplishments altered the modus operandi of the shipping market from one that was dominated by freight conferences to one that was free and fair with emphasis on better customer services.

Kenneth Brown egged me on: "What's your next target?"

"What target? My priority now is to consolidate our European services," I said.

He was obviously unimpressed. "No way!" he rejoined. "My guess is that Evergreen's fleet will span the Atlantic next."

As a matter of fact, though I had not told anybody about my scheme of things, I had already had plans to rationalise our existing services into a round-the-world operation. It surprised me that Mr Brown was able to read my mind so accurately.

Then he hit the bull's eye. "You're always full of ideas. I don't believe you are contented with what you have accomplished so far. In fact, I dare say you will break another maritime record with what you are going to do next!"

Gearing up for quality service

I formed special task forces in 1981 to carry out market studies and lay the groundwork for the launch of our round-the-world services.

The transatlantic trade was at that time dominated by nine conference carriers endowed with territorial advantage. They included Sea-Land, Hapag-Lloyd, US Line, ACL, Dart Line, Johnson Scan-Star, Lykes Line, Gulf-Europe Express and Euro-Pacific. Collectively, they constituted 69.61 per cent of total gross tonnage uplifted on this route or 772,000 TEUs. Non-conference carriers such as POL, TFL and CAST Line made up the balance 30.39 per cent or 337,000 TEUs. Competition could thus not have been any fiercer.

This market had all along been the monopoly of the USA, European and other Western shipping companies. Evergreen, as an outsider, was well aware of the obstacles that lay ahead. This was an entirely different ball game compared to our Far East-based services in which we commanded enormous territorial advantage.

We thus had to work doubly hard. We studied the operations of the conference carriers thoroughly. We also determined the specific requirements of cargo-owners. Our goal was to convince them to utilise the services of Evergreen, a newcomer without any credentials in this particular market but nonetheless backed by a solid track record in our European and American services. We followed up closely with our existing customers and promised to provide a consistent level of service.

The concept of a round-the-world service was first conceived in the 1980s. Although several shipping companies did venture into the field, none of them succeeded. This prompted me to figure out all the possible factors that could have contributed to the failures of these operations. I was eager to discover what the missing links were in a chain of interconnected parameters such as choice of berthing facilities, management of container movements, fleet deployment and sailing schedules, business strategies and information technology.

I remembered our US company and shipping agents in Europe were at the time under a lot of pressure to get the project off the ground. The agents and owner's representatives from offices around the world were summoned to Taipei to deliberate and fine-tune the plans.

I was mindful that if the intended round-the-world operations were to succeed, we had to have all the requisite back-up facilities. In this regard, starting from 1982, Evergreen commissioned Taiwan's China Shipbuilding and Japanese shipbuilding companies to build 24 of the most advanced G-type full-container ships.

G-type container vessels had a capacity of 2,728 TEUs. These ships were installed with state-of-the-art navigational gadgets and manned by crews of 17 each. They were considered the world's top-notch container ships at the time.

As Evergreen's fleet continued to expand, the demand for containers also rose sharply. To cater to the needs of cargo owners as well as for purposes of routine repair, retrofitting and maintenance of containers, it became necessary for Evergreen to set up its own container production facility.

The upshot was that in 1982, the company established Evergreen Heavy Industrial Corporation in Kaohsiung. The factory, reputedly the biggest container repair facility in the Far East, would initially only repair and retrofit used containers. At about the same time, Evergreen also set up a factory in Chungli to manufacture containers, container spare-parts, chassis and trailers.

Furthermore, in line with the rapid pace of containerisation in marine transportation and in anticipation of future limitations of Keelung Port's hinterland, we made preparations in 1983 to form Evergreen Container Terminal Corporation and to construct in Taoyuan the largest inland container terminal in the Far East. This facility would enable cargo owners to pick up and/or return the containers at their convenience.

As for inland haulage, Evergreen added more trucks and trailers to improve delivery efficiency and reduce berthing time of vessels. On yet another front, Uniglory Marine Corporation was to be set up specifically to provide regional and feeder services and to dovetail with Evergreen Line's global shipping network. Our aim was to offer a comprehensive one-stop customer-services centre so as to ensure quality and efficiency in our overall operations.

My plan was to start the twin services (concurrent eastbound and westbound sailings) in 1984 with an initial deployment of 16 G-type full-container ships. The duration of each voyage was tentatively fixed at 80 days with one sailing every ten days. A further 24 new G-type vessels were to be deployed on the service and the sailing frequency improved to a weekly basis. The eastbound service would take in the Far East-US-Europe-Far East route with the westbound service setting off in the opposite direction.

The mother-vessels called directly at major ports in Taiwan, Japan, Korea, Hong Kong, Singapore, Malaysia, England, Germany, Holland, Belgium, France, Spain, USA and Jamaica. Regional feeder services were expanded and strengthened to complement the major routes so as to form a shipping network that spanned many cities worldwide.

Another Evergreen first

With inaugural preparations over, I called a press conference in mid-1983 to officially announce Evergreen Line's pioneer round-the-world two-way services. The world's shipping community reacted in astonishment.

The news attracted banner headlines and was widely reported in professional shipping media around the world. Many in the shipping industry were sceptical of Evergreen's ambition and thought it a highly risky venture that was destined to fail.

Some operators bluntly told me: "Evergreen Line has already caused widespread discontent with its clobbering of the FEFC in the European market and its dominance in the US trade. As if this were not enough, you now want to encroach into the territories of European and American shipping companies in the transatlantic trade. They are not happy at all and are ready to hit back as soon as the service has been launched. They feel that Evergreen's finance, business, organisation and human resources are at their most vulnerable during this transitional period."

Soon after, baseless rumours claiming that Evergreen Line was financially strapped and could not pay its employees began to make their rounds. Indeed, some of our agents were so taken in by these lies that they even sought clarification from Evergreen about its financial health. Some detractors tried to dent Evergreen's confidence by suggesting that its round-the-globe service would flounder and fail miserably.

But I remained undaunted in the face of this flurry of veiled threats and admonitions from the shipping fraternity. I urged the staff to be vigilant and not be deceived.

Evergreen's existing US and European services were doing very well. Route rationalisation had reduced operating costs markedly and, as a result, we were actually able to amortise the capital outlay of the proposed transatlantic services right at the outset. I would be contented if the new service could break even. We were also prepared to make no profit in the initial stages of the operations. Nevertheless, I was confident that our firm foundation and inherent strength would enable us to provide a far superior service to cargo owners and, in the long term, carve out a niche in the market.

Thus in July 1984, Evergreen inaugurated its eastbound and westbound round-the-world twin services with the deployment of *Ever Garden* and *Ever Genius* respectively. A ceremony to commemorate this momentous occasion was held in Keelung Port on 22 and 31 July.

With this impressive achievement, not only did Evergreen Line manage to pen a new chapter in the annals of global marine transportation, it also became the world's largest container shipping company in 1985 with a fleet of more than 50 vessels and a total capacity of 100,000 TEUs.

Competitors turn nasty

Competitors were wary of Evergreen's transatlantic operations. They banded together in an attempt to maintain market dominance and to deprive Evergreen of any cargo through their price-cutting strategy.

But we were unflustered and went about our usual business. In fact, we were able to procure 1,500 20-foot containers on each voyage that generated sufficient revenue to sustain our operations. I steadfastly resisted cuts in our freight rates to avoid being drawn into a vicious circle of reductions that would only be detrimental to all.

Not surprisingly, incessant rumours designed to inflict maximum damage on Evergreen Line reared their ugly heads again just one year after the inauguration of the round-the-world service.

One particular rumour had it that Evergreen's load factor was fast dropping and that it was even carrying empty containers most of the time. There were bomb hoaxes on Evergreen vessels, which not only wasted the time of local firemen and bomb disposal experts but also disrupted normal services.

It was reported that Evergreen had deep financial problems and had to lay off workers as a result. Customers were therefore urged not to deal with Evergreen.

One shipping company even went to the extent of telling Sanwa Bank of Japan that Evergreen was facing severe cash-flow problems and it should therefore not extend any more shipbuilding loans to Evergreen. The bank was in turn encouraged to spread this false information to other banks.

There were also instances in which reports were made to the Customs claiming that firearms were found on board Evergreen vessels. Not only did such pranks waste Customs' and Evergreen's time, they also delayed deliveries of containers to customers. The corporate image of Evergreen suffered as a result.

One other ridiculous rumour that surfaced at the time was that Evergreen, due to overcommitment in its fleet expansion programme and in building the container terminal, had had to seek capital contributions from the employees and crews in order to avert the risks of imminent bankruptcy.

I was flabbergasted by the despicable behaviour of these people. Rivalry, I felt, was inevitable in any business. Indeed, competition, on a free and fair basis, would actually go a long way to enhance market efficiency that should in turn benefit society at large. On the other hand though, people who try to protect their selfish interests by causing harm to others through devious means would, I believe, one day receive their rightful retribution.

From foe to friend

Evergreen Line strengthened its regional shipping networks to com-plement the round-the-world operations with the inclusion of the Mediterranean-US East Coast service.

These moves further antagonised the FEFC, which had long con-sidered Evergreen their arch rival. In retaliation, the FEFC got the rumour mills churning overtime again in their futile attempts to prevent Evergreen from securing any cargo in the Mediterranean region.

"Evergreen was receiving huge financial subsidies from the Taiwan government which enabled it to compete by slashing its freight rates. Of the total freight movements on the Italy-Taiwan route in 1985 for example, the Italian state-run shipping company, Italia Line, accounted for a mere 8 per cent against the 70 per cent handled by the Republic of China (particularly Evergreen Line). And on the Taiwan-Italy leg, the percentage was 50 per cent and 7 per cent for the ROC and Italy respectively. In response, therefore, Italy, Spain, West Germany, France and England should pursue a common strategy to counter the insane pricing policy of Evergreen," it was alleged.

The allegation unnerved the Italian shipping line. After all, they had not exactly been doing well on their own over the years. This was an opportune moment to point their finger at Evergreen. It indeed wasted precious little time in urging the Italian government to take drastic actions against Evergreen.

The Italian government viewed with grave concern its shipping company's petition. To safeguard the carrier's interests, it announced, it would introduce tough legislation to curtail Evergreen's freight collection activity in Italy.

Amongst the measures that were proposed at the time was one which vested the Italian government with sweeping powers to take over complete control and supervision of cargoes carried by vessels belonging to countries deemed to have competed unfairly. We were perturbed by this turn of events. The extremes to which these people would go to attack the integrity of Evergreen simply defied imagination!

My concern was that should the Italian government be tempted to proceed with the legislation, it would do more harm than good to both sides and would further sour our relations. It would also result in greater confusion of the market. I immediately despatched a senior executive of Evergreen to Italy to clarify the situation with the Ministry of Transportation. We had ample evidence to prove that Evergreen was the innocent victim of a vindictive campaign of misinformation.

As a gesture of our sincerity towards the Italians, I decided that we might as well invite their carrier to join Evergreen in the Mediterranean-US East Coast services. Through this collaboration, the Italians were able to see clearly for themselves Evergreen's marketing strategies and pricing structures. They were soon to find out that there was no impropriety at all on the part of Evergreen.

Indeed, as Italia Line had by then discovered, it was the other shipping lines that were behind the whole price war. The truth of the matter was brought to the attention of the Ministry of Transportation. Only at this juncture was the Italian government fully aware that Evergreen was after all not the perpetrator and that Evergreen was not behind the financial woes of its own carrier. And on this note, we came to the conclusion of this unpleasant episode.

Originally a member of the FEFC, Italia Line's withdrawal from the cartel to tie up with Evergreen led to a huge outcry in the market. The FEFC's major concern was that the alliance would bolster the performance of the ailing Italian carrier, which would in turn strengthen the position of Evergreen. Worse still, other member lines might follow in the foot-steps of the Italian and form strategic alliances in order to compete and survive, thus ultimately threatening the FEFC's internal unity.

As for Italia Line, its business improved gradually. It even began to show profits, thus reversing the trend of years of continuous losses.

Evergreen enjoyed good relations with the Italian carrier. The Italian had by then a great deal of confidence in Evergreen. Not long after, its sister carrier, Lloyd Triestino, requested to join Evergreen's two services plying the Far East-Red Sea & Mediterranean Sea and Far East-US West Coast trades, with both sides deploying vessels on these routes, thus further cementing relationships between the two partners.

Striving for excellence

From Evergreen Line's inception in 1968 to its launch of the round-the-world services in 1984, it was a mere 15 years. But during this short span, the company achieved a number of firsts in both domestic and global maritime history. Evergreen, for example, was a pioneer in offering scheduled and fully containerised services to the Middle East, Central & South America, and the Mediterranean. It was the world's first shipping line to break the FEFC's stranglehold in the Far East-Europe trade. Evergreen was also the first Asian shipping company to have successfully broken into the transatlantic market.

Evergreen did not, however, equate its laudable achievements with unwarranted risk-taking. Our top priority was to maintain long-term stability. The company never over extended itself. With the management soundly on track and in spite of all the accolades, the company continued to strive for cost-effectiveness. We also paid particular emphasis on the nurturing of talent within the company.

With the eastbound and westbound twin services firmly in place, Evergreen proceeded to establish a global North-South network. As for myself, preservation of long-term competitive advantage was seldom far from my mind.

Spearheading
market study in
Europe, July 1978.

會茶航首輪生長綫航期定櫃貨全洲歐一東遠司公運海榮長

A reception was held to
mark the inauguration
of the Far East-Europe
full-container liner ·
services with the
deployment of the
newly-built *Ever Vital*
which set sail on her
maiden voyage on
10 April 1979.

Going separate ways:
Evergreen terminates its
"Gentlemen's Agreement"
with the Far Eastern Freight
Conference.

With the successful embarkation of the European services, I was ready to take on
the transatlantic trade.

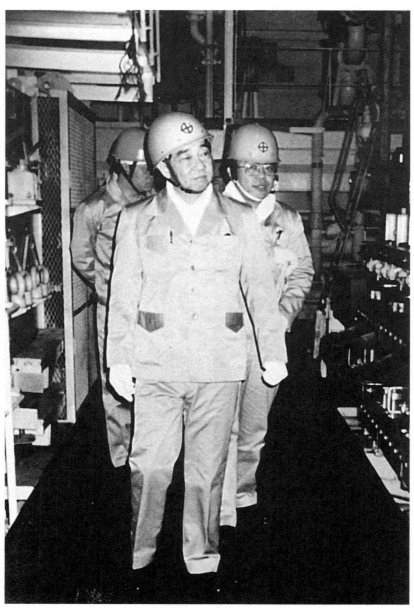

Taking Evergreen's G-type vessel on a sea-trial in Japan's Onomichi Shipyard.

The biggest inland container terminal in the Far East: located in Taoyuan, it was built by Evergreen to complement the launch of its round-the-world services.

The inauguration of the eastbound round-the-world service in Keelung Port on 22 July 1984 with the deployment of *Ever Garden*.

One for the future: Taking the world by storm with the launch of the round-the-world services in 1984.

The westbound round-the-world inaugural voyage was undertaken by *Ever Genius*.

Evergreen's unprecedented round-the-world twin services scored many firsts in the annals of Taiwan's and global maritime transportation.

170

[6]

The Sky is the Limit

EVA Air ultimately took to the sky as an airline par
excellence that did the Chinese proud despite being
pummelled by initial setbacks.

Evergreen's round-the-world services, launched in 1984, was a monumental feat that catapulted the company into an unassailable position with a worldwide network of marine and land transport operations. I was, however, not about to rest on my laurels. The firm foundations we had laid in shipping had placed us in a strategic position to establish an air transport business and, with it, the Evergreen Group was poised to offer an entire spectrum of sea, land and air services under one roof. But I had to scuttle the idea before it could really take root because Taiwan's aviation industry was at the time still highly regulated.

In the meantime though, rapid changes were taking place in the global arena. Governments of many countries were vigorously pushing for an "Open Skies" policy in a move to safeguard their interests in an increasingly competitive market.

The USA, for example, enacted the Deregulation Act in 1978 whilst Japan opened up its industry in 1987 which resulted in Japan Airlines and Japan Asia Airways being joined by the two domestic airlines, All Nippon Airways (ANA) and Japan Air System (JAS) in operating long-haul flights. In 1988, the Korean and Hong Kong governments also approved the setting up of a second international airline respectively, followed by many other countries in their footsteps.

To help their second long-haul carriers gain a firm foothold in an increasingly competitive environment, the governments were quick to extend preferential financing schemes to the newly established airlines and to renegotiate the air services agreements with their foreign counterparts accordingly.

It was, however, a starkly contrasting tale in Taiwan where flag-carrier, China Airlines, had long been a monopoly that controlled the country's international routes. Although the rapid growth of the country's economy since the 1980s had led to a sharp rise in the number of businessmen and tourists going abroad, China Airlines did not benefit from this trend due to its capacity limitations.

Meanwhile, airlines all around the world were feverishly stepping up efforts to sharpen their competitive edge. In the face of these challenges, and to keep up with the changing tides, Taiwan's transport ministry finally decided to deregulate the industry that had effectively remained closed to private enterprises for 40 odd years. An "Open Skies" policy was officially introduced in 1988.

The birth of EVA Air

For many years, the flight safety records of Chinese airlines on both sides of the Strait left much to be desired, which earned them the dubious distinction of being the world's worst airlines.

This infamous reputation notwithstanding, I was confident that the Chinese were fully capable of running a world-class airline. It was thus with this conviction and the blessing of Evergreen that I went ahead to make preparations to set up an international carrier that would provide the highest standard of services possible, which, I hoped, would alter the wrong perception foreigners had of the Chinese.

From a personal perspective, an international airline operation was an effective means by which we could offer the citizens of Taiwan quality in-flight services and better employment opportunities. It would, hopefully, also raise the standing of Taiwan's aviation industry to a higher level. The proposed undertaking was to all intents and purposes something of a national service.

Due to the magnitude of the venture, I felt it was only appropriate that I spearheaded the project myself. I wasted little time in setting up a task force within the company and began to draw up plans.

1 September 1988 was the twentieth anniversary celebrations of Evergreen Line. I chose to unveil my ambitious plan on this auspicious day in the presence of our colleagues and associates from around the world who had congregated in Taiwan to commemorate the occasion. I urged them to capitalise on the synergistic strengths of Evergreen and work closely together to plant our flag on the aviation map of the world. On that same day, we submitted to the Civil Aeronautics Administration (CAA) our proposal to operate a passenger-cum-freight airline.

Little did I foresee at the time that this would actually mark the beginning of an uphill battle. I was wrong to anticipate that competitive pressures would be the major stumbling block. In fact, soon after Evergreen's submission had gone into the CAA, we discovered much to our dismay that the real obstacle was Taiwan's archaic and inconsistent civil aviation regulations. Politicking within the legislature only served to exacerbate matters.

The government stayed fickle-minded from beginning to end. It dragged its feet and was certainly in no hurry to evaluate our proposal. When the decision finally came, the transport ministry stated that based on flight-safety considerations, the government would only consent to Evergreen operating a freighter service, initially at least.

I was flabbergasted. To me, the safety of every one on board, be it passengers or the crew of a freighter, is of equally paramount importance. I will never overlook flight safety whether it is a passenger airline or a dedicated freighter service.

From an economic standpoint, it is more cost-effective to operate a passenger-cum-cargo service as it offers a greater degree of operational flexibility than a purely freighter service. Whether in shipping or in aviation, critical mass is a precondition for achieving the benefits of economy of scale as it then allows the company's human and other resources to be more efficiently deployed, thus raising overall productivity.

A three- to four-year time-frame is normally required to get a new airline up and flying, from the moment aircraft orders are placed to manpower training to the installation of hardware, software and other facilities. By its very nature thus, our undertaking would obviously entail a hefty capital outlay. Although a detailed feasibility study was a prerequisite, good timing on the part of EVA Air was absolutely crucial as a miscalculation on the government's deregulation plans would cost the company dearly.

To add impetus to our application, as well as to show our unwavering commitment in the project, we held a dialogue session with the Ministry of Transportation in which we updated them on the prevailing trends in the global aviation industry. They were also told of our operational and financial plans.

Subsequent to this meeting, the transport ministry resubmitted Evergreen's proposal for evaluation to the Executive Yuan (Taiwan's Cabinet) who in turn delegated the task to the Council of Economic Planning & Development (CEPD).

The final evaluation report, together with input from industry experts and airline operators, was deliberated at great lengths by the transport ministry. The upshot was, on 17 January 1989, the government released the long-awaited criteria governing the incorporation of non-domestic passenger and cargo airlines. Evergreen promptly reapplied to the CAA in compliance with the new requirements. Its swift response at the time attracted unwarranted allegations that the ministry's decision to open up the passenger and freight sectors of the industry was designed to accommodate Evergreen.

In reality, however, although quite a number of domestic enterprises could easily have qualified under the new procedural guidelines, only Evergreen showed any overt desire and interest in investing in this business.

Almost five long months had elapsed since Evergreen's first

submission to the CAA. In the meantime, the cost of a passenger aircraft had escalated by 10 per cent, adding a further US$10 million to the price tag.

To add insult to injury, some people who were bent on seeing Evergreen fail in the venture stirred up further controversies by claiming that Evergreen had been accorded special privileges by the government whom it had supposedly pressured into submission.

I recalled a similar incident in Penghu where the provincial government was considering the county's future development and the Evergreen Group was invited to invest in tourist attractions there. But due to the dubious objections of a certain group of people, we had to abandon the plan in the end, putting paid to our desire to serve the broader interests of the community, and the county had to shelve the project indefinitely as a consequence.

In sharp contrast, Evergreen's shipping business fared considerably better. It had always been able to maintain a competitive edge by virtue of its track record as a steadfastly strong and trustworthy company. It, however, also owed much of its earlier success to the many governments around the world. Keen to bolster their economies, they welcomed Evergreen's investments in their countries with open arms and did all they could to facilitate the process. It was thus such an irony that Evergreen did not receive any form of assistance in her own country; instead, it had to grapple with so many obstacles. In such circumstances, I could only feel a deep sense of futility and regretted that we had committed such substantial investments in Taiwan over the years.

Tentative first steps

The transport ministry granted its official approval to EVA Air on 8 March 1989, after a lapse of more than six months. Sadly, despite the transparency of the entire process, some people still contrived to discredit Evergreen by claiming that the ministry had given the green-light due to the personal intervention of Mr Lee Teng-hui, the President of the Republic of China.

175

The fact was, if the allegations were true, Evergreen would certainly not have had to wait half a year for the approval to come through. It was regrettable that the President's name had to be dragged into the picture. I also had a sneaking feeling that we had not heard the last of this sort of baseless talk yet.

The CAA was in those days highly protective of China Airlines, with which it had an almost seamless relationship. The latter had long been a sinecure of CAA's top bureaucrats who had retired and were appointed senior executives in the airline. Also, as military ranks of senior executives in China Airlines were invariably higher than those of their counterparts at CAA, it was not unusual for CAA officials to address their "superiors" at China Airlines as "Commanding Officers". A more intractable problem though was the fact that CAA officials came mostly from the air force and were, therefore, not fully conversant with the nitty-gritty details of running a commercial airline. Overall thus, it was a diabolical situation in which the CAA appeared to be subservient to China Airlines when it should be the reverse.

As part of our overall efforts to lay the groundwork for a world-class airline, we entrusted Evergreen's global network of offices to collect as much information as possible about the industry. Task-force members were despatched overseas to carry out in-depth field studies and, to shorten our learning curve, we engaged foreign consultants to advise us.

Our progress was, however, severely hampered by the government's ineptitude. We were even belittled when we suggested that the aviation act be streamlined to keep the country's airline industry abreast of global trends.

I seriously doubted our prospects then, as I was certain that the government's red tape would unnecessarily constrain our ability to compete successfully in the international marketplace. It was perhaps better that we shelve the project, I told myself.

Although we had already sunk in two to three hundred million New Taiwan dollars in the project, I felt I had no choice but to bite the bullet. I conveyed my decision personally to the leaders of the task forces, including CC Cheng, Frank Hsu, Hanson Chen, KC Chang, Fu I-hsing, Tony Su, David Wang and Daniel Wu.

"I have decided to call it quits and stop all the ongoing activities forthwith, notwithstanding all the money and efforts we have put in thus far!" I told them, not without some pain.

I explained that I did not have any alternative, given the insuperable obstacles.

The task-force leaders, with tears welling up in their eyes, were devastated by the news. They had, after all, invested a considerable amount of their own time and stamina in the project.

They were angry that Evergreen's genuine desire to give Taiwan's languid domestic aviation business a much needed boost was repeatedly thwarted by an inconsiderate faction within the legislature. The government's incompetence was literally paving the way for airlines of other countries to forge ahead of Taiwan without any mercy.

I fully empathise with their collective sense of betrayal and injustice at the hands of our fellow countrymen.

Unwilling to yield to external pressure without a fight, the task-force leaders approached me a couple of days later and urged me to rethink my decision.

"Please leave this heavy responsibility to us young people. We have come this far and it would be a crying shame if we were to give it all up, especially now that we already have a good grasp of the business!" they implored, adding that I should not be the least concerned by any of the innuendoes.

"Oh yeah?" I responded, in mock surprise. "But do make sure that you don't come running to me when the going gets tough!" Still, I told them that I would give it a second thought.

At home that night, I related the story to my wife. She was sympathetic and agreed that I should indeed call it off especially when the project was mired in so many difficulties. Besides, she reasoned, I was already preoccupied with so much work and did not really have time to spare.

Deep down, I was struggling with myself. The diligence and

conviction of my people had struck an emotional chord in me. I was, however, concerned that, despite their youthful enthusiasm, willpower alone would not carry them very far in Taiwan's complex political labyrinth.

On the other hand, since they really wanted to have a go at it, I might as well let them try, although ultimately, I reckoned, they would still come to me in the event of any problems.

So on an early morning two days later, I summoned them to my office. Their undiminished passion and indomitable stamina had convinced me.

"Since you chaps have volunteered to take on the challenge," I said half in jest, "you'd better ensure that you stay committed till the end."

The truth was, I was just as eager to have the project revived. We picked up where we had previously left off and worked feverishly to recover lost ground.

Making it safe

To ensure the highest standards of flight safety, EVA Air invested almost 10 billion New Taiwan dollars in capital, manpower and equipment even before the actual operations had commenced.

Everyone in the company pitched in selflessly. We laid hands on all the pertinent books and reports we could find about the industry. Many of us criss-crossed various countries to learn about the latest technology, management concepts and other information.

From the upper echelon of the management to the employees on the shop floor, the company had a singularly unwavering conviction to practise what we had always been preaching – flight safety.

Businessmen, in my opinion, must never indulge in unethical or immoral acts, more so in an environment where human safety is at stake. It is in this light that both our management and employees have been instilled with the knowledge and understanding of their awesome responsibility from day one.

By its very nature, an aviation venture entails enormous investments in both capital equipment and manpower. But it is never a foregone conclusion that the operations will be commercially viable. In a sense, therefore, only fools would dare risk their money in this kind of business!

Just take the construction of our aircraft hangar as a typical example.

The government had decreed that all aircraft maintenance facilities be located within existing airport premises. In line with this ruling, EVA Air proposed to construct a state-of-the-art maintenance complex within Chiang Kai Shek (CKS) Airport. Several potential sites were chosen and evaluated based on such factors as the shape and size of land, accessibility, topography, weather and availability of public utilities, etc. Also assessed was whether the proposed hangar would impinge upon the air-traffic control systems, the airport's master development plan, airport security, regulations on noise levels and if it would obstruct the viewing gallery of the terminal.

We studied the hangar designs of other leading airlines and earmarked additional land for future expansion needs.

The outlook of Taiwan's aviation industry at the time had never looked so rosy. Rapid economic growth had led to a sharp increase in the number of both inbound and outbound air travellers. Many foreign airlines also picked CKS Airport as their regional hub. In view of this positive trend, we proposed that the government allow more leeway for the industry to grow by providing EVA Air and China Airlines with more land for both current and future development purposes. A more vibrant aviation industry would, in our view, contribute to the economic prosperity of the nation as a whole.

Our exhaustive appraisal showed that the southern corner of CKS Airport was the most ideal site to be developed into a second maintenance zone. The area, which was then used as a golf course, would not get in the way of any of the airport facilities nor would it impede the future development plans of the airport. An application to lease this piece of land was duly submitted to the CAA in March of 1989.

But although the transport ministry had in August 1989 consented to the siting of the maintenance zone to the south of the airport's transit hotel, it was not until the end of April 1990 that the CAA gave its green light for EVA Air to construct the hangar on the site where it still stands today. CAA would, it was agreed, fund the construction of the aircraft parking bays and the taxiway leading to the zone. The only catch was that they had not budgeted any expenditure for the project, unless we were prepared to wait till 1992. There was thus no way that CAA would be able to meet EVA Air's original deadline for the hangar to be operationally ready if we were to accept their construction schedule.

We had to make a decision quickly. Our aircraft delivery schedule and inaugural flight had already been postponed umpteen times. Any delay in the completion of the hangar would also adversely affect our future aircraft maintenance capability adversely. We were thus left with little choice but to proceed with the project unilaterally in November 1990.

Political obstruction

Little did we expect that the chaotic political scene in Taiwan at the time, with the ruling party split into the so-called "mainstream" and "non-mainstream" factions, would turn out to be such a huge stumbling block. The issue of EVA Air's land lease was fortuitously brought up for debate in the Legislative Yuan in April 1991 in which the New KMT Alliance unleashed a barrage of unwarranted criticisms against EVA Air. It argued that the piece of land should not be leased to EVA Air under the provisions of the airport's master plan. In reality, however, the land, which the airport authority had turned into a golf course for the exclusive enjoyment of its officials, was never earmarked for any development under the master plan.

The New KMT Alliance's verbal assault on EVA Air clearly bore the hallmark of a self-serving and vindictive motive and was obliquely targeted at those "mainstream" politicians of the ruling party who had resisted New KMT Alliance's attempts to cover up investigations into the Wah Lung scam. It went as far as saying that the transport ministry had amended the Civil Aviation Act for the sake of EVA Air.

The furore against EVA Air continued unabated and it eventually resulted in the freezing of expenses, which the CAA had originally earmarked for the construction of the taxiway. The New KMT Alliance had clearly exploited to its full advantage the ambiguity in the aviation laws and supplemental provisions, especially those relating to procedures which a prospective airline company must comply with in its application for an operating permit.

More than two years had elapsed since the day EVA Air was given the green light to set up the airline. In the meantime, agreements to purchase new aircraft were signed, aircraft leases sealed, our aircraft registered in the nationality of Taiwan and test-flights completed. EVA Air had complied fully with all the statutory requirements and it should by all accounts not have had any problems in securing the permit.

But some of the legislators, or so-called people's representatives, vexatious and belligerent as they were, had a different notion altogether. They maintained that EVA Air did not have the requisite credentials, much less the privilege to lease foreign aircraft. In short, they were bent on stopping EVA Air in its tracks.

I resented deeply all the aspersions cast on EVA Air. Had I not been of two minds earlier, I would not have needlessly exposed myself to all these ridicules. It was beyond my wildest imagination that, in our untiring efforts to start an airline company that the entire nation should deservedly be proud of, our very own elected representatives would turn out to be the most vociferous source of opposition.

Our battle cry

The trials and tribulations EVA Air's employees had to endure over the months only served to harden their resolve.

"We really cannot hold back our ire any longer," they clamoured, "we must not sit back and let these people freely trespass against our rights and interests. Otherwise, the public may misconstrue our reticence. We have to do something about it!"

It was demoralising to see that, amid all the hoo-ha, not a single government official came forth to put the matter in its proper perspective. Under no compulsion to appease the fomenters in the legislature and see our painstaking efforts over the last two to three years thwarted, I yielded to the hankering of my people and agreed that we should set the record straight publicly once and for all.

With my endorsement, they took out prominent full-page newspaper advertisements detailing EVA Air's predicament.

"Appeal to Our Elected Representatives Not to Kill Civil Aviation Business" appeared in banner headlines whilst "Our Cry of Anger" and "The Plain Truth" in bold print aptly portrayed the inner hurt of our employees and the whole truth about EVA Air's plight.

It is usual for the government to review the aviation laws periodically in line with changing circumstances. Such revisions are, however, for the benefits of all airlines, including Mandarin Airlines, in which China Airlines has a stake. So why was EVA Air always a target of unwarranted criticisms?

As a matter of fact, although glaring inconsistencies had existed in Taiwan's civil aviation laws for more than a decade, no one saw any compelling need to have these discrepancies rectified. So, why such a hue and cry when EVA Air had not contravened any statutory requirements to get its project approved?

Financially, as well as in various other aspects, most airlines in the world had received significant backing from their governments. Taiwan's flag carrier, China Airlines, was no exception. It enjoyed numerous privileges, the more notable of which I quoted below:

- The government purchased the aircraft and leased them to China Airlines at preferential interest rates.
- China Airlines' aircraft maintenance centre was leased from, and built by, the government.
- China Airlines paid 50 per cent of normal landing/take-off fees for its international routes.
- China Airlines received financial subsidies from the government for its Taiwan-New York and Taiwan-Holland routes.
- Traffic-rights fees paid by foreign airlines to the government went into the coffers of China Airlines.

- China Airlines was the sole provider of airport terminal and ground-handling services.

In the aviation business, traffic rights are the basic lifelines of any international airline company. Many governments around the world customarily realign the ownership of this precious commodity in order to nurture and assure the survival of their newly established long-haul carriers. In EVA Air's case, however, we had to rely totally on ourselves to secure the traffic rights, sometimes to no avail.

A case in point was the traffic rights for the Taiwan-Hong Kong route. This sector was at the time the exclusive preserve of flag carriers China Airlines and Cathay Pacific respectively. When EVA Air applied for rights to this market soon after its inception, the two incumbent carriers responded swiftly by forging a five-year alliance sooner than anticipated in a bid to keep EVA Air out of the loop. Our repeated appeals to the government to block the pact were in vain.

Financially, EVA Air had to fork out every penny of its entire capital outlay. Even in all other aspects, from the application to lease land to manpower training to the purchase of aircraft and to traffic rights negotiations, the government never offered EVA Air any assistance. Instead, we were the targets of a concerted smear campaign. In the circumstance, we could not help but feel a deep sense of futility.

I am all for constructive criticism. But, I believe people who criticise for the sheer joy of criticising never really have the welfare of the country and its citizens at heart.

The inaugural flight scheduled on 1 July 1991 was drawing near. It, however, ominously appeared that on-going politicking within the government machinery, with EVA Air unwittingly caught in between, would stall the planned launch.

Considering the numerous inquiries that had inundated us, we would most certainly end up with a less than auspicious maiden flight if we did not quickly get our advertising campaign going and start taking reservations. Besides, many people around the world had got wind of the impending launch and if the government's procrastination should cause the event to be abandoned yet again, Taiwan would inevitably become the butt of an international joke.

The transport ministry had meanwhile waited till June 14 to announce that EVA Air's maiden flight would proceed as planned. And it was only at the eleventh hour on 24 June that the CAA issued the permit to EVA Air.

More exasperating though, the bunch of troublesome legislators still did not want to give up their futile attempts even at this late hour. They demanded that the transport minister, Mr Eugene Chien, rescind the decision, failing which they would sue him for dereliction of duty.

But the truth was, Minister Chien had already made public his basis for approving EVA Air's proposal. He explained that EVA Air had complied fully in all respects with the statutory requirements of the transport ministry, notwithstanding the inadequacies of Taiwan's aviation laws. He said he had appraised the situation thoroughly and had arrived at his decision in the broader interests of the nation.

If the airlines in Taiwan had been refused permission by the transport ministry to operate aircraft with foreign registrations, China Airlines would have been compelled to mothball one third (or eight aircraft) of its entire fleet, resulting in some US$2 billion worth of losses to the company. As for EVA Air, the two aircraft we had leased had duly been registered in the nationality of the Republic of China.

EVA Air's plight raised many eyebrows both in Taiwan and abroad. Our friends and associates were bewildered as to why the government and the politicians would choose to frustrate the nation's very own airline instead of rendering support!

Across the seas to the north in South Korea, it was a picture of stark contrast. Asiana Airlines, the country's second long-haul carrier, was established on 17 February 1988. Barely a week later on 24 February, the company was issued the operating permit, followed shortly by its formal launch in December with eight leased aircraft.

Fortunately for us, in spite of all the setbacks, the launch went ahead triumphantly on 1 July 1991. Since the project was my brainchild, I thought it proper that I should continue to involve myself fully in running the operations with the same committed and vigorous style I had demonstrated in my many years in the marine transportation business. This Japanese proverb sums up my conviction succinctly: "Approach the bridge with caution but march bravely ahead once you're on it!"

EVA Air takes off

EVA managed to carve out an extensive route network spanning some 30 major destinations across Asia, Europe, USA and Australia within a mere three to four years of its launch. It was a monumental achievement, which in many respects could be attributed to the firm foundations Evergreen had hitherto laid down.

I had decided at the outset to transfer some of the brightest people from our shipping operations to EVA Air. Imbued with Evergreen's culture and traditions, they continued to work hard in EVA Air in pursuit of personal excellence. Their ability to grasp the complexity of various aspects of airline operations within a relatively short time took everyone by surprise.

Even for myself personally, although I had accumulated a wealth of experience in shipping over the years, the airline business, I must admit, was an entirely different ball game. Because I was starting virtually from zero base, I had to literally pore over stacks of reference books that I had brought back from Japan and elsewhere. I also visited many aircraft and plane-engine makers as part and parcel of my self-education process through which I was able to acquire an intimate understanding of the industry over the years.

In a way, I did not have any alternative but to upgrade myself professionally in tandem with the overall progress of the company if I was to continue leading the people into the future.

My guiding principle was since it was our own initiative to take on such a formidable challenge, we had better be fully committed. Due to Taiwan's "pariah" diplomatic status in those days, it was not easy for EVA Air to secure traffic rights. Against such formidable odds, the prospects of building EVA Air into the world's biggest airline appeared rather dim. Nevertheless, my ambition was still to add another feather to our cap by turning EVA Air into a global airline with the best safety records and the highest standards of customer services.

EVA Air invested heavily in terms of both capital and manpower in the critical areas of flight safety and passenger services from the outset, a bold commitment rarely seen in other newly established airlines around the world. Merely on aircraft purchases alone, EVA Air placed a one-time order with Boeing and McDonnell Douglas of the USA for 26 new aeroplanes that was worth some US$3.6 billion. Not only was this the biggest single private-sector deal that Taiwan had ever transacted with America, it was also unprecedented in that our purchase agreements with the two companies were signed concurrently in the same venue.

The reason I insisted that EVA Air purchase only new aircraft was because we wanted the planes to be custom-fitted with technologically superior navigational systems to ensure maximum flight safety. At the same time, we could send our people periodically to check the progress of the aircraft under production and to also learn the latest advances in aircraft repairs and maintenance. The knowledge and experience acquired in the process would place EVA Air in good stead to repair and maintain its own fleet of aircraft in the years to come.

With used aircraft, however, the main disadvantage was that the original equipment systems on board might not necessarily suit our needs unless they had been subjected to radical modifications, which, in themselves, might prove technically difficult to accomplish.

Most airlines in the world had invariably started off on a small scale with one or two new or even antiquated planes and their aircraft maintenance and manpower-training responsibilities were usually farmed out to external parties. Rarely would they see any necessity to expand their fleet or facilities until after the operations had become profitable.

EVA Air, however, adopted a drastically different approach. Not only did we acquire a fleet of brand new aircraft, we also spared no expenses on the construction of a state-of-the-art aircraft hangar and crew training complex. We committed investments of such a mammoth scale, even well before the commencement of actual operations and certainly prior to the realisation of any income, not because we craved "size" or status but, more relevantly, we wanted to ensure the highest standards of flight safety and customer services. It would be tough for me to run the operations effectively if I had to constantly worry about the critical issue of flight safety.

The best equipment and facilities by themselves would, however, not serve any useful purpose if we did not have dedicated and goal-oriented professionals around. In this regard, I often remind our flight crew to be always on their toes and to show an unwavering sense of mission and responsibility at all times.

"Never let your guard down even if you have flown a particular route umpteen times. Rather, treat each flight with the same care and attitude as you would the very first flight. Execute every procedure and manoeuvre with precision and never allow yourself to slacken off," I would tell them.

Indeed, this same spirit of personal commitment had long been entrenched among the captains of Evergreen vessels and it kept the rate of shipping accidents to the barest minimum. After all, the fate of a vessel and its entire crew and cargo rest squarely on the shoulders of the captain alone, especially in times of trouble.

I require our flight crew to ensure that every single navigational device is functioning perfectly prior to each flight. If any fault is discovered, even if it is a minor one, which would normally not impinge upon the safety of the people on board, I still insist that the flight be grounded immediately. It will only be cleared for take-off after exhaustive checks have been carried out. Faulty parts or components have to be duly replaced no matter how costly they are. In business, there is a natural tendency to keep costs down and stay competitive. But profit should not be an end in itself. This is why we enforce a rigid maintenance schedule in EVA Air, as I demand absolute dedication as long as flight safety is involved.

Nurturing talent among flight crew

The first batch of 16 flight cadets was despatched to the flight training centre in the University of North Dakota, whilst a further two batches with a total of 26 trainees were enrolled in the International Air Service Company in California.

The first batch comprised employees whom we had picked from amongst the second and third-ranked officers of Evergreen Line as well as from other affiliates of the conglomerate. This was an unprecedented move as never in the history of the aviation industry had any company inducted en masse people with only shipping knowledge into an airline operation.

Although some people were cynical of our decision, I was confident that the conviction and endurance of our young and fit Evergreen colleagues would stand them in good stead. In fact, there is actually a great deal of similarity between shipping and flying particularly in the areas of navigation, geography, meteorology and terminology. Besides, people in shipping, which truly transcends national boundaries, often possess tremendous foresight and a high level of professionalism. These are qualities that would enable them to switch in midstream to a new career, say, in aviation, without any difficulty at all.

I recalled sharing with the boys my long-held maxim before they left for their training stint in the United States: "A pilot must possess the requisite skills but, more importantly, he must be seen to be morally incorruptible. He must ensure that the safety of every person on board is uppermost in his mind and, as such, he must discharge his duty to the best of his ability, especially if it's within his control to pre-empt any problems arising."

The flight cadets cherished their training opportunity. They worked hard and emerged from their course literally with flying colours, scoring an impressive 98% on average. Upon graduation, they were sent to several leading airline and plane-engine companies for further training as well as to familiarise themselves with handling different aircraft types. Only after they had gone through the entire programme and passed a series of stringent tests were they commissioned assistant co-pilots, followed by continual on-the-job training in order to acquire more practical experience.

On average, we need to spend some US$300,000 to train a first officer from scratch, excluding salary, food and lodging, transport and other miscellaneous expenses. It is a hefty investment but nevertheless well justified in the long run. A well-structured training programme not only goes a long way towards raising the standards of flight safety in the profession in general, it also helps nurture talents, the value of which cannot be quantified in monetary terms.

Although it is expensive to groom a pilot, finding qualified people to fill these demanding positions is an even greater challenge. Pilots must be healthy and physically fit at all times, must possess good vision, be free from any heart ailments and must not be predisposed to serious illness.

Not many young people can fit the bill nowadays going by these stringent standards. If they do not have bad eyesight, most probably they are afflicted with some kind of health problems. As a result, out of the droves that turn up for recruitment interviews, only a handful eventually make the grade. Successful candidates are required to undergo many long hours of arduous training and have to pass a gamut of gruelling tests before they can eventually qualify as co-pilots. Promotion to the rank of captain would probably take them a further ten years or so, depending on experience. The nurturing of talent is thus a laborious process, as one can see.

In those days, Taiwan did not have any professional schools or institutions that catered to the training of civilian pilots. It was, therefore, not uncommon that the flight crew of airlines comprised mostly former air-force pilots. Pilot shortage became even more acute following the introduction of the "Open Skies" policy under which Taiwan's airlines witnessed an unprecedented rate of fleet expansion.

In the face of this untenable situation, EVA Air swiftly implemented a comprehensive programme with a view to accelerating the pace of pilot training and to nurture a self-sufficient pool of flight crew in the long-term. The company invested in a state-of-the-art training facility.

Meanwhile, foreign pilots with the right credentials were hired to alleviate the manpower crisis. Their invaluable experience and expertise helped bolster our training procedures considerably, paving the way for the establishment of our own in-house training capability eventually.

EVA Air also installed an array of flight simulators so that pilots could upgrade themselves and hone their skills in handling emergency situations based on a multitude of variables including weather conditions and air currents. Regardless of nationality or track record, it is compulsory for every pilot to undergo a fixed simulator training schedule and to pass all the required tests if he wants to continue flying.

In view of their heavy responsibilities, I always encourage our pilots to learn to manage their time judiciously. I believe our moods are influenced more by our mental well-being rather than by such extraneous factors as people, objects or events around us. A balanced and decent life style leads invariably to a relaxed frame of mind that in turn makes work seem so much more effortless and enjoyable.

What really pleases me is that all these years, the entire flight crew, which comprises both locals and foreigners, have been able to work hand in glove together. Their spirit of camaraderie and faithful devotion to the company is a real source of joy to me!

Aiming for "zero defect" maintenance

Although pilots are a vital link in the propagation of air safety consciousness, we must never overlook the critical importance of a well-maintained aircraft. Engine troubles in mid-air could prove disastrous, no matter how skilful or responsive the pilots. As a simple illustration, a stricken vessel can possibly stay adrift on the high seas, awaiting rescue. But a distressed plane cruising at an altitude of some ten thousand metres in the sky presents a totally different scenario with unthinkable consequences.

It is thus essential for an airline to possess in-house maintenance capability if it aims to achieve a high standard of air-safety. Because of the varying degree of complexity of equipment, fittings and components found in different aircraft types, there is no guarantee that the required checks or repair work will be attended to thoroughly if these responsibilities were entrusted to third parties. It would actually amount to an act of negligence on the part of the airline should any of its planes encounter serious mishaps. "Safety First" is thus not simply a catchy slogan; it is a matter of life and death that no one should take for granted.

In view of the gravity of the safety issue, EVA Air deemed it necessary to invest some NT$3 billion in a maintenance hangar right at the outset. Although this commitment was a heavy burden on the company's finances, I was convinced of its long-term justification. Apart from producing skilled technicians and engineers, which in itself was an integral part of the company's overall air-safety management, the facility also benefited the community at large as it offered ample employment and vocational opportunities.

To shorten our learning curve, I hand-picked 24 senior engineers from amongst the ranks of Evergreen's shipping and related operations and packed them off to Oklahoma's Spartan School of Aeronautics in the United States for an initial 13-month apprenticeship. The boys spent half of the time on theory and the remainder on practical sessions in the school's maintenance hangar in Tulsa where they learnt hands-on to strip and reassemble different makes of aircraft engines.

Driven by a passionate sense of personal responsibility and the desire to excel, they treasured the opportunity and did exceptionally well in their assessments, obtaining an average score of 95 per cent. Some of them even achieved a perfect score!

I was thrilled when I learned of their outstanding results. On my visit to Los Angeles some time later, I invited them all to dinner. The school's instructors heaped lofty praises upon the boys whose discipline and esprit de corps, and above all else, their academic brilliance had enabled them to achieve the highest score ever in the entire history of Spartan.

"Although aircraft's equipment systems and their functions are much more complex compared with those of a ship, we had had no problems in coping at all," they enthused.

Not only did the boys manage to improve their mastery of the English language, they were also able to acquire the much desired FAA (Federal Aviation Administration) licenses that qualified them to repair airframes and engines.

With the completion of the programme's first module, the trainees were sent to several aviation companies in America for a specialised 9-month course in the repair and maintenance of different aircraft types, followed by a further three-month on-the-job attachment with ANA of Japan.

They were later to tell me of their deep apprehension and fear, especially of making inadvertent mistakes, whenever ANA maintenance crew assigned them an aircraft. They related how their worries would give way to tremendous relief and jubilation when they witnessed their custodial plane take to the skies without any hitch.

Responsible and meticulous in their tasks, the engineers' collective motto was to achieve a standard of maintenance that promised virtually no risk of any negligent acts arising. Credit must indeed go to the maintenance team whose diligence in the hectic months gone by had made possible the inaugural flight, a historic occasion I was sure they would all cherish for a long time.

It is customary for the maintenance crew to line up and bid a confident "Bon Voyage" to the pilots as the plane taxis away for take-off. This simple but thoughtful gesture is a testament to the maintenance team's undivided attachment to the importance of every person's safety aboard.

Because of the highly demanding and complex nature of aircraft repairs and upkeep, I insist that the technicians and engineers keep a thorough record of all their activities. They must adhere to standard operating procedures as an integral part of our stringent quality control measures system-wide. Every minute detail, including the identity of the person responsible for executing the task, must be logged into the computer whenever any rectification has been carried out. This is to ensure that the proverbial buck stops where it should and that there are no wilful cover-ups.

Rome, as they say, was not built in a day. Likewise, it takes years of hard slog to establish the fine reputation of an airline. EVA Air has finally reached an admirable stage in which other airlines are seeking its help in improving the quality of their in-flight services. It also ranks among the tops as the preferred airline of many travellers. This recognition by the public and the aviation fraternity is a huge boost to the morale of everyone in the company.

I have often said that airline business is a highly-strung venture to be in. It does not matter how much effort you have put in previously, you must still ensure that every single one of the ensuing flights is handled with the utmost of attention and care. There is absolutely no exception to this rule.

Whenever the scheduled take-off of any planes is held over by more than an hour, or if any unexpected problem should arise, regardless of the hour of the day and night, I insist that it be reported immediately to me. That is why my mobile phone is on a 24-hour standby and my heart often skips a beat or two whenever the phone rings in the middle of the night. It is thus not an exaggeration to say that running an airline operation is a nerve-racking experience!

Top class in-flight service

I have personally had the privilege of travelling on most of the world's leading airlines. As far as the standard of in-flight services is concerned, I would generally rate Japanese airlines ahead of others. This was the reason I struck a deal with All Nippon Airways under which ANA would train our flight attendants as a first step towards establishing our own criteria for quality services.

The first batch of trainee stewardesses was picked from the offices of Evergreen Line and Uniglory Line. Together with fresh recruits, they underwent a three-month training stint in ANA. Most of the girls had just graduated from their universities and had never been out of the country before. They thus found it tough initially to adjust to a foreign land. To make matters worse, it was coincidentally December at the time, the coldest month of the year in Japan, and virtually all the girls came down with flu. Furthermore, they had to grapple with their hectic and strenuous training schedules. As a result, some of them were reduced to tears and longed to go home.

I have always been a disciplinarian. The girls' naivete and lack of determination infuriated me initially. Nevertheless, I thought it was my duty to boost their flagging morale. When I visited them shortly later in Japan, they were so relieved that tears of joy literally welled up in their eyes, as though it was an emotional family reunion of some sort.

I explained to them that the course, deliberately designed to be rigorous and tough, was meant to give them a solid grounding to prepare them for their upcoming roles. It would be such a waste if they did not learn anything from their experienced instructors. I admonished them not to underestimate their own ability or, worse still, make fools of themselves. Be conscious of the heavy responsibility ahead, I said, in view of the large numbers of passengers they would have to serve on each and every flight. Only through sheer determination and continuous self-improvement would they be able to turn into reality their cherished goal to be the best in the industry, I reminded them.

I was happy to see at the end of their three-month course that not only did the girls manage to acquire the necessary skills, they had also matured in stature considerably. As for those one-time loathsome instructors, they became the girls' idols!

But when the time came for them to put their knowledge to the test, ANA flight attendants flatly rejected the girls' expressed desire to help out. Instead, they were made to just stand around. Their Japanese colleagues feared that the relative inexperience of our girls would upset the passengers and tarnish ANA's image as a result. To add insult to injury, no sooner was the plane airborne than their in-flight announcement would make it abundantly clear that there were trainee attendants from EVA Air in their midst, as though they were more of a liability than an asset.

Not prepared to be snubbed indefinitely by their Japanese colleagues, some of the girls plucked up their courage and asked for a chance to serve the passengers.

"We are confident that we'll manage all right. Please let us try as we'll surely not let you down," they begged.

The girls' earnestness convinced some of the ANA in-flight supervisors to change their minds. Others, however, turned a deaf ear. Those who were fortunate enough to have a go at it were delighted that their performance far exceeded their own expectations. Shuttling back and forth along the aisles in the distinctive attire of EVA Air, their friendly and diligent dispositions won the adulation of many a passenger. Their commendable performance certainly dispelled any lingering doubts the Japanese chief pursers might still have of them.

Back in EVA Air, the first batch of graduates promptly set out to compile a handbook on various aspects of in-flight services they had learnt in ANA. But although EVA Air is primarily an international carrier, 80 per cent of the passengers it carries comprises Taiwan nationals. As such, it was inappropriate to transplant ANA's culture in its entirety on EVA Air. Where ANA's practices were deemed unsuitable in EVA Air's context, they were modified and improved upon to cater to the specific needs of our countrymen. This way we were able to gradually establish our own in-flight service procedures and the handbook has since become a standard training tool in EVA Air.

Personally, when flying on other airlines on my frequent trips overseas, I always pay particular attention to the variety of in-flight food and beverages they serve. As far as we are aware, the majority of our countrymen have an overwhelming preference for oriental cuisine. ANA had, however, suggested that cold foods are more ideal on short-haul routes as there is insufficient time to heat up the meals on these flights. But to me Chinese food does not taste good if it is not served piping hot. We were hard-pressed to find a way out of this problem.

EVA Air sought Boeing's assistance in this matter. In collaboration with our senior flight attendants that I had sent to Seattle earlier, Boeing conducted a series of experiments to see how meals could possibly be served hot on short-haul flights. Their efforts were duly rewarded as they soon discovered a practicable solution that was subsequently adopted successfully on EVA Air's short-range flights. Even the hitherto sceptical ANA later sent its people to learn from our experience.

As part of our overall objective to develop an in-house capability in cabin-crew training, EVA Air invested heavily in a dedicated and modern facility offering a vast array of programmes.

Trainee stewardesses have to undergo an intensive and rigorous three-month course which covers a myriad of subjects including language proficiency, deportment, etiquette, meals presentation, personal grooming, first-aid, emergency evacuation and communal living, among others. With the exception of public holidays, it is compulsory for students to stay back in the hostels throughout the course of the training.

Some trainees in the past were not able to endure the rigours of the course and dropped out halfway. The majority of them, however, persevered and performed well. The parents of many of the students were grateful that EVA Air had practically transformed their children into mature, sensible ladies overnight. They said that not only do their daughters now help out in household chores, they have also become more caring and filial.

EVA Air swears by this training formula with missionary zeal. It is our fundamental belief that if we are to maintain continuity and consistency in the standard of our in-flight services in the long term, we must groom our chief pursers from within the rank-and-file of the company. Rather than resorting to poaching people from other airlines, it is, therefore, logical to promote the more senior flight attendants to fill these positions in the company.

Generally speaking, it takes some seven or eight years for a flight attendant to acquire enough experience to become a chief purser. Given the long gestation period, these positions in newly established airlines are often filled by people hired from rival carriers. The problem with such a practice is that the "recruits", coming as they do from a different background, may not necessarily fit into the new workplace, given the fact that no two companies are ever the same in terms of culture or management philosophy. Thus if EVA Air were to deliver a consistently high standard of service at all times, it must deploy only those people whom it has trained and groomed for the tasks they are capable of. In this respect, I was confident that our girls would measure up.

Again, to shorten our learning curve, we specially invited six senior chief pursers over from ANA. Over a three-month period, EVA Air's designated chief pursers learnt the ropes under the supervision of their Japanese peers who later told them how very impressed they were by the girls.

"They have all done impeccably well," our ANA colleagues beamed, "and there isn't anything else we can teach them."

The first batch of home-grown chief pursers did not disappoint us. Indeed, graduates of the earlier batches have all since risen to the rank of either chief purser or training instructor, thus promulgating the tradition of nurturing cabin-crew talent internally at EVA Air.

As in the case with other areas of EVA Air's operations, the company enforces a strict code of conduct in its in-flight services so as to pre-empt the possibility of standards slackening. Before leaving together for the airport, flight attendants are required to attend a pre-flight briefing during which they are also assigned specific tasks they have to perform on board.

Again upon the flight's return to base, the crew have to get back to the office first for a round of debriefing in which any untoward incidents, the crew's responses as well as passengers' reactions are discussed and minuted. Where necessary, the reports are submitted to the senior levels of the relevant departments to be used as a basis for improvement, thus raising the overall service standards of EVA Air to an even higher plane.

Evergreen deluxe – a class without peers

Most airline companies of the world operate a largely similar configuration of aircraft types in their fleets. They thus have to be highly innovative in their products and services in order to differentiate

197

themselves in a cluttered and competitive marketplace. Given this situation, personalised services of the highest order and maximum passenger comfort are indispensable in winning over and retaining customer loyalty.

The choice of cabin and seating configurations of our aircraft were a major preoccupation of mine. I made it a point to travel on different types of aeroplanes with different airlines on my regular trips overseas so that I could study the layout, fitting and furnishing of the various classes of their cabins. I went as far as taking measurements of the legroom and the spaciousness and pitch of the seats.

Whenever a new idea or concept came to my mind, I would call for a brainstorming session with my colleagues from various departments, in which computer simulations of different cabin configurations were created until an optimal layout was found.

Our fastidiousness with the quality of the plane's interior furnishings and fittings, even down to the fabric and colour scheme of the seat covers, often put the aircraft makers in a quandary. Whenever something was not within our expectations, and as long as the plane had not been delivered to EVA Air, we would require the manufacturer to make the necessary changes accordingly. Although modifications of this nature would entail additional costs and could even disrupt the aeroplane production schedule, I insisted that they be carried out nonetheless. My rationale was, whilst timeliness of aircraft delivery was important, it should not be an end in itself, more so if it should result in shoddy workmanship.

Traditionally, most airlines in the world adopt a three-class configuration: first, business and economy. However, as I observed on my numerous trips overseas, often only a handful out of the 32 first-class seats were taken up regardless of peak or lull seasons. This is contrary to the popular industry notion that businessmen travel on business class only if the first-class cabin is full and that they fly economy as a last resort when both first and business classes are not available.

I was baffled by this apparent phenomenon which I later discovered to be a legacy of the Persian Gulf wars. The global economic contraction that occurred in the wake of the Gulf conflicts prompted companies to drastically cut back on their budgets for overseas travels. As a result, business travellers who would normally have flown first-class were compelled to fly business-class instead.

The economic hardships at the time also led to a sharp decline in the tourism trade in Taiwan, resulting in airlines slashing their prices. When economy-class fares, which were usually about half the price of first-class ticket, were reduced to a mere quarter of the latter, many businessmen opted to travel economy instead for obvious reasons.

This development inspired me to re-think my strategy.

From what I observed, although FIT's (free and independent travellers), who are mostly businessmen, generally pay more for their economy-class fares than passengers in tour groups, they all enjoy the same level of in-flight services, which seems somewhat unfair to the FIT's.

I thus came up with the concept of a "hybrid" class. It was something of a cross between the business and economy class but which mirrored the business-class standards of the industry in terms of service and spaciousness. FIT's only had to fork out slightly more than an economy-class ticket to enjoy the better service and greater comfort of this new class of cabin.

EVA Air's first and business-class cabins were already more luxurious than those of other carriers. Our innovative hybrid class, called "Economy Deluxe Class" or YD in short, not only offered passengers a level of in-flight comfort available only to business-class travellers of other airlines, it was also more affordable.

The service was well received by the market and attracted a popular following within a rather short period of time. Many travellers would actually not settle for anything less than YD.

In May 1995, more than two years after its introduction, EVA Air renamed YD Class "Evergreen Deluxe Class" (ED) and the service was further revamped in line with the rising expectations of our customers.

Although EVA Air was at the time a relative newcomer to the industry, our goal was to be the best in the world offering the highest standards of services. Thus, whether it was in cabin designs, seating layout, in-flight entertainment or in-flight meals and beverages, EVA Air's products and services all bore the hallmarks of ingenuity and originality. Passengers were assured of a truly unforgettable experience flying with EVA Air!

Our fully reclined seats in the "Super First-Class Cabin", personal audio-video in ED Class and in-flight announcements, which we provided in a variety of local dialects, did not just bring about reverberations in the market. These trend-setting innovations also indirectly contributed to the vast improvements in the cabin services of many airlines in the world.

Coming of the 747 Combi

Boeing 767-300 ER (extended range) planes were the mainstays of EVA Air's fleet in the initial stage of its operations. But when the wide-body 747s were introduced later, I observed that, given a choice, customers generally preferred to travel in jumbos on international routes.

The problem was, with a capacity of around 400 passengers, a 747 was not exactly an economically viable option, particularly in lull periods when load factors are consistently low. I was thus eager to find a win-win way out of this dilemma whereby customers' needs could be met on the one hand and the surplus capacity of the jumbo gainfully utilised on the other.

Because of Taiwan's relative small geographic size, there was little scope for EVA Air to develop a domestic route network. International air traffic rights, on the other hand, were difficult to come by. These constraints, coupled with a slow growth in passenger traffic as well as drastic seasonal variations in load factors, convinced me that a passenger-cum-freight mode of operation, the "Combi", was the direction I should aim for.

My immediate plan was to convert some of our 747 passenger

aircraft into Combi's in which the number of seats would be limited to some 200, with the rest of the capacity earmarked for carrying cargo. The Combi was an ideal option to maximise capacity utilisation, more so during seasonally lull periods. In peak seasons, the aircraft could be reconfigured to cater to greater passenger demand. This way, we could maintain the average passenger and cargo load factors of our jumbo jets at reasonably high levels throughout the year.

You could say I "borrowed" the Combi concept from the Dutch Airlines, KLM. But my decision also rested on the premise that freight operations are relatively unaffected by seasonal factors and that Evergreen Group's considerable experience and expertise in marine transportation and logistics would stand EVA Air in good stead to secure sufficient cargo for the Combi operations to be successful.

EVA Air had earlier placed a firm order for eight Boeing 747-400 planes, of which four had already been delivered. When we notified Boeing that we wanted to convert the remaining four aircraft into Combi's, we were met with howls of protest. They argued that, coming at such a late stage, these major and costly engineering changes would invariably disrupt production and result in delivery delays.

But I was assertive. Although it would take us quite a while to recoup the expenses incurred as a result of such changes, I explained that the opportunity costs were far greater in the long run if we did not carry out the conversion at the outset; considering the average 15-year life span of an aircraft, I was certain that the long-term growth of EVA Air would be stifled without the revamp. Boeing finally gave in to our insistence and proceeded with the modifications.

I subsequently made a drastic decision to also convert two of the 747s that were already in service into Combi's. Although these were major rectification works which would cost us some US$10 million for a single aircraft, not counting two months of downtime when the aeroplanes had to be grounded, I nevertheless decided to bite the bullet for the long-term benefit of EVA Air.

My decision to go for the Combi's was vindicated by a vast improvement in EVA Air's air-cargo business since the introduction of these services. Their regular and frequent schedules were a boon to shippers who welcomed the convenience not available to them previously. From the standpoint of operational efficiency, the Combi's offered greater flexibility, thus enabling the company's fleet of aircraft to be put to more optimum use.

With an extensive network and a consistently high standard of service, EVA Air deservedly earned itself a global reputation for excellence within a few short years of its launch. It was also largely instrumental in raising the profile and status of Taiwan's aviation industry internationally.

Despite the accolade, I continued to find ways to strengthen and broaden the ꞌscope of EVA Air's existing services by investing in in-flight catering facilities, airport terminal services and other related activities. The development and management of an international chain of resorts and hotels was a complementary project I championed.

EVA Air's creative and innovative approach, which ensured that the company was always one step ahead of others, literally propelled Taiwan's aviation industry into the next millennium. It played a major role in instilling in the industry a high level of awareness concerning the critical importance of flight safety and quality services. The relentless push to extend the international frontiers of its operations also served to broaden the scope and horizons of Taiwan's businessmen and leisure travellers alike.

Although the mammoth scope of Evergreen Group's multifaceted sea, land and air-based activities had by then traversed the globe, we were not about to rest on our laurels, particularly in the critical area of quality improvements. I continued to travel extensively, racking my brains and exploring new frontiers. I also devoted more of my time to community service: a token of my gratitude for what society had generously provided me with over the years.

Evergreen Line's 20th anniversary celebration, during which I officially announced that we were applying for an aviation licence to establish an international airline company.

New KMT Alliance's legislators tried in vain to derail EVA Air's plan to build the aircraft maintenance facility on leased land.

EVA Air's staff took out newspaper advertisements to air the truths and to implore the politicians not to snuff out the civil aviation business.

EVA Air's inaugural flight took off smoothly on 1 July 1991, having successfully overcome a series of obstacles.

You can say I am an expert in airline operation today, the result of tireless self-study, an inquisitive mind and a keen sense of observation.

THE SIGNING CEREMONY OF
PURCHASE AGREEMENTS
FOR
B747-400/B767-300ER AND MD-11
BETWEEN
BOEING & EVERGREEN AIRWAYS
DONNELL DOUGLAS & EVERGREEN

Two separate agreements to purchase 26 new aircraft from both the Boeing Company and McDonnell Douglas were signed concurrently not long after EVA Air was established.

"Safety First – the No. 1 Priority" is not just a catchy slogan. On the contrary, EVA Air invests heavily in an in-house aircraft repair and maintenance centre.

To ensure flight safety, EVA Air spares no expenses in the training and education of its technical crew.

掛牌宣言－飛安保證！

EVA Air's engineering personnel are required to log in their names onto the computer whenever they carry out any maintenance or repair jobs.

Maintenance crew bidding a reassuring "Bon Voyage" to a departing EVA airplane.

In-flight crew being put through their paces in this NT$3 billion training centre.

The quality of in-flight food and beverages are constantly under scrutiny in an untiring effort to improve standards.

An industry first: EVA Air's trailblazing "Economy Deluxe Class" revolutionised the global standard of in-flight services.

Considerable thought went into the design and arrangement of aircraft seats to provide maximum passenger comfort.

The wings of Taiwan: EVA Air, pride of the Chinese people, also won the widespread recognition of the global community.

With my wife in Seattle, USA, for the delivery by Boeing Company of EVA Air's first two new B747-400 jumbo aircraft.

A bold and decisive move: two existing B747 passenger aircraft being retrofitted into "Combi's" to enhance operational flexibility and efficiency.

Evergreen Laurel Hotel: an international chain of hotels established by the Group to provide customers with its unique brand of fine services.

[7]

Evergreen's Management Philosophy

A strong desire to put on one's thinking cap and to stay well-informed are indispensable in ensuring a company's sustained competitiveness. Employees, on the other hand, are the backbone of an entrepreneur's long-term survival.

A successful enterprise must have a ready pool of talented people, besides management quality and foresight, to ensure long-term growth and survival. Indeed, I believe people are the most precious asset of a company, although talent scouting and nurturing is easier said than done.

In Evergreen, recruitment exercises are targeted at fresh graduates and those who have just completed military service. These are the people who, we feel, have not imbibed the bad influences of modern society and can better fit into the culture and demands of the company.

However, we do not necessarily recruit only people with high academic qualifications. In fact, more than anything else, greater emphasis is placed on the malleability, work attitude and moral bearing of the candidates. To this end, we had developed a reliable technique to ensure that only those who are suitable are selected.

In the earlier days, job applicants had to pass a written test before

I interviewed them together with my colleagues. The technique has been fine-tuned in recent years to prevent any inadvertent omission of those who possess what I consider the "Evergreen quality". In some situations, a written test is preceded by an interview, while in others applicants have to go through several rounds of interviews. Even though each person spends only a few minutes with us, we can roughly gauge his or her suitability.

We are careful not to overrate applicant's performance during the interviews; this is because people generally try their best to make a good impression. Instead, we rely more on our carefully crafted questionnaire to size up their inclinations, besides keeping an eye on their demeanour while they wait their turn to be interviewed.

I sometimes ask an interviewee if he drinks, and if he says no, he is told that he cannot be a sales person, prompting him to quickly change tack and admit that he actually drinks a little.

"How little is little?" I would prod further.

"Just a couple of beers really!" some of them would rejoin, while others would cook up all kinds of stories. No two answers were ever the same. But there was nothing cynical about these questions as all I wanted to find out was how they would react.

The first five batches of EVA Air's flight attendants were interviewed by me personally, in the hope that people I had selected could be groomed to help develop a customer-services system we could call our own, as well as to train future recruits.

I normally interviewed five girls together at any one time. Though I might appear to be talking to just one of them, I was actually also keeping an eye on all the others. This approach enabled me to study their mannerisms, composure and other personal characteristics all at once, a case of "killing five birds with one stone". Some people jokingly said that I did it my way because I admired pretty girls!

In the area of written examinations, besides the usual general knowledge and language proficiency requirements, applicants were also subjected to "Mental Agility" and "Job Compatibility" tests.

In the "Mental Agility" test, candidates had to solve several relatively complex numerical problems. Some job seekers quibbled over the relevance of this test in relation to the jobs they were applying for. In reality, this test is the best way to gauge people's ability to focus on a given task. I believe a person who lacks concentration is not capable of doing a proper job.

The "Compatibility" test was devised with the aim of understanding the applicants' inner qualities such as their notion of values, attitude towards work and moral uprightness, through which we could judge whether they would fit into the corporate culture and management style of Evergreen. Candidates were, for instance, asked if they would accept any overseas posting or whether they would be willing to work overtime, should the need arise.

Not all who excelled in the written tests are deemed suitable though, particularly those whom we felt would not fit into Evergreen's style of doing things. These were people who would usually quit their jobs shortly after joining. The compatibility test was thus almost a "make-it-or break-it" hurdle that dashed the hopes and aspirations of many a candidate.

Although the technique was later streamlined to keep with changes in society and to meet our own manpower requirements, one thing never changed – our uncompromising stance on the moral uprightness of employees. I believe that people with good moral behaviour usually lead a normal, decent life style and are thus less likely to be distracted in their work, which is particularly crucial in the case of EVA Air, where the highest level of flight safety must be maintained.

Evergreen prohibits any influence peddling or string pulling when recruiting staff. Our job ads clearly state that any one trying to use his or her personal connections to seek employment with us will have their applications rejected forthwith. We have no choice but to be strict lest people we hire later become a liability to the company. Unfortunately, those who do not understand our position feel that we are being high-handed, and although I unintentionally offended many of them in the process, I did not budge.

Training and education are priorities

A person who excels in school is often called a "scholar", but it does not necessarily mean that his scholastic talent can be transferred to work. Formal education does not automatically equal success in life. I often look upon a business enterprise as being some sort of a university, charged with the burden of educating and training employees. Indeed, if a company desires to groom talent successfully, it must first of all have a sound training and management programme, over and above the existence of a conducive environment. Thus, it is in the area of nurturing talent in Evergreen that I have devoted much of my effort.

Employees who have just joined Evergreen are promptly inculcated with the awareness to improve themselves continually. They are encouraged to work hard for themselves, not just because the company hands them a paycheck at the end of the month, but also to broaden their knowledge and skills, and to cultivate good work ethics, so that they can realise their full potential and succeed in life.

Evergreen does not spare any effort, time or money on nurturing talent. But training is rigorous, in fact so much so that out of the one hundred odd employees we had hired on one particular occasion, only a meagre ten remained a year later. These were the ones whom we regarded as having made the grade.

In our experience, people who have joined us from other companies do not usually stay on for long, mainly because they are simply unable to fit into Evergreen's culture. For example, out of the ten people we recruited from several American and European shipping companies in conjunction with the launch of Evergreen Line's European services, more than half of them quit their positions in the first year.

Training of recruits, impressionable people that they are, is particularly emphasised in Evergreen. But our training is not merely restricted to the acquisition of knowledge or inter-personal skills; we adopt what is in pugilistic parlance a "master-student" relationship, in which recruits are tutored by their supervisors to have the correct values and mindset from the outset.

The "master" is vested with a heavy responsibility in this mentoring

215

relationship as his own future in the company very much depends on the progress of his "students". In other words, he can ill-afford to withhold any skills or knowledge from his wards, unless he does not aspire to move up the ranks himself.

We customarily send our staff for overseas training in order to meet the personnel requirements and the high professional standards of new ventures we embark upon. The training of EVA Air's flight, cabin and maintenance crews in Japan and America was a good example, as was the strong team of 19 people we despatched to SHATEC – Singapore Hotel & Tourism Education Centre – for a one-year attachment in connection with the launch of our international chain of hotels.

Evergreen maintains a long-term goal in nurturing talent, an important criterion particularly in the IT (information technology) age that we live in today. We provide a wide variety of courses to enable employees to continually upgrade themselves. Even our experienced seamen must undergo specialised training before they are deployed on new-generation container vessels. Seagoing staff of foreign nationalities are not exempted either; they are encouraged to learn new skills, in the hope that they will feel happy working for the company for as long as possible.

By virtue of Evergreen's extensive operations around the world, employees have the opportunity to serve in different subsidiaries and offices of the group both in and outside of Taiwan under our job rotation programme. Besides offering employees the benefit of wider international exposure, the programme is a perfect antidote not only against professional fatigue that is associated with a prolonged attachment to a particular job, but also against the siege mentality of incumbent managers who insist on doing things in their established ways.

Some of our managers have since had the opportunity to work in numerous other countries besides Taiwan – Japan, the US East and West coasts, Panama, England and Germany – as part of management's overall objectives to groom them for higher positions in the Evergreen Group.

The nature of the job function an employee in the Evergreen Group is given depends on his personality and ability. Those who have just joined Evergreen Marine Corporation, for example, spend two to three years in the commercial section before they are assigned to suitable positions.

I believe we all have our strengths and weaknesses, and as such we should refrain from instantly writing a person off merely because he fails to live up to the expectations of a certain department head. On the contrary, we should endeavour to find out what his inherent strengths are; perhaps he has certain previously untapped qualities which he can be put to good use in some other fields.

Moreover, courses that some people elect to study in school or college may not necessarily match their personal predilections, a problem that is compounded in Taiwan by its joint-examination system. Some students, on the other hand, choose to enrol themselves in any school regardless of the curriculum it offers.

Many young people are attracted to work in Evergreen due to the conducive environment and excellent career prospects it offers. As long as these youngsters are willing to strive, they have every chance to succeed and become useful citizens. It would indeed not be hyperbolic to liken the Evergreen Group to a huge intellectual cradle from which many of our society's elite have emerged.

The "Sea-Land" orientation programme

I was a seafarer for 15 years before I struck out on my own and am, therefore, not unaccustomed to the rough-and-tumble world seamen live in. Hence, crew management and sailors' welfare are amongst my top priorities now that I am the boss of my own shipping company.

Evergreen Line had a fleet of 600-, 800- and 1200-TEU fully-containerised vessels in the early days. A 1200-TEU vessel could complete its discharging and loading operations at a port within a matter of a few hours, thus leaving sailors with precious little time to spend with their families.

I also observed that sometimes the cargo we had collected was in excess of what our vessel could normally accommodate without being overloaded. The conflict of interests between the port captain and the ship's master pertaining to the vessel's loading plan would often result in heated exchanges between them.

The problem was, although our sales staff would normally stop accepting cargo once they had met their quota, it was sometimes difficult to turn down customers' last-minute requests. When that happened, we would end up with more cargo than what our vessel could ordinarily carry.

Let's take an 800-TEU vessel as an illustration. Say, we already have in hand 780 boxes of cargo but must decide whether to accept another consignment of 30 containers. If we do, the ship's capacity will have been exceeded by 10 boxes; if we do not, the shipper will not be happy and we will also end up the poorer with a dead-freight of 20 containers.

In practice, every container vessel has a built-in tolerance to permit overloading to a reasonable extent as long as its overall safety is not compromised. Nevertheless, the question of overloading is the sole prerogative of the ship's captain and not even the chairman of the shipping company can overrule him. After all, the captain is solely responsible for the safety of the entire vessel and its crew.

To help alleviate the problem, crew members were given an opportunity to work on land for a length of time so as to have a better appreciation of the sort of operational constraints their shore-based colleagues had to face all the time, and vice-versa. Besides, fostering a climate of mutual understanding and close cooperation, the scheme also allowed crew members to have more time with their families.

This so-called "sea-land" job orientation programme was a first in the industry and soon became a popular object of emulation by other shipping companies.

In the past, the literacy level of Taiwan's sailors was very low and many of them, especially those who had spent weeks on the high seas, tended to squander all their money as soon as they hit dry land, thus often leaving their families to fend for themselves.

Although seamen are generally better educated these days, they are still often away from home, sometimes for two or more months on end. To ensure that the livelihood of their families is taken care of in the meantime, I require seamen to have their family members draw a portion of their wages each month.

Because of the perilous nature of seafaring in the past, not many people were willing to work on the ships even though seamen generally earned three times more than their counterparts on land. With the passage of time and coupled with the advent of new technologies, however, sailing has become a much safer profession these days.

Nevertheless, the welfare of our crew, their educational and training needs, as well as their career prospects remain high on the list of my priorities. We also provide a conducive and stimulating environment in which employees can carve out a lifelong career with us. Indeed, many senior managers in the Evergreen Group today were once captains of the Evergreen Line.

Managing change

Besides the ready availability of talent, a company has to have a strong management system in order to ensure progress. A business can safely count on the leadership of its founders in the initial years, but long-term, sustainable growth is only possible if it has a formal organisational structure and a sound management system from an early stage.

A well-conceived system ensures that the company does not lose sight of its objectives, much like the way a new employee has to be inculcated with the right and proper work attitude from the outset. An improper grounding or a weak foundation breeds bad work habits, which are difficult to change later, unless the company starts on a clean slate altogether with an entirely new workforce.

When we first started the Evergreen Line in 1968, the company had one rickety general-cargo ship and a handful of employees. Business was tough and we had to push ourselves doubly hard. But, because my mind was already set on the future, I did not have any qualms at all about instituting the necessary operational procedures and guidelines.

It took me exactly six months to draw up, in the Japanese language, the "Management Rules & Guidelines" and "Principles of Crew Management", as well as the corporate and management structures.

For the compliance of everyone in the company, I laid down precise directives governing such matters as the hiring and assessment of employees, delegation of authority and responsibilities, reward and punishment, among other things. They formed the basic management framework within which necessary changes in the future could be made in line with the growth and expansion of our operations.

The bounds of authority and responsibility of every level of employees in the company are clearly defined so that employees know exactly where they stand, apart from ensuring that what needs to be done gets done, perfectly and efficiently, and that the company's operations stay steadfastly on track.

In terms of organisational structure, the basic consideration in my mind then was the total number of departments and sections that had to be set up, both initially and in later stages, including their potential manpower and office needs. I envisioned that as business grew, and as headcount increased, a formal corporate structure complete with all its functional scopes would eventually emerge.

Evergreen's corporate structure is organised along the line of divisions and sections, with each division led by a Senior Vice-President and his or her assistant. Sections, coming as they do under the wings of divisions, are the most fundamental operating units. They each have a manager, whose duty it is to manage the section's operations and to supervise the work of his subordinates. Not only is he answerable to the senior management, he also acts as a conduit through which the feedback from those in the lower ranks can filter up to the top.

In terms of staffing, the headcount of each section is largely determined by its growth potential. In my experience, a section should ideally comprise eight to 10 people, maximum 12, beyond which it becomes an unwieldy group. On the other hand, a smaller group entails a more compact office layout, which makes the supervisory role of the section chief much easier. In any case, some people simply do not have the ability to manage a bigger group of, say, 12 workers.

My guiding principle when I set out to draft the management rules was that the system remain current and relevant at all times. Where change to the system or in the manner of its execution is due, it must be effected promptly so that the company does not lose track of the mission the system was originally designed to accomplish.

Rules are after all laid down by people for people, so that employees are aware of their personal as well as collective responsibilities. But if rules are applied inflexibly or dogmatically, they soon become a burden to workers, and a source of resentment, thus stifling the company's progress.

In the past, for example, employees going away for business received a fixed lodging allowance, with the quantum pegged to his seniority. But due to unforeseen circumstances, like when they had to put up in a more expensive hotel because the place they could afford happened to be full, they incurred extra expenses, which could amount to quite a significant sum in some cases, but which they nevertheless had to bear personally.

The problem was rectified when the rules were changed to allow employees the discretion to stay in any hotel, depending on their ranks, with expenses incurred by them reimbursed in full.

Yet another example of change we saw in Evergreen concerned its remuneration system. In the old days, male and female employees in Evergreen were paid different wages even if they were of the same rank. But when it later became a social norm for women to go to work, we promptly instituted an equitable pay system under which employees, regardless of gender, received the same wages for the same type of work they were doing.

A management system is not unlike the constitution of a sovereign country, the rule of law that every citizen has to uphold and respect. But in a world of shifting values and expectations, even a nation's legal system has to stay relevant and current by doing away with antiquated or obsolete statutes which may otherwise hinder the progress of society.

In this context, although a strong management system is indispensable, how it can be creatively and flexibly applied is an intellectual challenge in itself.

Consider Evergreen's retirement policy as an example. Many of our experienced senior managers who had reached the company's mandatory retirement age of sixty were still hale and hearty; they certainly did not relish the prospect of languishing at home, having led an active working life for decades.

Although I empathised with their plight, extending the retirement age was, however, not a panacea either. It would result in fewer career openings for the younger managers, the "rising stars" of the company as it were, who would bring their youthful enthusiasm and innovative ideas to the jobs.

A win-win situation, I felt, was to retain those senior managers who still had a strong desire to work for the company while moving others to one of a number of companies I had specially set up for them with my own funds. The main purpose of these companies was to provide the retirees with some work to do in a less stressful environment, and since they were old friends, they could frequently meet up to talk shop, thus making post-retirement life so much more invigorating. They were even urged to take equity in the company, which they also had a free hand in running, in the hope that they would experience a sense of pride and achievement.

Many of those due for retirement were moved to tears when they learnt of my deep concern for their personal well-being. Of course, there were also those whom I did not ask to stay; some of them, much to my abhorrence, had no hesitation in discrediting their erstwhile colleagues in front of me just before leaving, in a final test of their true moral principles, I suppose!

I believe a sound management approach does not only promote discipline in the workforce, it also produces an environment in which innovative ideas can flourish. The Evergreen Group, with thirty years of experience in the transportation business, can certainly boast of a fairly complete management system with all its pertinent controls, checks and balances firmly in place. Fledgling enterprises in the group can readily draw on existing management know-how and practices, thus helping to propagate the established traditions of Evergreen in the process.

When I first started out with EVA Air, I racked my brain in trying to come up with an ideal organisational structure and management system for the company. It was after all the group's maiden foray into the highly capital and people-intensive airline business, and I had to tread very carefully to ensure that we started out on a firm footing, with a strong management.

The last five years have been devoted to strengthening the foundations of EVA Air's personnel administration, training and education, as well as long-term strategic planning. The little leisure time that I had was spent on poring over numerous professional airline publications and on countless study trips, prompting some people to jokingly brand me a workaholic chairman.

Once the corporate structure and rules and regulations have been clearly established, education or employee awareness assumes a crucial role in their eventual implementation. It is through continuing education that the management is able to instil the aspirations and ideals of the company in the minds of the employees; only when everybody is pulling in the same direction that management objectives and policies can be realised.

On hindsight, I am relieved that Evergreen has had a consummate management system from the very beginning, otherwise, I reckon I would still be chipping laboriously away today.

From dictatorial to democratic management

I believe a businessman should not allow himself to be bogged down with the nitty-gritty of day-to day operations; the burden of ensuring growth after all rests with everybody in the company. In this respect, it is important that an entrepreneur knows when to delegate more responsibilities, and hence greater authority, to his peers, provided of course he has the right people.

The development cycle of a business can be divided into several stages, with the initial phase usually led by an individual who wields the power of a "dictator". But once the operations are on track, the businessman must start grooming people for management roles at the same time that the company gradually moves towards a "democratic" system. The second phase of a company's growth thus assumes a semi-autocratic, semi-libertarian management style, ensuring that people who are competent are entrusted with greater responsibilities to run the operations.

In this context, a businessman must know how to spot, use and groom talent, besides the need to be professionally competent; he must pave the way for employees who are capable to move up the ranks so that they can be trained for even bigger roles ahead.

However, an employee who has risen to a higher position but does not live up to his ability should not be promoted further or given any more responsibilities than he can handle. This is because some people are capable of leading only a small team, say, a section, but lack the quality to cope with bigger groups.

Employees' advancement prospects in Evergreen are based strictly on merit and only those who meet the criteria are promoted. Although our management staff is comparatively still very young, they are nevertheless an experienced lot; in fact the average age of our section chiefs is barely over 30.

The authority that Evergreen entrusts to its management staff of various ranks, from section heads upwards to vice-presidents and beyond, is clearly defined, as is the jurisdiction of every operating unit in the company. The end result is that we see a heightened sense of involvement and responsibility among all the employees, who know exactly where they stand and what the management expects of them.

For a system to be effective there must be trust between management and workers or else it can at best only exist in form rather than in substance. It is folly, for example, to delegate certain responsibilities, and with them authority, to a section chief and then worry about his integrity behind his back. Instead of being self-contradictory or trying to hold onto power, management staff must be magnanimous enough to impart skills and knowledge to subordinates unselfishly.

Indeed, considering the scale and scope of Evergreen's operations, I would not have been able to cope had I not delegated the bulk of my responsibilities to my colleagues, with myself playing the role of a "Supreme Commander", providing leadership and guidance. After all, it is not individual effort but collective strength that counts at the end of the day.

Unlike most other companies, management staff in Evergreen is personally responsible for the proper conduct of their subordinates. Where employees have fallen short, or when they have committed wrongs, it is the duty of the superiors to counsel, teach and provide guidance. But just as management staff is answerable for the mistakes of their subordinates, we expect the latter to toe the line and obey the instructions of their superiors.

We often asked job seekers in our recruitment tests how they would react if they felt that the boss had given them an unreasonable assignment. The correct action, I feel, is to voice your views on the matter, but ultimately, comply with the superior's orders. The reason is because although you may feel you have good reasons to disagree, the boss has had the benefit of experience and a wider perspective of things, and if he still sticks to his guns despite your cogent arguments, it is better that you listen. If indeed employees think it proper to quibble over every job they are asked to do, the company will be reduced to a state of chaos and ineffectiveness in no time, with management and employees constantly at loggerheads.

But I hasten to say that although we do not condone insubordination in Evergreen, it does not also mean that our employees have to be "yes" men. On the contrary, we have always advocated a democratic, participatory style of management. Also, my notion of "democracy" is definitely not one that lacks cohesion, and coherence, much like a handful of loose grains of sand, but one that strongly emphasises collective effort and wisdom so that the company's growth momentum can be sustained.

Advancement based on merit

Staff performance appraisals in Evergreen are a perennial exercise. Their respective deputy managers and higher-ranked superiors assess employees several times a year on their overall achievement, skills, conduct, attitude and diligence, among other things. The outcome of these assessments will determine workers' annual increments, year-end bonuses and promotion prospects.

To ensure impartiality and fair play, each employee is assessed not only by his or her immediate superior, but also by their indirect bosses, with the results channelled directly to the personnel department where they are compiled into an average score. The appraisers are not allowed to discuss, consult or influence each other on the outcome of their assessments.

The fact that each employee is appraised by two or three people not only ensures that the end results reflect more accurately his or her overall performance, it also pre-empts attempts by any boss to use the appraisal process to discriminate against his subordinates. A manager may, for example, hold a grudge against his subordinate and give him a poor assessment. However, if the low score is averaged out with that of, say, the VP's, the true status will eventually emerge.

The reason employees are assessed a few times a year is because this is the only way to ascertain accurately their overall performance over the one-year period. I personally took part in the appraisal exercises in the earlier years, through which I was able to know the strengths and weaknesses of our employees like the back of my hands. In the past, the appraisal was conducted on a quarterly basis, which compelled employees to be on their toes at all times.

Some companies assess their employees perfunctorily once a year whilst others make it a year-end exercise just before they pay out the bonuses or review the employees' salary. This, in my opinion, is not exactly a good method as there are always people who only work hard to impress their bosses round about the time the appraisal is to take place. Such a situation can occur especially if the person responsible for the appraisal has just joined a particular section and does not, therefore, have a good feel of the workers' year-round performance.

Now that Evergreen's operations are firmly on track and the group's workforce has also grown considerably over the years, the appraisal frequency has been reduced from four to two or three times a year. But the exercise is still conducted in the strictest confidence.

In Evergreen's formative years, employees usually came to visit me at home during the Chinese New Year or on other festive occasions, bearing gifts and with their wives in tow. It was a custom I put a quick stop to as I did not want to subject myself to any emotional blackmail nor did I wish to encourage people to curry favour, thinking that everything would be all right if they lavished me with presents. If indeed these things were allowed to happen, it would have been most difficult to justify myself to those who were genuinely diligent and committed in their jobs. It was therefore imperative that I set a personal example so that our managers would also deal with their staff fairly and objectively.

Unsurprisingly, not a single employee has since dared turn up at my doorstep during Chinese New Year or on other occasions, leaving me in relative peace and quiet. My former schoolmates and friends were initially curious, or even suspicious, about the whole thing, unbeknown to them that employees who breached the standing instruction risked being sacked from the company. But they soon came to appreciate my stand, although I still jokingly told them that perhaps it was because I was such an unpopular boss in the eyes of my staff that they did not want to visit me anymore!

Discipline with a human touch

The culture and other special attributes of a company, born directly of the very system it has instituted, manifest themselves in the overall corporate image or style. Hence, characteristics ranging from the manpower structure and commercial functions of the various departments, to office design and layout, interior lighting, and even down to office ambience, all reveal something about the disciplinary nature of a company.

Evergreen Group's worldwide offices adopt a consistent open-style layout, with the section chief seated at the front end of two tightly-aligned rows of desks, while his subordinates occupy the two lateral sides.

This layout has several advantages. Apart from economy of space utilisation, it enables a section chief to monitor his staff closely. It also compels employees in the section to have more than just a superficial knowledge of their colleagues' responsibilities so that when one of them is away on business or on leave, somebody else can cover his duty in the meantime.

Such matters as the precise arrangement of our office chairs, desks, cabinets and light fittings may seem trivial at first glance, but the fact is that office ambience does have an effect on the staff's mood and efficiency. Furthermore, by being attentive to these details, we also show ourselves to be a methodical and disciplined lot. Just like in everything else we do, we must always strive to achieve the best instead of displaying a sloppy attitude.

Visitors to Evergreen often wonder why they do not see any cups, ashtrays or other personal effects on employees' desks. These neat surroundings are in fact the result of our ongoing effort in instilling a deep sense of discipline in the company. To me, a person sipping tea at his workplace not only makes him appear so lethargic, and incapable of concentrating on his task, he is likely to make a mess of the documents if the drink gets spilled. If workers want to have a drink or a snack, they can always go to the pantry, which is found on every floor of the office building.

Smoking is also strictly prohibited inside the office building and visitors are not exempted either. A person sitting at his workplace with a cigarette sticking out of the corner of his mouth is not only an obnoxious sight, the tobacco fumes will foul up the air in the entire office and upset non-smoking colleagues.

Ever since the ban was imposed, we have been enjoying those hitherto elusive refreshing breaths of clean air each time we walk through the doors of the building. Many people were envious of our accomplishment because similar measures taken by other companies had not produced the same result. In fact, in our case, many smokers actually kicked the habit altogether after some time.

I have always been a stickler for a clean and neat office environment as I believe it does a lot of good for the mood, vitality and even the health of a person, which in turn has a positive effect on employees' work and general attitude indirectly. It is a habit that I feel is worthwhile preserving.

Employees in Evergreen are also urged to be civic-minded, to take proper care of things in the office. This, I am happy to note, is something they are more than willing to oblige with. Staff will, for example, clean up the vanity-tops in the washroom with the very paper towels they have just used to dry their hands; not only does this simple gesture reduce wastefulness and save cost, it also helps keep the place generally clean and tidy.

To reinforce my message, the company organises a big spring-cleaning at the end of each year, during which everybody, regardless of rank, joins in to spruce up literally all the nooks and crannies in the office. Not that we do not normally keep our office clean and tidy, but by getting employees involved in these activities, I hope they have a better appreciation of their personal responsibility in maintaining a spick-and-span office surrounding.

Office attire is one other area I am very particular about. But as long as what they wear is presentable, as I would often tell them, they need not put on a new dress every day. Like it or loathe it, we often judge a person by what he or she wears, and a good first impression goes a long way towards establishing a smooth and fruitful relationship in business.

I believe a proper dress code is also essential in promoting discipline. In Evergreen, ladies don a green outer suit while men are dressed in their signature white shirtsleeves and a tie. If employees were free to wear whatever they fancy to come to work, the office would very soon be reduced to a venue for fashion competitions of some sort. Unlike men's, ladies' fashions change overnight, and in trying to keep up with the Joneses, the girls may get overly engrossed with dressing themselves to the nines, thus neglecting their work. Requiring employees to wear uniforms at work is, therefore, the most effective way to deal with such a potential problem. In fact, when our employees were asked their views on the need for wearing uniforms in a survey some time back, the majority of them voted in favour of carrying on with the tradition.

Personally, basic courtesy dictates that I put on a formal suit whenever I have to receive visitors. Particularly in a business of an international nature like shipping, we can ill-afford to be sloppy or ignorant of universally accepted norms of etiquette. Appropriate attire after all helps project a respectable image, both for the businessman and his company.

Actually all these rules of decorum have been in force in Evergreen since the very early days, as evidenced by the impressive white shirt and Western suit attire of Evergreen Marine Corporation's business executives whenever they are out visiting customers. Similarly for the flight attendants of EVA Air, whether they are on board or in the airport terminals, they are always immaculately attired in the company's uniforms.

One area of discipline that the Evergreen Group has never had any problem with is the punctuality with which employees report for work. In fact, most workers have cultivated the commendable habit of clocking in early and leaving late in the evening, and of not attending to personal matters during office hours. As far as personal conduct is concerned, the management takes a stern view on such unruly behaviour as fighting, gambling or an indiscreet private lifestyle, with those breaking the rules taken to task.

I recalled when I was a first mate in my seafaring days, the sailors called me a "policeman" by dint of my reputation as a disciplinarian and a demanding taskmaster. Nevertheless, I did not hold them in contempt; on the contrary, I was the one who spurred them on whenever their morale was down, especially during the vessels' loading and discharging operations which I expected to be carried out with the greatest of efficiency and little or no damage to the cargo. I even forked out my own money to buy quayside labourers beers to thank them for their hard work.

In the final analysis thus, while it is important for the management to be unambiguous on the concept of reward and punishment, it should also be seen to be sensitive and compassionate towards the employees, as only then can we instil discipline without having to be callous.

The Evergreen spirit

The so-called spirit of Evergreen embodies the 3 C's: Challenge, Creativity and Cohesion which my peers and I conceived during our start-up years.

I often urge our employees to face up to challenges boldly and to overcome them with panache, for there are ample rewards to be reaped. To beat a hasty retreat without even trying is to be blatantly irresponsible and it will not get anybody anywhere in life.

A person with a positive, and proactive, attitude often also shows an irrepressible appetite for the pursuit of excellence. This quality, coupled with a readiness to adapt to changes, would help ensure that the company continues to grow unencumbered.

But however creative a person's idea may be, his lone effort will not suffice. He must instead tap the wisdom and effort of his colleagues in order to bring about the fruition of his ideas.

In ancient times, Chinese physicians were often in possession of so-called "secret formulae". A formula's mystique lay in its being a closely guarded family recipe which one generation of the family would hand down to the next. But if a situation arose in which the family was unable to find a suitable heir to perpetuate the tradition, the recipe could in fact do more damage than good. It is for this reason that I am against anybody in Evergreen holding onto any secret formula; instead of employees concealing any skills or knowledge, I want them to foster a spirit of sharing and teamwork (or cohesion) so that the company can thrive in the long run.

Besides the 3C's, I also stress the importance of good moral behaviour in Evergreen.

As far as I could remember, schools in Taiwan offered lessons in moral education during the Japanese Occupation. Students were taught the fundamental principles of morality and propriety, a valuable concept that remained indelibly imprinted on my mind and has become part of my life's guiding principles. Which, of course, is one of the reasons Evergreen's training programmes also emphasise moral education, besides imparting skills and knowledge. Indeed, forums expounding the virtues of rectitude are regularly organised for the benefit of employees, in the hope that they will carry the message back with them to their families.

In my view, one of the most important attributes of a person is to have an indefatigable spirit in the pursuit of one's goals. If an individual has determination and drive, coupled with a passionate desire to learn and assimilate new ideas, he can overcome any obstacles in his path once he has put his mind and heart to the task. Ultimately, his achievements will not only benefit the company, they will stand him in good stead throughout his entire lifetime.

Harmony, equality and honour

Some people claim that Evergreen's management approach is based on the Japanese management model, which of course cannot be further from the truth. In reality, ours is a system I have personally developed with ideas culled from the best management models available.

But whatever model a company adopts, it must most importantly be compatible with the overall environment in which it operates vis-à-vis its own needs and expectations. We should not apply the so-called Harvard or Japanese models blindly without first considering their relevance under what could be a totally different set of conditions.

Nowadays, many young people with foreign university degrees in business management like to think they know the subject only too well and thus aspire to be their own bosses. In practice though, running a company is not as simple as just dogmatically applying all the theories that one has picked up in college, at least not in an environment that is in a constant state of flux.

In this respect, it is naive to think that academic experts who hail from the world's renowned business schools are naturally capable of running an enterprise successfully. In the hustle and bustle of the real business world, which is in sharp contrast with the relative serenity of an ivory tower, nothing can replace the valuable experience that one can acquire only through sheer hard work and self-sacrifice.

In the context of management appointments, the president of a Japanese corporation, for example, is appointed to a four-year tenure, just about long enough for him to have a reasonable feel of the overall business. Aware that his term of office is limited, he would be contented with just maintaining the status quo, and because he is averse to risk-taking, it is unlikely that he would accomplish anything memorable at the end of his tenure. The situation is not helped by the fact that the retirement age of the chairman is fixed at sixty-five. Hence, if the chairman were already in his sixties when he is appointed to the position, he would be inclined to be even more conservative in his management approach.

In Japan, I thus observed, the top management of every successful corporation has invariably had a long-term mandate to pursue its goals. Similarly in my own case, I have remained at the helm of Evergreen Marine Corporation, taking on challenges and providing strong leadership, since the very day it was founded by me when I was 42 years old. In simple terms, a management that is to all intents and purposes on a fixed short-term contract will not help the growth of a company.

Compared to other companies in Taiwan, the management hierarchy of the Evergreen Group comprises mainly young people. This is because our employees have by and large joined us straight after leaving college, and many of them have risen to their senior positions at a relatively young age of just over forty through a combination of hard work, experience, and verve.

In any case, if we want to keep up with the pace of progress in the technology-driven age that we live in today, it is essential that we allow young people, particularly those in the computer and IT industries, more leeway to express themselves. Ideally, if a company were to stay constantly innovative, it must be endowed with talent that comes from combining the experience of the older-generation managers with the enthusiasm and fresh ideas of their younger brethren.

It is, however, quite a different scenario in Europe and America where job-hopping seems to be a widespread phenomenon; workers there commonly work for a company for only one or two years before heading for greener pastures elsewhere.

In a way, our European and American counterparts have only themselves to blame. Theirs is a system that does not offer workers long-term job security; in fact, employees can be fired from their jobs anytime. Given the insecurity, workers naturally do not have any desire to stay longer than absolutely necessary, and would quit from the company whenever attractive opportunities elsewhere beckon. It is a vicious circle that is detrimental to the interests of both the employer and employees themselves in the long run.

In contrast, Evergreen's management emphasises harmony, much like the cordial atmosphere that permeates a big but close-knit family. We invest generously in our people. Besides being paid a favourable wage, our workers also enjoy a whole host of munificent perks, a decent working environment, as well as excellent prospects for career advancement. Employees in return feel secure enough about their future to want to stay put and grow with the company.

Traditionally, Evergreen has a low staff turnover. In fact, in a poll of Taiwan's "Most Desired Employer", the young and educated generation had consistently ranked the Evergreen Group tops. People who ask me what it is that makes Evergreen tick would invariably be told that, compared to their counterparts in other companies, our people are definitely more proactive and industrious. They are also better able to identify themselves with the company's vision. On the other hand, we care about their well-being, and together we forge a close alliance and share a common destiny. This is the secret of our success!

I really long to see our workers treat Evergreen as one big, warm family, with everyone showing mutual affection and concern, thus engendering a conducive environment that they feel comfortable working in.

Evergreen Line, as I recall, started providing free lunch to employees soon after it was founded, when the office was still situated along Chang An East Road. Before that, workers packed their own boxed lunch, which they would then heat up in the office pantry during mealtimes, causing the food to lose its original flavour and nutritious value. It was worse in the winter when the food tended to get cold very quickly, rendering it unhealthy to eat. I also observed that some workers often took their lunch in solitude, which, as I later discovered, was because they, coming as they did from less well-off families, were ashamed of the meagre lunch they had brought from home.

It was this generally unsatisfactory state of affairs that subsequently prompted me to engage a restaurant near the office called Umeko, to cater lunch for the employees. This particular restaurant was not exactly a well-known name in the trade at the time, but business boomed when news spread that it was being patronised by Evergreen.

The catering arrangement had to be discontinued, however, when we relocated from Chang An East Road to Sung Chiang Road because we could not find any decent restaurant in the vicinity of the office. In its place we introduced a cash-subsidy scheme instead. But I soon noticed much to my dismay that employees were trying to save money by having their lunch at roadside stalls, despite all the dust and exhaust fumes. Not only were these places unhygienic, going out to eat was also such a hassle, especially on rainy days. That was when I thought it proper that Evergreen set up a kitchen and hired our own cooks to prepare the meals. The facility would also be useful to those who had to stay behind to finish their work late into the night.

Since then, the kitchen has become a standard feature in every subsidiary company of the Evergreen Group, providing a wide variety of foods, including vegetarian meals. For reasons of hygiene, our cooks and kitchen hands, whom we recruit directly, are required to undergo regular health screening.

What is worth mentioning perhaps is that I apply what I preach on good morals whenever I have the opportunity. For example, our employees are provided with cheap buffet breakfasts, which they have to pay for voluntarily by leaving their money on an empty plate left by the side of the counter. But whether they actually pay the required amount or not, we leave it entirely to their conscience, since there is no cashier around to collect the payment. All that we want to inculcate is a spirit of honesty and integrity among the employees.

The health of our employees does not escape my attention either. For this reason, we have an in-house medical clinic providing basic treatment and consultation. A screening programme was instituted in 1982, requiring our workers to undergo periodic health check-ups conducted by visiting doctors engaged by Evergreen. The clinic had its facilities enhanced in 1992 when we acquired state-of-the-art equipment such as X-ray, ultra-sound and cardiogram machines.

I often impress upon our cadres to capitalise on the strengths of people we employ, rather than dwell on their shortcomings. If employees are weak in certain areas, it is the duty of the managers to teach and guide them with patience and understanding. After all, nobody is perfect and if we get overly engrossed with people's defects, we will never be able to accomplish anything.

A responsible manager must also treat his subordinates with compassion and magnanimity, imparting his knowledge and experience to them unselfishly. He should not abuse the authority of his position by compelling his subordinates to submit to him; respect has to be earned and it is only via exemplary conduct that other people will look up to you.

I used to be very stern with my employees due to my high expectations. But although they often incurred my wrath when they made mistakes, I did not hold them in contempt. On the contrary, it was my fervent hope that all the admonitions they received from me would help turn them into the company's mainstay someday.

Times change and societal values shift in tandem. Compared to our generation, people these days are a vastly different breed. They seem to lack the tenacity to take hard knocks, probably because they have grown up in a totally different environment. Given this background, managers need to be even more sensitive and patient towards their subordinates, ungrudgingly instilling in them the right values and attitudes from the outset. This is the only way to encourage workers to be committed to the company and to groom a ready pool of talent to ensure managerial continuity and long-term survival.

To this end, our managers are constantly reminded of the importance to unwaveringly propagate the spirit and moral principles of Evergreen, while adopting a flexible and adaptable management approach at the same time.

In short, not only must a businessman be nimble in responding to change swiftly, he must also be seen to be fair and sensitive to the needs and expectations of his workers, to establish a close rapport, as well as create a pleasant and harmonious environment for all to work in.

It should indeed be the ambition of every budding entrepreneur to run a business competently, while at the same time not neglecting the needs of society at large, so that his employees will feel a deep sense of pride and honour working for the company and that other people will look up to them wherever they go. Only in this manner is running a business, and being a part of it as an employee, a worthwhile pursuit.

Know the market

I was often asked why it was that everything Evergreen touched seemed to turn to gold. The truth is our success had neither been a miracle nor a fairy tale; it was a culmination of sheer hard work and an unflappable spirit of a great many people in the company, as well as our practical, down-to-earth attitude. What people see now is the obvious side of things – the success of Evergreen – little do they appreciate the amount of mental anguish and painstaking labour that went into every single stage of our metamorphosis.

Evergreen does not believe in luck or opportunism, nor do we tolerate shoddiness. What we emphasise is a management that is not only forward-looking and decisive, but one that is at the same time nimble, meticulous and efficient in the execution of all its plans and strategies.

I invariably insist that we undertake a detailed and comprehensive feasibility study as a basic requirement for any project that we embark upon, for it is only through such an exercise that we can truly feel the pulse of the market and make accurate decisions.

Although market studies are costly, grave mistakes arising from committing investments rashly without the benefit of a proper evaluation can be even costlier. In the worst-case scenario, wrong decisions can even bring down a company.

Due to the global nature of Evergreen's shipping and airline business, the need for in-depth field research becomes all the more compelling. Because political and economic situations, as well as investment regulations vary widely from country to country, they carry with them different risks which must be thoroughly evaluated, notwithstanding the huge expenses that have to be incurred, before committing ourselves.

Our decision to enter international liner services was a case in point. In the old days, although Taiwan's shipping companies mainly plied the regional routes, my assessment of the island's economy, however, convinced me that our future lay in international shipping. Although getting into this business was an uphill battle, I was nevertheless determined to press ahead, establishing in the process the springboard from which we were to launch our ambitious fleet containerisation programme sometime later.

It was for the containerisation exercise that Evergreen Marine Corporation spent US$1 million over two years on its feasibility study alone, by no means a paltry sum, considering the relatively modest scale of our operations then. On the other hand, had we not had the benefit of a detailed market study, we might not have had the courage to undertake this mammoth project, let alone be where we are today.

In market studies, speed is of the essence, over and above the need to be thorough. The market is never static, and competitors will always have an upper hand if we are not nimble enough.

Generally speaking, once an investment target has been identified, we will quickly establish a task force to plan our strategies and delegate responsibilities. Members of the task force will be on the first available plane out of the country for their assignments as soon as their travelling arrangements have been completed. Their job is to gather as much firsthand information and data as possible, including such parameters as the prevailing local conditions, industry and market trends, existing laws and regulations, manpower and other resources, as well as the costs of doing business.

This information is then collated and analysed. The feasibility study is not considered complete until all the pertinent issues have been thoroughly dealt with and the investment costs quantified. Should any doubts arise during the course of the study, the onus is on the task force to promptly sort out any discrepancies, leaving no stone unturned. Finally, if the prognosis is favourable, the team will proceed to draw up the detailed action plans, including visiting potential customers, placing orders for vessels and equipment, setting up a customer services network and looking for potential partners and associates, among other things. From then on, everybody in the company, from the top management down to the most junior staff, will join hands to push the project through to fruition.

Compared to other companies, Evergreen always had a head start in the various projects it undertook. With no precedent to fall back on, we had to rely heavily on our own market research to lead the way. Each project had its own unique problem areas which called for different solutions, as was the case with Evergreen Marine Corporation and the many obstacles it had to overcome each time a new service was launched. At times the challenges seemed so daunting that they threatened to overwhelm the financial and manpower resources of our modest operations then.

I spearheaded all the market studies in the initial years, meticulously and earnestly, something that rubbed off on my colleagues in the company. These days, even if I do not have the time to get involved in every investment detail, I need not lose any sleep over it, as I am confident that my colleagues will adopt the very same attitude and initiatives in getting things done without me.

Keep eyes open, ask questions

I often urge my staff to be observant, to have an inquisitive mind. Whether we are on business or simply vacationing, ample opportunities exist for us to explore the unique characteristics of the various places we are visiting. Not only does a meticulous attitude towards learning enrich us in terms of knowledge and creativity, it also broadens our horizons, thus laying the foundation for a better future.

Those of us on overseas business trips can easily see the different cultures and infrastructures that exist in different countries, from which we can, for example, learn something about the rationale behind their policies on street planning, building designs or environmental protection. To use an analogy of a pretty lady, we can tell what it is that makes her attractive – her good sense of fashion maybe or is it the manner in which she carries herself that makes the difference? The answer is there, if we probe deep enough.

Perhaps not many people know the extent of my personal involvement in the design and creation of the wide range of products and services that the Evergreen Group offers: Evergreen's fleet renewal, EVA Air's aircraft livery and cabins, the planning and design of our hotels and commercial buildings, even down to our corporate gift items, you name it, I have had a hand in it. A lot of my ideas and inspiration came from the numerous books and publications that I read and from observations gleaned on my countless overseas business trips.

I still travel extensively these days, visiting Evergreen's various global operations and keeping myself in touch with the latest news and development. In a dynamic world in which the only constant is change, we have to stay current and keep up with the pace of development if we do not want to lag behind competitors.

This keenness to observe and learn is something that I had always impressed upon my staff to emulate. Personally, as the initiator and prime mover of most of Evergreen's investments, I had to work doubly hard in areas ranging from the initial desk research to gathering data from overseas, to seeking advice from other companies. I shall cite a few typical examples here.

As part of our overall effort to put EVA Air on the world's aviation map, I visited Boeing and McDonnell Douglas of America several times to acquaint myself with the aircraft production process. General Electric, which designs and manufactures aircraft engines, was another company that I called upon.

I even went to the extent of measuring the pitch of the aircraft seats in the first, business and economy classes of the various airlines I flew with on my many business trips overseas; their different standards of in-flight services, as well as the attitude of their cabin crew also did not escape my attention. Information I gathered from the observations was used as a reference in the planning of our own services subsequently.

When we first started out on our international hotel chain project, I organised a task force to study the market on the one hand, while personally traversing some ten countries across Europe and America in order to have a better feel of the global hotel industry myself.

Very often, the moment I checked into a hotel, I would quickly set out with my measuring tape in hand to find out for myself the size of the guestroom, its bath, the passageway, as well as the height of the ceiling, among other things. These are the basic features of convenience and comfort that guests pine for when they first check in a hotel. I would also take pictures of the bathroom fittings and fixtures, as well as note the different varieties, packaging and fragrance of the toiletries provided by the hotel, some of which, like the soap, shampoo and body lotion, I would keep as samples for reference purposes.

Other features of the hotel, no matter how minor they were, did not escape my attention either. Like the room's soundproofing quality which, if it were poor, would result in the noise of bath waters being drained off late at night disturbing guests sleeping in adjoining rooms.

It is a seemingly trivial detail that guests may not necessarily notice immediately, but which is nevertheless a reflection of a hotel's genuine commitment in providing a high standard of customer services.

All in all, this down-to-earth, conscientious and hands-on approach has served Evergreen well. It is in fact a major contributory factor to the success of the group at sea, on land and in the air.

Managing costs

People generally think of budget cuts, retrenchments, wage restraints or suppliers being unfairly squeezed, whenever the subject of cost controls is mooted. But such measures, if adopted without careful consideration, are bound to adversely affect quality standards and employees' well-being, which may in turn damage a company's credibility and long-term prospects.

My notion of effective cost management is one that stresses the vital importance of reining in unjustified expenses at all times, while keeping direct costs in check. It will be too little too late if we only get cracking when the company has fallen on bad times or when competition has reached an unbearable level.

I believe keeping a tight lid on cost is a necessary evil if we are to maintain a competitive edge in the long run. Indeed, we constantly remind our staff to be conscious of all aspects of our costs and not be lured into any futile price wars. It does not make any commercial sense, for example, to fill up a plane or a vessel if it does not generate any profit for the company.

In the past, competitors regularly accused Evergreen Marine Corporation of price undercutting in their forlorn attempts to sully our reputation or even to destroy us. But if indeed Evergreen had been guilty of such practices, how was it possible that we were able to stay consistently profitable year after year?

Cost structures vary widely from business to business and from company to company, depending on the scale and efficiency of each operation. Which was why I strongly objected to the shipping industry's blanket proposal to eradicate the so-called "over-tonnage" by curtailing the freight capacity of individual carriers. The quality of services differs from carrier to carrier and it is surely the prerogative of customers to do business with whichever shipping company they choose; it is also the only way to ensure free and fair competition, as well as safeguard the progress of the industry. Business enterprises must, in my view, rid themselves of a parochial mindset, and strive to maintain a minimal acceptable standard of services for the sake of their own survival.

From the perspective of a shipping company, its cost structure, and hence competitive strength, is a direct function of the design of its vessels as well as its total container capacity. As a general rule of thumb, a shipping company has to have a minimum box capacity that is 2.5 to 3.0 times the total dead-weight capacity of its entire fleet. Evergreen, however, has managed to pare the supply factor down to a low 1.9 to 2.0 times.

The movement of every Evergreen container is closely tracked by computer to ensure a quick turnaround and to prevent any loss from occurring. This, coupled with a high level of operational flexibility, has enabled us to keep the capital costs of our containers much lower than those of other carriers.

Furthermore, not only are our container vessels designed with the optimum cargo-carrying capacity, and with the best fuel efficiency, they are also highly automated. Automation reduces crew size to the barest minimum, a radical breakthrough in containing costs. In fact, Evergreen has always had the leanest crews among all the shipping companies in the world.

Take, for example, the 2,728-TEU G-type container ship that was first deployed in Evergreen's round-the-world service launched in 1984. It had a full complement of a crew of sixteen (seventeen, if we included the one cadet engineer on board), against the 25-member crew found on similar vessels of other carriers. Even our current R-type 4,229-TEU vessel has a relatively small crew of thirteen. It is an effective crew management model that has since been adopted by many other shipping companies.

One other cost containment measure is to ensure that the market demand justifies the investment cost of a new vessel. The key consideration here is design flexibility. Take, for example, our S-type vessels that were deployed on Evergreen's first container route. Although each vessel was designed with an initial capacity of only 600 TEUs, there were provisions for the ship's hull to be lengthened should there be a subsequent increase in demand. Known in the industry as the "Jumbo" process, which takes only a matter of months to complete, it is a cost-effective strategy that also enhances operational flexibility and efficiency.

In the case of EVA Air, it has long had a policy of acquiring only new planes and of enforcing a stringent maintenance programme from the outset. Aircraft parts or components that have reached their prescribed life cycle are replaced even if they are still serviceable. This strategy ensures a minimal rate of breakdowns, which in turn results in a smooth and efficient operation.

What is also worth mentioning is that procuring only similar types of vessels, as well as aircraft and aircraft engines, not only obviates the need for huge inventories of spares to be maintained, the strategy also allows manpower to be trained and deployed more cost-effectively.

I was asked why we routinely consigned our decommissioned but nevertheless well-maintained vessels to the scrap-yard instead of selling them to other operators. The reason is quite simple. In the shipping business, freight rates are uniform across the industry regardless of the age of the vessels that are deployed in the carriage of goods. Thus, if our older vessels, which can costs tens of millions of dollars (US$) each to build originally, were sold off at, say, some US$3 to 4 million each, they could well turn out to be the very lethal "weapon" other operators use to compete detrimentally against us. Hence, in the context of cost management, we cannot afford to be penny-wise and pound-foolish.

There are actually many areas in which we can cut costs as long as we have the resolve. How stringently we manage our cash flows, for example, can be a critical tool in itself. Indeed, a sound financial management system is the cornerstone of a company's growth strategies whilst imprudence can easily result in it facing even heftier cost burdens.

I devoted a great deal of energy to raising capital for Evergreen Marine Corporation in the early days, for the best plans and talents in the world would be rendered useless if we lacked funding. I also saw the crucial need for a tight financial management system, including subjecting the expenses of all our branches, representative offices and agents to stringent audits. It was for this purpose that we set up an internal audit department to monitor closely the books of the group's network of domestic and overseas operations, culminating in a 10 per cent decline in operating costs since its inception.

It generally takes shipping companies some three months to collect back the freight revenue from their agents, which, I feel, is too protracted a period as it can result in severe cash-flow problems for some carriers. To improve the situation, Evergreen laid down precise accounting procedures for the compliance of its agents, who also have to recover any outstanding freight charges from their customers within a specified time frame. Agents cannot offset the expenses they have incurred, and which Evergreen must pay for, against the freight income they have collected; these expenses have to be verified by Evergreen before agents are reimbursed the money. This accounting practice of treating the receivable and payable separately not only shortens the recovery period of our freight revenue, it also strengthens our cash-flow positions considerably.

Besides vigorously curtailing wasteful expenses, management must also have the courage and conviction to take swift actions in the face of adversity, changing course or even abandoning the plans in mid-stream if necessary in order to prevent the company from incurring potentially bigger losses.

For example, when it became clear that the "Combi" was the best option for EVA Air, we wasted precious little time in persuading the Boeing Company to reconfigure the aircraft's cabin according to our requirements. Although the change was to cost us much more per plane, procrastinating over the matter or not proceeding with the modifications would have resulted in lost opportunities, or even jeopardised our long-term growth prospects.

EVA Air had invested heavily in manpower training and flight safety even before its operations came on stream. Although the company did grow rapidly over the years, hefty investments up front became a drag on near-term profitability. To alleviate the situation, I pressed for a reduction in the share capital of the company by NT$6.3 billion, a drastic financial revamp by any means.

Losses incurred as a result of capital reduction had to be borne by shareholders themselves, and since I was the majority shareholder, I stood to lose the biggest amount. Had it been somebody else in my shoes, I believed the restructuring exercise would not have materialised. But I had to bite the bullet in the wider interests of the company.

As far as I am concerned, a businessman must have the gumption to act resolutely when faced with an issue of strategic importance, setting aside any personal motives for the sake of the company at large. We must not be blinded by short-term gains lest we miss out on other growth opportunities that would otherwise safeguard the future of the business.

Moreover, we must never allow ourselves to be lulled into complacency and let costs run out of control when times are good; we must also desist from hiring surplus workers only to find ourselves resorting to laying them off in the event of an economic downturn. Provide for rainy days instead, so that the future of the company and that of workers can be safeguarded. Cost containment in general, and keeping a tight lid on wasteful expenses in particular, must be an on-going exercise, which together with a policy of retaining sufficient earnings in better times will see the company through lean periods.

Several companies in the Evergreen Group are listed in the stock exchange of Taiwan, and although shareholders regularly clamour for bigger dividend payouts, I have steadfastly resisted the pressure. Financial prudence requires a company to have strong reserves in order to weather any prolonged periods of economic downturn and to emerge from the experience relatively unscathed. Indeed, a company's long-term growth prospects will be severely compromised if whatever profit it makes is unreservedly paid out to shareholders year after year.

Personally, as majority shareholder of these companies, I stand to gain much more financially if we were to adopt a liberal dividend policy. But as a responsible businessman, I have to place the long-term interests of the company above those of my own.

Managing diversification

Whether in business or in life, we must always uphold a spirit of consistency. In other words, in everything that we do, there has to be a proper beginning and a proper end, which, in business, may mean the provision of a comprehensive range of quality services under one roof.

The Evergreen Group was founded on shipping and while it was essential that it quickly build up a critical mass in its core business, it also had to ensure that all the peripheral activities as well as its entire network of domestic and overseas offices supported and complemented each other well.

Evergreen Marine Corporation entered the transoceanic liner trade one year after its founding in 1968; it opened offices in strategic locations around the world, following the inauguration of services to the Middle-East, and Central and South Americas. We also appointed more agents and had a greater number of our own people posted overseas to take charge of the local operations.

The launch of our container services in 1975 also saw us set up affiliated companies and offices in the USA to beef up the operations there. In Europe and the Mediterranean countries, however, by virtue of their vast cultural diversities, we had to depend on our agents to take care of the operations in these places.

Evergreen Marine Corporation presently has more than two hundred offices in some sixty countries in Asia, the Americas, Europe, Australia and Africa, with their operations inextricably linked to each other, thus making it a truly multinational company. Some people even say that the sun never sets on Evergreen's business empire.

I established Evergreen Transport Corporation in 1973 to handle container trucking in Taiwan, as part of our overall strategy to reinforce the wholesale containerisation of Evergreen Marine Corporation. Further diversification into other related activities took place following the launch of our round-the-world services in 1984 – Evergreen Heavy Industrial Corporation produces containers and trailer chassis; Evergreen Container Terminal Corporation operates a fully integrated container terminal; and Uniglory Marine Corporation serves regional and feeder routes. Collectively, the Evergreen Group offers customers the convenience of a wide range of marine and land transport as well as other related services under one roof.

To add another feather to our cap, which in the process also transformed Evergreen into a giant providing a fully integrated system of sea, land and air transport services, EVA Air's inaugural flight took off triumphantly in July 1991, three years after an application to launch the operation was filed in 1988. That EVA Air had been able to achieve impressive growth over the years was due in no small measure to the credibility and sound reputation of Evergreen Marine Corporation throughout the world.

In keeping with Evergreen's spirit of diversification, EVA Air embarked on a string of related activities to strengthen its core business. Among the first to come on stream was an aircraft maintenance hangar, as well as a flight and cabin crew training centre. These were followed by Evergreen Airline Services Corporation (it provides airport terminal-handling services); Evergreen Multi-Service Corporation (a general cleaning and laundry services company); Evergreen Sky Catering Corporation (supplies in-flight meals); and Evervoyage Transport Corporation (handles ground tours).

Evergreen also developed its own hotel management expertise to facilitate the establishment of a global chain of quality hotels catering to both business and leisure travellers. The Evergreen Laurel Hotel chain, with its distinctive laurel-wreath logo, quickly made its mark in Taichung, Keelung, Bangkok, Penang, and Paris. It proudly offers a standard of service that rivals the best traditions top hotels embrace in Europe.

I later established Evergreen International Corporation with the primary purpose of overseeing the group's manifold operations, as well as to champion and coordinate our overall diversification and growth strategies.

Evergreen Group now has more than 20 affiliated companies scattered all around the world. Even though investment opportunities abound, I still maintain a cautious and conservative approach, and only those activities that add value to our core business or which fit into our overall diversification plans are likely to attract my attention.

Looking to the future, I expect growth strategies to still revolve around the three main pillars of the group – Evergreen International Corporation, Evergreen Marine Corporation and EVA Airways. Shipping and aviation will retain their roles as the two major driving forces, under the direct control and supervision of Evergreen International Corporation.

Managing succession

People in the Orient tend to hand management controls of family-run businesses to their children regardless of the youngsters' merit or personal inclinations. In some cases, once the young people joined the company, they would hastily be installed in senior management positions.

If the children do in fact show a keen interest or are suitably qualified, they should of course be nurtured, starting from the lower ranks. But if their minds are somewhere else, I feel we should not force them; make them shareholders of the company instead, and leave the critical task of running the day-to-day operations to the professionals. A company can sustain growth and scale new heights only if it has a truly committed and unprejudiced management team, appointed by and answerable to the board of directors.

The fact that many century-old European and American multinationals, such as those automobile and oil majors, have not seen their vast fortunes wane over the decades is exactly because they have vested the management of their companies in the hands of capable professionals whom the board of directors has hand-picked.

Even if a company's majority shareholder is not necessarily involved in its day-to-day operations, he can still play a crucial role in helping maintain a steady course by leaving his board of directors to carry out their tasks unencumbered.

From the perspective of Evergreen Group's core shipping and airline businesses, since they are highly specialised fields in their own right, and also because there is a dearth of suitably qualified manpower around, we have always had to depend on people whom we have groomed ourselves, as well as our own management model, to run our operations efficiently.

We could, out of expediency, have appointed outsiders to the board, but the trouble is, firstly, these people may not be familiar with the sort of business we are in, and secondly, we have to be absolutely convinced that they are committed and are not driven by any ulterior motives. For this reason, therefore, I insist that the main shareholders of every company in the Evergreen Group hold a majority stake.

For a businessman to be able to safeguard the future of his company, it is essential that people who will succeed him are not only professionally competent, they must also be well acquainted with the culture of the company.

Management succession in the Evergreen Group is well-defined and only people who possess the requisite experience, ability and leadership qualities are considered. I have successively relinquished to my senior colleagues the chairmanships of all the subsidiary companies within the Evergreen Group since 1993, retaining only my role as the Chairman of the group.

Presently, the positions of chairman, vice-chairman and presidents in the three principal subsidiaries of the group – Evergreen International, Evergreen Marine, and EVA Airways – are occupied by truly outstanding professionals who have risen through the ranks in the twenty odd years they have been with the group.

I was practically managing the affairs of the Evergreen Group single-handedly in the early days. But as operations took on the scale and dimension that we see today, it became necessary for me to gradually delegate management responsibilities to my peers and adopt a collective approach towards accelerating the growth momentum of the Group.

I am the sort of person who derives tremendous joy out of the work I am doing. Indeed, I have never grown weary of any of the businesses I have carved out literally with my bare hands. As Group Chairman now, not only do I have a firm grasp of our major growth directions, I am also able to ensure that the development of the various enterprises within the conglomerate take place on an even keel. At the same time, the experience that I have tirelessly imparted to my successors will hopefully inspire them to take over the reins of management sooner rather than later.

Personally invigilating the personnel recruitment tests in the early days.

Cream of the crop: These are highly experienced employees who have gone through Evergreen's rigorous management and training systems and stayed.

My immersion in the maritime transportation industry since leaving school, including a 15-year seafaring career, have given me a profound understanding of ships and shipping operations.

倫理道德教育

Moral principles and education are strongly emphasised among Evergreen's employees.

A congenial atmosphere: Evergreen values cordial relationships with employees.

One big family: Evergreen takes care of employees' career paths and creates a harmonious and happy working environment.

Conferred an honorary doctorate degree in Business Administration by the University of South Carolina, USA.

No substitute for hard work: Evergreen's success is built on a steady and earnest approach to business.

Studying the aircraft manufacturing process in Boeing Company

On an inspection trip to the shipyard where the hull of an Evergreen vessel was
being extended (jumboised) to increase its capacity.

Presiding over the keel-laying ceremony of *Ever Right* in Japan's Onomichi Shipyard.

Factors such as dead-weight capacity, fuel efficiency, crewing requirements, as well as market trends are all taken into account when designing a new vessel-type.

To ensure Evergreen is responsive to an ever-changing market, provisions are made during the construction process to enable the vessel's hull to be extended in the future.

Personal motto: a long-term vision for the company must remain the top priority of a responsible entrepreneur.

The shipping business transcends national boundaries, and as such, a shipping executive is a truly "international" businessman.

The Evergreen Group: a truly diversified conglomerate.

[8]

The Way for Evergreen

The more successful a person becomes, the more he should remember his origin; he must be thankful to, and repay, society for all that he has benefited from the community. "Tao" ("the Way") is the truth; cultivating Tao enhances morality and righteousness in man.

I always liken a humble and grateful person to a willow tree; the bigger and stronger it grows, the further downwards its branches will droop. Similarly, the greater the achievement of a person, the more he should remember his origin; he must be thankful to and repay society for all the benefits he has received from the community.

There are many opportunities and ways one can repay society – by running a business diligently, by nurturing talent, by providing employees with a secure livelihood, and by showing a positive outlook in life, among others.

I have been in the shipping business for a long time and am thus deeply aware of its contribution to the development of trade and industry in Taiwan. But if we were to lift our shipping industry to an even higher plane, we must systematically groom a ready pool of senior maritime talent.

Towards this end, I have established bursaries in a number of schools and university colleges since 1970, three years after the inception of

Evergreen Marine Corporation to help those students from poor families eager to pursue a career in seafaring to finish their maritime studies.

These study grants were aimed specifically at bright students with poor family backgrounds; the money was disbursed every semester (each student received NT$5,000 per semester in 1970) to cover the beneficiaries' school fees and miscellaneous expenses, as well as their food and lodging for the term. Students could thus concentrate on their studies without having to worry about their finances.

The bursaries did not come with any strings attached; recipients, for example, did not have to be bonded to Evergreen Marine Corporation after their graduation. Higher institutions of learning in which Evergreen established bursaries over the years include the National Taiwan Ocean University, China Junior College of Marine Technology, National Kaohsiung Institute of Marine Technology, National Chiao Tung University College of Engineering, among others.

In addition, we also offered beneficiaries hands-on training in Evergreen Marine Corporation as well as on its vessels during their winter and summer vacations. Students made use of these opportunities to earn allowances to help lighten the financial burden of their families on the one hand, and bolster their knowledge and experience of shipping operations on the other.

Most shipping companies in the past were reluctant to accept any students from the universities and colleges for training with them. In our bid to support the development of higher levels of maritime studies in Taiwan, Evergreen Marine teamed up with Tamkang University to establish a purpose-built school; two disciplines, in navigation and marine-engineering, were offered beginning in 1976 and 1977, respectively. I personally funded the construction of one block, the Merchant Ship Hall, and had it equipped with state-of-the-art navigational gadgets, equipment and instruments, as well as other facilities for both teaching and training purposes.

Mr Lin Tien-fu was at the time the Chairman of the Board of Directors of Tamkang University. I remember we literally had to scour the world together to gather the necessary information, and visited several maritime schools in Japan to learn from their experience. I also came up with the design of the building exterior and planned all the attendant facilities within.

Construction of the building, costing some NT$20 million and located within the premises of Tamkang University, commenced on 30 March 1977 and was completed in early April 1978. It bore the familiar facade of a merchant ship's cabin and living accommodation area.

The entire building consisted of five floors; besides offices and classrooms, there were also facilities that simulated a ship's open deck, the wheelhouse, the charting room, the library, among others. A 200-room cabin and a life-size engine room were also incorporated.

In order to inject more realism into the teaching of navigational and marine engineering studies, Evergreen Marine had donated to the school the latest global positioning systems, loran, radio direction finder, omega navigation aids, radar, depth sonar systems, gyro and magnetic compasses and other navigational gadgets. Besides, we also had relevant American, European and Japanese maritime books translated into Chinese by our own experts so that they could be used as both teaching materials and student's reference books.

But because maritime studies is a unique and highly professional discipline, and the government at the time stipulated that only those who had attained the status of a professor or a lecturer were eligible to teach in the school, people who were qualified were in very short supply. Of the lecturers and professors adjudicated to have possessed the relevant qualifications, half of them did not have any practical experience in maritime navigation.

I originally planned to second some of Evergreen's experienced and skilled captains and chief engineers to teach in the school. But, much to my regret and frustration, the plan had to be aborted when the inspectors from the department of education deemed the qualifications of our people unsuitable.

As a matter of fact, not only did our professionals boast impeccable credentials, and had passed all the requisite national examinations, they also possessed a wealth of operational experience. I had no doubt that the students would benefit immeasurably from the skills and knowledge of these seafaring elders.

It was only after much lobbying by myself that our captains and chief engineers eventually were given the go-ahead to share their valuable experience with the students.

Ever Training – a school at sea

Students had to undergo a compulsory training stint on a vessel after their four-year course in the school. While it was normal for the government in other countries to provide such training vessels, the relevant authorities in Taiwan did not offer any similar facility for a variety of dubious reasons.

The situation prompted me to propose to Evergreen Marine that we explore the possibility of providing such a training vessel so that students pursing maritime studies in Taiwan could apply what they had learnt in schools in actual practice.

The upshot was that Evergreen Marine Corporation purchased a 2,050-tonne second-hand passenger liner in 1979 and had it retrofitted into a maritime training vessel at a total cost of some NT$36 million. Christened *Ever Training*, Taiwan's first maritime training ship was ready to set sail at the end of the same year upon completion of the retrofit.

Ever Training was equipped with classrooms, study rooms, laboratories, as well as a well-furnished living area that could accommodate 100-odd students, with training in a variety of subjects conducted by their teachers who accompanied them on the trip. The vessel was also designed to carry some general cargo so that students were able to experience firsthand how loading and discharging operations were carried out in various ports in Taiwan and overseas, besides familiarising themselves with the working of the myriad instruments found on board the vessel. All the expenses incurred by the students during training were borne in full by Evergreen.

From end-1979 to 1985, when the programme was scrapped, *Ever*

Training made a total of 63 voyages, churning out 1,668 graduates. All in, students from six maritime colleges comprising National Chiao Tung University, Tamkang University, National Taiwan Ocean University, National Kaohsiung Institute of Marine Technology, China Junior College of Marine Technology and China Commercial Maritime Vocational Senior High School benefited from our free service.

In September 1983, in a move to enhance the functional capability of training vessels, Evergreen Marine Corporation decided to have its 15,000-tonne general-cargo vessel *Ever Safety* retrofitted into a modern container ship that could accommodate 200 students.

The retrofitting works were entrusted to Japan's Onomichi Shipyard. Completed in March 1984 at a total cost of NT$160 million, and rechristened *Ever Trust*, the vessel was equipped with the latest navigational gadgets and engine control systems; it also contained a wide range of facilities catering to the diverse needs of the students. All the instruments on board were installed in duplicate, so that students could make use of one of the sets for training purposes without interfering with the normal operations of the vessel.

It was due to this special built-in facility that *Ever Trust* was able to circumnavigate the globe on two separate occasions, crossing the three oceans and calling on 15 countries along the way. Wherever it went, the training ship was welcomed and valued by the local government and maritime colleges.

The educational services Evergreen Marine Corporation provided at the time to students of maritime-related studies in Taiwan were all free of charge. Those who had graduated from the training course did not necessarily have to work for Evergreen either. Not surprisingly, the response from students who had had a chance to sail with either *Ever Training* or *Ever Trust* was overwhelmingly positive; they stated unreservedly in their final report how they had benefited enormously from the experience in terms of knowledge and exposure.

But things were not looking good. The government of Taiwan changed the national education policy in 1985 to preclude all other universities, except National Taiwan Ocean University, from offering any maritime-related courses. This ruling thus put paid to Evergreen's collaborative efforts in maritime education with Tamkang University. We stopped taking in students in 1986, and the last batch graduated in 1989. *Ever Trust* gradually unwound its mission in 1990, by which time it had already provided navigational training to several thousand students.

With maritime education in Tamkang disbanded, I accepted Mr Lin Tien-fu's proposal to turn the academy, which was located on the grounds of the university, into Taiwan's first Maritime Museum at my own cost for the benefit of society at large.

The museum was officially opened to the public on 6 June 1990. Besides displaying the various navigational and mechanical paraphernalia of a vessel, as well as mock-ups of actual scenes, it also showcased miniature models and pictures of vessels of various styles and origins of both the past and present era. A library and an audio-video room, containing a huge collection of maritime-related books and films, including technical shipping literature of various advanced countries, were also featured. All said, the elevation of the role of maritime education in a formal school setting to educating society at large by way of the museum could be considered as the manifestation of my unbridled love for fostering this particular field of knowledge and expertise.

Charity and public service

My long-held conviction is that we all live to do good deeds and earn merits. Whether we are dealing with the less fortunate people around us or employees or even strangers, we are duty-bound to show love and compassion.

Besides sheer hard work, I believe the accomplishments of a successful businessman can largely be attributed to the seed of kindness that has been sown over many generations. For this reason, an entrepreneur who has made it must not forget his roots, but be humble and charitable, and return something back to society.

I have always embraced this principle myself. In my earnest desire to help even more people, I conceived the idea of setting up a dedicated charitable and public welfare organisation, combining our resources with the effort of a greater number of other people in order to actively promote community services. Through our activities, we hoped to encourage the public to be kind-hearted, more caring, leading to a more peaceful and harmonious society.

Thus was born the Chang Yung-fa Foundation on 5 December 1985, with a three-pronged mission – providing charitable medical care to the poor and needy, promoting cultural education, and establishing a think-tank on national policies.

Medical aid was primarily extended to low-income families or victims of disasters, who had been identified by the foundation's staff. In order to do a good job, I had our staff at the foundation trained by professionals at the outset on the correct approach to dealing with needy people. Liaison bases were also established in various big hospitals, community services centres and other public welfare associations so that we could respond quickly in times of emergencies. Many doctors and nurses volunteered their services, promptly getting in touch with the foundation whenever there were cases of penniless patients requiring urgent medical treatment.

There was one occasion when we had to donate several coffins to a home for the aged. Residents of these homes were generally destitute, without kith or kin; the homes themselves often lacked sufficient funding and could not afford to bear the funeral expenses of inmates who had passed away. The only way out was for them to approach the foundation for assistance. ·

Taiwan had a highly developed economy and its citizens were generally well provided for financially. But there remained a significant minority of families still living in abject poverty and deprivation. We often scoured the length and breadth of the country, including the outlying islands, to have a better feel of the problems so that every dollar that we gave actually went to helping the less privileged.

The foundation kept me informed of some of the dire situations its staff encountered on their field trips. The magnitude of suffering endured by the multitude of the sick and poor prompted me at one stage to think of building a hospital to serve their medical needs. A hospital would not only benefit more of these people directly, employees of the Evergreen Group and their families could also make use of the facilities provided. Besides, I was planning to have the hospital conduct research on occupational diseases more exhaustively.

In those days, the Evergreen Group had an ideal piece of land in Taoyuan on which a hospital could be built. As the location was also near to the city of Taipei, the facility would be well placed to serve the population of the metropolis as well. With this idea in mind, I engaged a consultant to come up with the conceptual design for a large, state-of-the-art medical centre; we spent almost NT$10 million on these preliminary designs alone.

Much to my surprise, however, our venture ran into strong opposition from the local medical clinics; worried that Evergreen would rob them of their business, they teamed up to boycott our plan.

I was extremely upset by the temerity of these doctors, who had no scruples in safeguarding their self-interest by ignoring the well-being of the public at large. In the face of their boycott, I was reluctant to force the issue, but let the proposal lapse.

The primary focus in the area of cultural education was for the foundation to grant financial aid to those high school, college or university students who came from low-income or destitute families to finish their tertiary education. It also sponsored group activities organised by various cultural associations.

The reason why the foundation only gave out bursaries, and not scholarships, was because the latter targeted those who excelled academically, whereas the former were designed specifically to help teenage students who aspired to progress in life, but lacked the financial means because of their poor family background.

Many talented music students received grants from the foundation in the early days to further their studies abroad. We owed the origin of this financial assistance scheme to a professor from a college of music in America who had heard of my passionate concern for Taiwan's education. He made a deliberate trip to see me and encouraged me to sponsor some of Taiwan's promising musicians to study overseas.

He told me that Taiwan had a number of very fine fourteen and fifteen year-old music students who possessed great potential. But because their families were poor, and also financial grants of this kind were not available in Taiwan, most of them could not afford to carry on with their studies. As I also felt then that the country was really short of talent in this field, I agreed to establish a musical bursary under the auspices of the foundation. Each year, a number of students selected by a panel of renowned professors of music in Taiwan were sent abroad to pursue their interests under this scheme.

These bursaries were awarded for the last time in 1995. With the rapid development of Taiwan's economy, most families had become reasonably well-off financially. The fact that parents could now afford music lessons for their children evidently showed that it would not be too much of a problem for them to send their children abroad for further studies.

As was the case everywhere else, in the course of helping the indigent, the foundation often came across some impostors who unabashedly sought financial assistance even though they were quite well-to-do people. Such regrettable incidents brought out in the open the boundless avarice and moral frailties of mankind.

Besides actively rendering help to the sick and destitute in society, the foundation did not neglect the needs of the families of Evergreen Group's employees either. Of the 15,000 employees in the group, it was invariable that some of them would at times encounter misfortune in their families; even though workers had a steady income, they had to reckon with heavier financial burdens in the event of any unforeseen circumstances. Their reluctance to seek any assistance from the foundation often exacerbated the difficult situation they were already in. It was against this background that I urged Evergreen's senior staff to take an active interest in the welfare of their subordinates, and to help them seek pecuniary aid from the foundation should they face any unexpected problems at home.

From a personal standpoint, a businessman must take care of his employees, even treating them as part of the family. The purpose of my establishing the foundation was to help others, regardless of their colour, creed, or race. But if we could not even help those around us, how could we possibly profess our desire to reach out to strangers in the name of charity?

The foundation gave out a few billion NT$ in aid each year. My plan was to continually expand its role so that a bigger cross-section of the population could benefit from the services.

Some people suggested to me that the foundation publicise its activities in order to make it a bigger name in town. But to me, charitable acts are an expression of our inner desires, our willingness to do good deeds without expecting anything in return. Otherwise, the original meaning of charity would be lost.

A private think-tank

Politics should be a concern of every businessman in a democratic country; if entrepreneurs only mind their own interests, ignoring the political issues of the day, the country is bound to face difficulties of calamitous proportions. Japan's Keidanren, for example, an organisation comprising the country's major business corporations, takes an active interest in the affairs of the country. It expresses its views and offers constructive suggestions and advice to the government, in the hope that Japan's political and economic developments would be even sounder, leading to peace and harmony in society.

It had been my lifelong belief that Taiwan should have a genuinely trustworthy public-policy research body, offering its impartial and objective analyses and views on the affairs of the nation. This was why I decided to establish a policy research and resource centre (the Institute for National Policy Research, or INPR, in short) under the patronage of the Chang Yung-fa Foundation. It would bring together academics and experts in the country to carry out research on political, economic, educational and social reform issues, but leaving shipping and aviation out of its scope.

Although I am a politically conscious person, I never sought to influence the opinions expressed by researchers at the INPR, which was essential in maintaining its independent and above-board stand. The centre also does not accept any funding from the government; many foundations had not been able to achieve their desired missions because of unwarranted interference by benefactors.

Political affiliations of the INPR's staff members are inconsequential; what I require of them as intellectuals in their own right is to carry out their tasks conscientiously, ensuring that their work is in keeping with the welfare needs of the public in general. By and large, the research fellows are accorded a free rein to pursue their interests, doing what they enjoy most.

Some people asked me why I elected to set up the research institute instead of spending the same largesse, which amounted to several tens of million of dollars annually, on helping those in need of food and shelter. In reality, the work of the institute is also one form of community service, yielding results and analyses that the government and politicians can use to help them shape their policies. It also acts as a catalyst that helps speed up socio-political reforms in the country, and if as a result of which the government were compelled to implement its policies more soundly, the people would ultimately have benefited too.

The INPR was set up with the primary objective of doing something useful for society on a voluntary basis, without hoping to receive anything in return. Unfortunately, it was accused by some people, whose motives were best known to themselves, of being a tool of Taiwan's pro-independence stance, even a think-tank of President Lee Teng-hui's. The truth is, the foundation was already carrying out this sort of work well before Mr Lee became president.

The malicious attacks against Evergreen went on for some time, forcing me at one stage to consider closing down the centre. The alternative, I thought, was to open it up to the involvement and patronage of other members of the business community, with myself staying on as one of the directors, so that people would no longer cast aspersions on its integrity.

News of my intention to close the INPR drew the attention of people in the academic and business circles, both in Taiwan and abroad, many of whom rang up or wrote to me, expressing their support for its continued existence, citing its valuable contribution to the country. They were concerned that many idealistic scholars would be deprived of an important avenue to express their opinions if the centre were to be disbanded.

Although some businessmen, in response to my invitation to participate in the activities of the research institute, did declare their support and agreed to contribute some funds towards its operating expenses annually, they were slow to act on their promises. In the end, when I sensed that assistance was not forthcoming from other quarters, I decided to carry on alone.

My fervent hope is that the INPR continues with its autonomous approach, winning the recognition and the voluntary support of a wider section of the public, including those in the business community. A time will come when it can then solicit contributions to gradually expand its organisation, paving the way for it to break out of the Chang Yung-fa Foundation's shadows and establish itself as an independent legal entity. This way, everybody would have an opportunity to help build a better future together. INPR eventually became independent on 20 December 1997.

Honesty is the best policy

People always describe me as something of an enigmatic person, which cannot of course be further from the truth. I am not one who craves fame and wealth, nor do I seek to bathe myself in the limelight; instead, I am a low-profile person, which, when taken together, I suppose, is why they consider me an enigma.

Everybody in this world has his own attitude or style of doing things; some people thrive in the limelight, while others prefer to plod away silently. As for me, I strive to be honest and earnest in all that I do; what matters most to me is that my determined efforts, especially in

271

business, will bring about the betterment of employees' well-being, as well as strengthen my resolve to give something back to society.

Perfecting the art of cultivating influential government officials has never been my style, nor do I harbour any selfish desire to befriend politicians for personal enrichment. To me, fate decides whether people become friends, and an intimate friendship is possible only if it is predestined.

The thing is, as a businessman, it is inevitable that I get to know politicians through some official functions, which, due to the sensitive nature of my status, often result in unwarranted speculation and sheer conjecture. My ties with President Lee Teng-hui, for example, often set many tongues wagging, conjuring up speculation of impropriety on my part.

In fact, I am well acquainted with many of the world's leading political figures, among them Baroness Margaret Thatcher, the former premier of Britain, as well as prominent politicians in America, Italy, France, Germany, and other countries. But the reason I know them is largely due to the demands of our shipping business, and not because I went all out to court their friendship deliberately. On the other hand, as the majority of the vessels in the Evergreen Group are Panama-registered, the host country derives enormous benefits from increased tax income, over and above the investments that Evergreen had injected into the local economy, thus contributing to the nation's wealth and prosperity. It was as a result of this long association that I got to know the Panamanian president and his top government officials very well.

My ties with President Lee also started off quite by chance; I could not possibly have predicted then that he would one day become the president of Taiwan.

Mr Lee was at the time the mayor of the city of Taipei. One day, I was having a round of golf with the then president of Evergreen Line, Mr Yeh Fu-shing at the club where, coincidentally, Mr Lee was also playing, and we introduced ourselves. But it was much later after that fateful encounter on the golf course that we got in touch with each

272

other again. He was by then the provincial governor, and was convey-
ing to me the invitations of some foreign maritime authorities to have
Evergreen Line call at their ports.

Unfortunately, Taiwan's domestic politics was at sixes and sevens
soon after Mr Lee was elected the country's president, and our
relationship became the subject of much baseless speculation and
innuendoes. President Lee's remark at the press conference upon his
return from visiting Singapore only stoked the flames of unbridled
imagination when he was asked whom he considered as some of his
closer friends in Taiwan's business community.

"Chang Yung-fa and Wang Yung-ching, of course," President Lee
let it be known, unhesitatingly. But everybody knew that President
Lee's circle of good friends was far more extensive than just Wang and
myself.

It was to achieve their own political ends that some of these
people had gone on a smear campaign against their opponents on the
pretext that they were targeting certain unscrupulous enterprises in
the country. They were absolutely devoid of any regard for the existence of legitimate and honest businesses, let alone the importance
and contribution of these enterprises to the development of Taiwan's
trade and economy.

In reality, the government and the ordinary man in the street, as
well as business enterprises, have an inextricably linked, inseparable
relationship. In any case, it is expected of the government to look
after the welfare of the citizens, and to consciously support legitimately
run businesses. Therefore, it is perfectly justified for the government
to prosper the common people, but no individuals should be tempted
to enrich themselves dishonestly.

There isn't any country in the world whose economic prosperity
and entrepreneurial development do not depend on the support of
the government and the presence of a sound legal framework. On the
other hand, a country will not be able to raise the standard of the
people's living, as well as its international stature, if it lacks a strong
business sector to underpin the overall economy. In short, the gov-

ernment and businesses are interdependent.

Take, for example, the aviation business. The government must pave the way for the entrepreneurs by ensuring that policies it enacts are conducive, and that it has the basic infrastructure in place. It must also muster the strength of the people to fight for, and secure more air-services rights, so as to propel the development of the aviation industry, as well as the international profile of the country, to greater heights.

In the case of shipping, Evergreen's vessels call at numerous ports around the world, bringing about greater economic prosperity to the local people, as well as ample employment opportunities. As a result, many countries welcome Evergreen's presence with open arms, and often strive to improve their logistics facilities and investment environment in order to create a life of abundance and riches for the local inhabitants.

Only when the government actively supports the businesses of the common folks, and entrepreneurs in return commit themselves to running their businesses as best they can, as well as reciprocate what society has provided them with in the first place, will the country experience the true meaning of progress.

Staying apolitical

Taiwan was in the grip of martial law in its early days, and the majority of businesses were urged to join the Kuomingtang (KMT) if they desired to get things done smoothly. Fortunately for Evergreen Line, as the bulk of its operations were internationally oriented at the time, the pressure for the company to follow suit was not too great. Anyway, I have not found it necessary to join any political party till now.

In fact, Mr Lin Jin-shen, tried very hard to persuade me to join the KMT when he was Transport Minister; many senior government officials also encouraged me to do so. But I was not moved.

"It would suffice if I were a friend of the party instead of becoming a full-fledged member," I told them, in an attempt to fend them off. "Anyway," I rationalised, "it's easier for a friend of the party to maintain a politically neutral stand, which makes his words much more

274

convincing to people. Besides, people might misconstrue me as a mouthpiece of the KMT if I become an official member."

They thought my explanation reasonable, and have since refrained from bothering me with the idea again.

Following the transformation of Taiwan's political landscape in later years, and because I thought it unnecessary to join the KMT, plus my preference for the native Taiwanese language, there were persistent rumours that I supported an independent Taiwan, alluding to the green corporate logo of Evergreen as the tell-tale sign of my political leaning. What could I say except to mention that people bent on tarnishing the reputation of others could always trump up charges to achieve their ends? Since I was born and raised in Taiwan, what was wrong with my speaking the vernacular? These rumours had obviously originated from people who were out to stir up trouble.

I do not discriminate against or favour any political party. I also do not look at people's political affiliations, and thus form preconceived ideas about them, when making friends. I see people as who they are, not their political background, and treat them with the same attitude as I would everybody else. As long as we can click, we can become friends.

Every citizen must have a sense of patriotism and service for his country irrespective of his party affiliations. In other words, there is absolutely no relationship between a person's political views and his desire to serve the nation; it is the responsibility of every political party to safeguard the interest of their country, and to work for the common good of society at large.

I would not dare to claim any credit for myself, nor would I expect anything from the government just because I have worked hard for my business and have contributed to society; it is after all my duty to do my part for the people. I thus found it a bit of a bitter pill to swallow when EVA Airways was accused by some quarters of having received special privileges from the government, when in fact we had sacrificed so much of our money and effort to bolster the aviation business of the country.

Special privileges? I would have been most thankful had the

government not given us any trouble in the first place!

In my mind, the process of democratisation in Taiwan had proceeded at too rapid a pace, so fast that in fact people did not understand the true essence of democracy. Worse, some people took it as their right in the name of democracy to abuse those who did not share their views.

For Taiwan especially, democratic freedom could have come more slowly, in a number of stages; the fact that so much of it arrived in so short a time probably did more harm than good. Look at some of the economic and social ironies that prevail in Taiwan today – difficulties in financing domestic infrastructure projects even though the government coffer is flush with foreign reserves, and a democracy that is not necessarily accompanied by a truly sophisticated society – two glaring examples. One could thus imagine the chaos that would reign in a country which is not exactly "civilised", but in which the democratic process occurs at a breakneck speed. If we want to forestall this problem, we have to start with the wholesale revamp of the people's mindset through a combination of family, school, and social education. But above all, the moral fabric of the society must be strengthened.

I believe the democratisation of a country must be in keeping with the various cultural, social and environmental peculiarities that exist domestically instead of blindly following the so-called Western style of democracy, which may not necessarily be suitable in the local context. As Chinese, therefore, we must develop a model of democracy, and at a pace, that is compatible with our expectations and moral sense, so that we do not transgress the bounds of correctness.

The meaning of friendship

I have built up my business painstakingly, and am, therefore, not unaccustomed to the vagaries of human feelings and disposition, which in fact stood me in good stead as I am seldom ruffled these days by the constant changes and uncertainties that surround us.

We ought to treasure, and be grateful for, whatever that we have, be it happiness or material wealth; we must especially not forget the kind deeds of other people, so that we can return the favour when the opportunity arises. This, after all, is the fundamental prerequisite for the existence of mankind; a person who is devoid of goodwill and compassion will, I believe, not earn the respect of others.

I recall when we first started out, Evergreen Marine encountered some cash-flow problems on one occasion and had to turn to the boss of Formosa Shipping Agencies, Mr Loh Yao-fon, for help. He agreed to give me a loan of NT$100,000 on the spot without so much as muttering a word. Although it was a relatively small sum of money, and I paid it back to him shortly after, I was eternally grateful to him for the help he rendered in the hour of need.

The year 1984 saw the birth of Uniglory Marine when Evergreen's regional shipping operations were hived off to become an independent business entity. Mr Loh's company was then facing a tough time due to intense competition, and by virtue of his intimate knowledge of the shipping business, I invited him to join Uniglory as a shareholder, and appointed him chairman of the company's board of directors, contrary to the usual practice. Until then, I was, without exception, the chairman of every single affiliated company in the Evergreen Group.

Coming to the aid of people in times of emergencies or hardships is a lot more worthwhile and heart-warming than striving for perfection, as judged by the traumatic experience I had personally gone through before. In this context, I have learnt to cherish friendship dearly, to treasure and be contented with what we have, in the course of our everyday life.

With the rapid development of the Evergreen Group from a virtually unknown entity to the behemoth that it is today, some people asked me whether I consider myself a successful person.

To me, a person deserves to be revered only if, by virtue of his moral integrity and conduct, he earns the sincere approval and recognition of others, and at the same time selflessly devotes himself to the service of the masses. As for those people who relentlessly pursue fame and fortune, and who gauge their worth by their wealth and title, these unbridled desires to gratify themselves frankly seem somewhat ignoble, and even morally unethical.

Some people might perhaps feel that I am biased in my thinking as I have already achieved fame and fortune myself. But the reality is that no two people share the same destiny. I work hard not because I crave more wealth, but rather it is my duty, and obligation, to look after the livelihood of the more than ten thousand employees and their families in the Evergreen Group. Were it not for the fact that so many people depend on Evergreen to provide them with a stable job to feed their families, I would not have to devote so much of my time and energy to constantly trotting around, attending to the affairs of the company.

You could say I am now established in my business and have accumulated considerable wealth over the years. But I also have to pay a heavy price for these achievements in that I have to forgo my personal freedom. Besides the official duties that practically occupy all of my time day in and day out, I also have to travel extensively both within and outside of Taiwan. On the other hand, in spite of all these sacrifices, I feel a deep sense of fulfilment and gratitude; I am gratified that my business has contributed in no small measure to the well-being of society, and at the same time provided for the livelihood of the employees' families.

I still constantly urge myself to work harder to fulfil my foreordained mission and destiny, and to not take for granted the fame and wealth I have been blessed with. I must cherish these dearly, and put them to good use for the benefit of people and society.

Discovering spiritual fulfilment in "Tao"

I have been exposed to Buddhism and Tao since young. My mother was a deeply religious person, and I occasionally tagged along when she went to pray at the temple. But I never embraced any form of religion seriously, even though many people tried very hard to make a proselyte of me, all to no avail.

It was mainly because a lot of doubts were lingering in my mind then

278

as to who God is, and whose God is the greatest among all the deities.

Soon after my marriage, however, my mother and I got our first taste of Tao through the influence of my wife, who had incidentally been a devotee long before we tied the knot. But, because I had received Japanese education since I was a small boy, I found it rather difficult to understand all the Tao literature written in Chinese. Hence, I did not really try hard to delve into the subject more deeply.

Then in 1975, my mother died and religion took a stronger hold of me. I remember she passed away on the eve of Tien Gong's ("God of the Cosmos") birthday. The day had started off routinely enough for her; she was about to leave the house for Keelung's Tien Gong Temple when I saw her in her usual alert and radiant self. I asked my chauffeur to give her a lift to the temple. Little did I realise then that I was seeing her for the last time. She passed away peacefully that morning at the temple on the chair she was sitting on, without any hint of trouble at all.

Just before she was laid to rest in the casket, workers putting the makeup on her at the funeral parlour noticed that her skin was supple and her body soft; it was as if she had fallen into a blissful slumber.

Chang Sheng-tu, my close friend from Keelung, was at the wake and he told me later that it was because my mother had done penance that her body had not turned stiff at all even though it was already several days into the funeral.

Indeed, I later came across cases in which the corpses of devotees who had sought penitence and pursued enlightenment did stay unusually supple instead of turning rigid. I was profoundly mystified by this phenomenon, which prompted me to take a more serious interest in the religion from then on.

Later when I was in Japan, I discovered by chance that there were many books written on the teachings of Tao, and I bought a number of them to read. I was so captivated by the contents of these books that I read them over and over again, which gradually enabled me to have a better understanding of the true meaning of this particular religion.

The ensuing pursuit of the significance of Tao, in the hope of eventually attaining enlightenment, drastically altered my perception of life.

Tao teaches righteousness, thus enabling believers to discern right from wrong, leading them onto a road of self-discipline, compassion, kindness (doing good deeds), and enlightenment, which in turn result in inner peace and a natural desire to walk life's straight paths. In this context, people who do not know the truths are more likely to go wayward and succumb to acts of wrongdoing. On the other hand, I believe if a person devotes himself to attaining spiritual enlightenment, he will be blessed with an even greater sense of morality and righteousness.

A merciful and benevolent heart

I understand from Tao that everything goes through a cycle of cause and effect; we only have to look at our present plight and experiences to know what previous lives were like. Hence, whatever our present fate, we should not blame anybody, because ultimately we reap what we sow; in short, good will be repaid with good, evil with evil.

People who did good deeds in their previous lives are unlikely to encounter too many hardships in their present existence. Even if bad fortune or dangers should befall them, they can easily deal with the situations, rendering an adversity harmless. If we were made to understand this karmic cycle of human existence, we could perhaps refrain from nitpicking or grumbling, and devote more of our energy to doing charitable deeds instead.

Deeds of kindness and charity can never be enough in this world, and everybody can play an important part in making society a more comfortable place for all to live in.

For instance, whenever charitable organisations or public welfare groups approached me to contribute to their good causes, I deliberately turned down their requests although I could have single-handedly supported all their financial needs with my personal resources. This was because I wanted others to also have a chance to do good and to donate whatever amount they could afford. If at the end of the day the money collected was still not enough, I undertook to top up the shortfall.

On the other hand, our acts of benevolence should not be driven by any selfish motive to seek public recognition, just because we can afford it, without any regard for the ability and desire of others to help. Those of us with money can give generously, and those without can always volunteer our services, so that together we can derive the satisfaction of seeing society benefit from our contributions.

Personally, I always uphold the highest standard of morality in my daily living. I feel we should cherish our happiness and be contented with our lot; rid ourselves of envy and greed, but imbue ourselves instead with honesty and propriety, so that we can live happily with peace of mind.

Some people asked me whether it was because of my devotion to Tao that the Evergreen Group has been able to achieve the huge success that we see today. The truth is, my spiritual pursuit was not an act of sacrificial offering for all the wealth and fame that heaven has endowed me with. On the contrary, it was my sincere desire to arouse the innate propensity of every human being to be honest and kind-hearted, and to do more good deeds in my lifetime.

People will naturally accumulate both genuine reputation and wealth if they work hard, earnestly and conscientiously. If, however, this status had been attained through some unscrupulous means, not only would it not stand the test of time, these people would also not earn the respect of others.

There is definitely no such thing in the world as a life that is guaranteed to be plain sailing and peaceful, just because a person pursues a spiritually enlightened path. It is inevitable that even devout believers will encounter difficulties and setbacks in their lifetimes just like everyone else, for there is no way that the destiny of mankind can be detached from the unremitting cause-and-effect cycle.

Although I enjoy sharing my faith with others, I am also fully aware that different people have different affinities towards religion. While some people are happy to know more about Tao and devote a lot of their time to studying the teachings, others may not necessarily be able to grasp the subject. There is no way we can coerce them into accepting the faith. Hence, I never compelled any of my employees to also seek spiritual enlightenment; neither would their religious beliefs have any implication on their promotion prospects in the company.

I became an avowed vegetarian after turning sixty. It was my way of showing gratitude for the heavenly realm's abundant mercy on the existence of every living creature on earth, and for allowing both man and animals to coexist in the universe. As a result, my respect for life was greatly aroused, and I could no longer bear to snuff out any living things. Since making the choice, I have lived a pure and refreshing life, comfortably at ease with myself, without the slightest feeling of any inconvenience or privation at all.

A lifelong dedication to the sea

I am one of those people who enjoy work tremendously, in fact so much so that I often lose my sense of time, and despite the long hours, I also do not feel fatigued. Although I have to go abroad regularly because of my numerous business commitments, I seldom have the time to take in the sights in the many countries that I visit, preferring to pour all my energy into work. On public holidays, apart from playing an occasional game or two of golf with my senior colleagues and my close friends to relax, I spend the bulk of my time reading books and trade publications concerning the shipping and airline industries.

Marine transportation has always been my pet profession, and one that has aroused the greatest interest in me. Indeed, I have never grown weary of this business even though I have been in it for the past few decades, dealing with shipping-related affairs day in and day out. On the contrary, I feel all the more emotionally attached to it as time passes, as though we are inseparable. That is why, whenever and wherever I see ocean and ships, a gust of affection would course through my veins, as if I have just bumped into my long-time bosom friends. My long association with the oceanic realm with all its attraction and majesty, has not only enriched my soul, I have also been able to draw

282

a great deal of inspiration from the experience.

I recall nostalgically those seafaring days when the practical experience I gained from all the hard work enabled me to mature in stature steadily. With almost every single day of my life spent in the warm embrace of the infinite vastness of the mighty ocean, my dream was one of hope and promises for the future. Looking back, it was indeed a time of happiness and great joy. For me, I feel that taking in the panoramic view of the scenery on land from the distant seas is always an especially beautiful and moving experience.

You might say a ship is a ship by any other name. In reality, we can also look at it as an object that possesses life, exuding charm and feelings. I still remember there was one occasion during my seafaring days when I had to accompany a certain vessel for a very long period of time. Because of the many months we sailed the mighty ocean together, it was as if the ship and I were inseparable working partners with a good tacit understanding of each other's style. Even till today, I can still remember vividly every minute feature of the ship.

Traditionally, ladies have always had the honour of smashing the bottle during the launching ceremony of a new vessel. This symbolic act, marking the launch, can be likened to the bestowing of life on the vessel; indeed, the lady personally responsible for this ritual often regards the vessel as her own flesh and blood, with a special affection for it. After a useful life span of twenty, thirty years, when the vessel has to be consigned to the breaking yard to be scrapped, it is not unusual for the "mother" to even shed tears, as though bemoaning the loss of a loved one.

For me, a ship is just like one of my children; from the commencement of its construction, to its christening and launch, to the sea trial, and the eventual delivery, I want to know what is happening at every single stage of the entire process.

No matter how tight my schedule is, I will find time to preside over the launching and christening ceremony of a new ship. Usually a sea trial would be conducted for the vessel three months after it has been launched. I would, without exception, personally take part in these manoeuvres whenever the first of a new series of vessels is launched; from eight o'clock in the morning to around eight at night, the vessel would be put through its paces, subjecting its various capabilities to stringent tests.

My many years in the seafaring profession have enabled me to understand the ins and outs of such aspects of a vessel as its construction, the materials used, its design, as well as the functional capability of the various types of navigational instruments. Hence, if and when during the sea trial I come across anything in the vessel that can be further refined, I will have the improvements incorporated in the next series of new ships to be built.

Whenever an old ship from among the Evergreen's fleet was due to be scrapped, I ensured that its major navigational gadgets were kept aside, to be used as exhibits later. I also have a collection of maritime-related paintings as well as works by local artists in Taiwan. All these, together with artefacts bought from world-renowned auction houses, are part of my preparations to set up a hyper-scale maritime museum in Taiwan.

The museum is to adopt a leisurely but educational approach towards exhibiting various cultural relics of Taiwan's, and the rest of the world's maritime industry of both the past and present era. On display will be realistic mock-ups of vessels and their engines, as well as other paraphernalia, scale-models of ships, paintings, films and books, among other things, so that the community at large would have a better understanding and knowledge of maritime history and civilisation for generations to come.

This project has been on my drawing board for many years; it is a forum through which I hope to share the fruits of my long association with the maritime transportation business, as well as my passion for the ocean, with society.

The ocean and the ships have been an extremely important part of my life. To say that the seas and I have a uniquely special relationship is to understate the truth somewhat; that I was born the son of the mighty ocean would perhaps be a more fitting description!

A tablet presented by President Chiang Ching-kuo in 1981 in appreciation of my passion for promoting education.

Receiving a plaque from a graduate student representative from Tamkang University's faculty of maritime studies in May 1989 for contributing to maritime education.

A gift to the people of Taiwan: Tamkang University's Merchant Ship Hall. I also helped conceive the architectural design of the facade.

Ever Training, Taiwan's first navigational training vessel.

Evergreen spent NT$160 million to convert *Ever Safety* into a container training ship and renamed it *Ever Trust*.

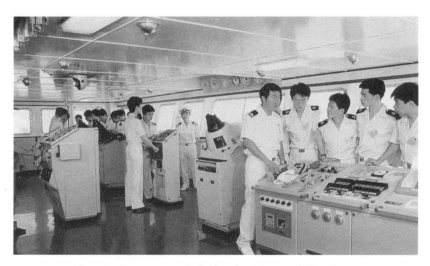

A session in progress on the bridge of training vessel, *Ever Trust*.

A sampling of the numerous plaques and tablets presented by well-wishers and beneficiaries of the Chang Yung-fa Foundation in appreciation of its immeasurable contribution to society.

Former British Prime Minister, Margaret Thatcher, launching Evergreen's new-generation container vessel, *Ever Result*.

Shuttle Diplomacy: Evergreen's vessels call at numerous ports around the world, contributing to the prosperity of the local economies. The company also maintains cordial relations with host governments.

We must be thankful to, and repay, society for all that we have benefited from it.

My religious faith has drastically altered my perception in life.

I want people to be morally upright, but I never impel employees to do penance
or seek enlightenment.

291

An "ascetic" ceremony held on my sixtieth birthday
during which I vowed to become a vegetarian.

Relaxing over a round of golf.

I personally participated in the sea-trials of every first new-generation vessel.

Putting a new D-type vessel through her paces.

EVERGREEN GROUP
長　榮　集　團

 長 榮 國 際 有 限 公 司（巴拿馬）
EVERGREEN INTERNATIONAL S. A.

 長 榮 美 國 有 限 公 司
EVERGREEN AMERICA CORPORATION

エバーグリーン・ジャパン株式会社
EVERGREEN JAPAN CORPORATION

 長 榮 英 國 有 限 公 司
EVERGREEN U. K. LIMITED

 長 榮 德 國 有 限 公 司
EVERGREEN　DEUTSCHLAND GMBH

長 榮 菲 律 賓 有 限 公 司
EVERGREEN PHILIPPINES CORPORATION

 長 榮 香 港 有 限 公 司
EVERGREEN STAR HONG KONG LTD.

長 榮 重 工（馬）有 限 公 司
EVERGREEN HEAVY INDUSTRIAL CORP.(M) BERHAD

 長 榮 造 船 株 式 会 社
EVERGREEN SHIPYARD CORPORATION

長 榮 桂 冠 酒 店（曼谷）
EVERGREEN LAUREL HOTEL
(BANGKOK)

 長 榮 桂 冠 酒 店（檳城）
EVERGREEN LAUREL HOTEL
(PENANG)

 長 榮 桂 冠 酒 店（巴黎）
EVERGREEN LAUREL HOTEL
(PARIS)

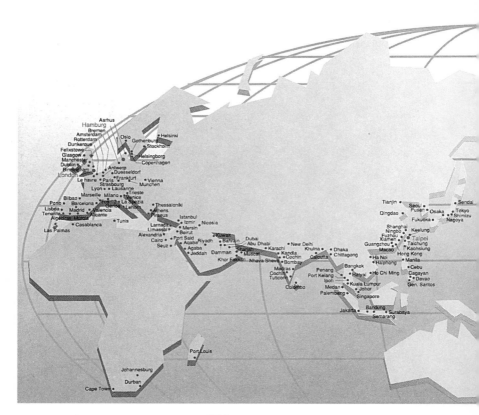

294

長 榮 國 際 股 份 有 限 公 司
EVERGREEN INTERNATIONAL CORP.

 長 榮 海 運 股 份 有 限 公 司
EVERGREEN MARINE CORP. (TAIWAN) LTD.

 長 榮 航 空 股 份 有 限 公 司
EVA AIRWAYS CORPORATION

 立 榮 海 運 股 份 有 限 公 司
UNIGLORY MARINE CORPORATION

 長 榮 重 工 股 份 有 限 公 司
EVERGREEN HEAVY INDUSTRIAL CORP.

 長 榮 貨 櫃 股 份 有 限 公 司
EVERGREEN CONTAINER TERMINAL CORP.

 長 榮 運 輸 股 份 有 限 公 司
EVERGREEN TRANSPORT CORPORATION

 台 灣 碼 頭 服 務 股 份 有 限 公 司
TAIWAN TERMINAL SERVICES CORP. LTD.

 長 榮 航 勤 股 份 有 限 公 司
EVERGREEN AIRLINE SERVICES CORPORATION

 長 航 通 運 股 份 有 限 公 司
EVERVOYAGE TRANSPORT CORPORATION

 長 榮 空 廚 股 份 有 限 公 司
EVERGREEN SKY CATERING CORPORATION

 長 榮 清 勤 股 份 有 限 公 司
EVERGREEN MULTI-SERVICE CORPORATION

 長 榮 航 太 科 技 股 份 有 限 公 司
EVERGREEN AVIATION TECHNOLOGIES CORP.

 長 榮 保 全 股 份 有 限 公 司
EVERGREEN SECURITY CORPORATION

 長 榮 桂 冠 酒 店 (台中)
EVERGREEN LAUREL HOTEL
(TAICHUNG)

 長 榮 桂 冠 酒 店 (基隆)
EVERGREEN LAUREL HOTEL
(KEELUNG)

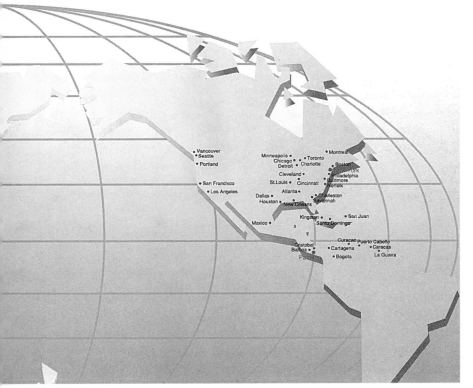

Chronology

6 October 1927	Born in Suao, Ilan County, Taiwan.
1934	Entire family moved to Keelung, enrolled in Keelung "Shou" primary school.
1941	Employed by the Keelung representative office of Minami Nippon Steam-ship, attended night classes at a vocational secondary school in Taipei.
8 December 1941	World War II broke out.
end 1943	Seconded to Taipei General Corporation's ship department, promoted to staff employee.
early 1944	Deployed on first seagoing assignment as a purser onboard the passenger/cargo ship *Kishu Maru*.
end 1944	Posted back to Taipei General Corporation's ship department and tasked with crew assignment duties.
	Evacuated mother and four younger siblings to Ilan's Kung Liao village; moved with eldest brother and his wife to Shijr.
	US Allied forces attacked and sank *Shonan Maru*, the ship that father was working on. After father's death, took sole responsibility for family's livelihood.
1945	Seconded to Sempaku Uneikai.
15 August 1945	World War II ended following Japan's unconditional surrender to the Allies; China regained sovereignty of Taiwan.
	Relocated mother and four younger siblings back to Keelung.
1946	Kuomin government took control of all Japanese vessels in Taiwan.
	Found employment on a Taiwanese vessel *Fung Shan* through the assistance of Lin Tai-san. Lin Tien-fu was captain of the ship.
	Successively obtained third, second and first officer's license through painstaking self-study.
1953	Tied the nuptial knot.
June 1961	Established New Taiwan Marine with Liao Wen-liang and Chu Shiang-zong.
July 1962	Represented New Taiwan Marine for the first time to Japan to arrange for the purchase of a 1,600-tonne second-hand vessel (later named *Shin Tai*).
1964	Proposed the idea of newbuildings to shareholders of New Taiwan Marine, thus became the first person at the time to advocate and make the building of new banana and timber carriers a reality.
1965	Quit New Taiwan Marine.
	Initiated by Tien Jiu-jing, proceeded to jointly establish Central Marine with Hsiao Yi-hsui and Hsiao Ju-hsui.
April 1968	Central Marine took delivery of its first ocean-going vessel, *Central Trust*, at Tsuneishi Shipyard in Japan.
	Time-chartered to Showa Line, *Central Trust* was disabled by a failure in its water feed pump enroute to Seattle, the resultant delay led Showa Line to serve a notice of cancellation for the charter party prior to its expiration.

296

end August 1968	Expelled from the company's board and made to assume the liability of *Central Trust* following a board's decision passed during an emergency meeting convened by Hsiao Yi-hsui in my absence.
1 September 1968	Evergreen Marine Corporation, located at 24-1 Chang An East Road, Section 1, Taipei, was established.
April 1969	Evergreen Marine entered a Buy/Leaseback deal with Showa Line for a bulk breaker, *Ever Glory*.
15 August 1969	Evergreen Marine purchased a second-hand general-cargo ship, *Ever Island*, from K Line to ply on its newly opened Far East/Arabian-Persian Gulf regular liner service.
7 September 1969	Fire broke out on *Ever Island* in Keelung.
early October 1969	*Ever State* encountered engine failure enroute to the USA.
17 November 1969	*Central Trust* collided with a Swedish container ship off the American port of Norfolk.
1970	Evergreen Marine Corporation established bursaries in a number of maritime schools and university colleges to help elevate Taiwan's shipping industry and nurture maritime talents.
July & Sept. 1971	Evergreen Marine acquired its first two second-hand diesel engine vessels, *Ever Fortune* and *Ever Lasting*.
31 January 1972	Evergreen Marine's first newbuilding, a general-cargo vessel *Ever Safety*, was delivered to inaugurate the Far East/Caribbean Sea route.
February 1972	Established Evergreen Japan Corporation in Tokyo.
September 1973	Established Evergreen Transport Corporation to provide inland container haulage.
March 1974	Established Evergreen America Corporation in New York.
July 1974	Evergreen Marine Corporation relocated its headquarters to the Evergreen Building at 63 Sung Chiang Road in Taipei.
1974 - 1976	Evergreen Marine commissioned the construction of 5 H-type bulk carriers for lease to NYK Line on a time-charter basis.
February 1975	Established Evergreen International S.A. (Panama) to own and manage Evergreen Group's ships registered under the Panamanian flag as well as provide support to operations in Central & South America.
March 1975	Mother's demise.
26 April 1975	Evergreen Marine's first full container ship, *Ever Spring*, was launched in Japan.
17 July 1975	*Ever Spring* inaugurated the Far East/US East Coast route, the company's first full container service. Evergreen Marine was the first shipping company in Taiwan to offer containerised services.
March 1976	Evergreen America Corporation established its branch office in California.
October 1976	A regular full container service from the Far East to the US West Coast was launched and inaugurated by *Ever Spring*. Evergreen Marine collaborated with Tamkang University to establish two disciplines, navigation and marine engineering, in 1976 and 1977 respectively. Solely funded the construction of the Merchant Ship Hall.
24 March 1977	Containerisation of Evergreen Marine's Far East/Caribbean Sea liner service. *Ever Mercy* was deployed on the inaugural voyage.

297

26 June 1977	*Ever Promoter*, a general-cargo vessel, inaugurated the Far East/Red Sea-Mediterranean Sea liner service.
25 May 1978	Containerisation of Evergreen Marine's Far East//Red Sea-Mediterranean Sea liner service. *Ever Humanity* was deployed on the inaugural voyage.
10 April 1979	*Ever Vital* inaugurated the Far East/Europe regular full container service. Evergreen Marine provided free training for maritime navigation and engineering students from the maritime schools in Taiwan on board its own, also the country's first, training vessel, *Ever Training*.
November 1979	Established Evergreen UK Limited.
21 May 1982	Evergreen Marine and Far Eastern Freight Conference signed the Gentlemen's Agreement which remained in effect between July 1982 and end 1985.
August 1982	Established Evergreen Heavy Industrial Corporation to manufacture, repair and retrofit containers and container parts as well as produce chassis and special trailers.
November 1983	Founded Evergreen Container Terminal Corporation and built Asia's largest inland container terminal in Taoyuan, Nankan.
July 1984	FEFC unilaterally announced the premature termination of the Gentlemen's Agreement, following which Evergreen Marine also swiftly made known its decision to end the pact with FEFC. Established Evergreen International Corporation to provide full support to and propel the diversification of the Evergreen Group of companies. *Ever Garden* and *Ever Genius* inaugurated the unprecedented round-the-world eastbound and westbound services respectively.
August 1984	Established Uniglory Marine Corporation to operate container service in the intra-Asia trades.
1985	Evergreen Marine is the world's largest container shipping company.
May 1985	A regular full container service was inaugurated between the Western Mediterranean and US East Coast.
5 December 1985	Established the Chang Yung-fa Foundation.
April 1986	Opening ceremony of Evergreen Building situated at 166 Minsheng East Road, Section 2, Taipei.
October 1986	Established Evergreen Deutschland Gmbh in Hamburg to oversee operations in Europe and the Mediterranean. Became an avowed vegetarian following sixtieth birthday.
1 September 1988	Submitted application for the establishment of an international airline; set up EVA Air task force.
8 March 1989	EVA Air granted approval to operate international passenger cum cargo services.
June 1989	Established Evergreen Heavy Industrial Corporation (M) Berhad in Johor to manufacture containers.
6 October 1989	EVA Air signed purchase agreements with the Boeing Company and McDonnell Douglas for a total of 26 new aircraft worth some US$3.6 billion.
13 September 1990	Conferred the Honorary Doctor of Humane Letters by The California State University.
October 1990	Established Evergreen Airline Services Corporation to provide ground handling services, laundry as well as cleaning and maintenance of office

	blocks. Evergreen Multi-Service Corporation was established in October of 1996 to take over the laundry and cleaning services.
1 July 1991	EVA Air formally took to the skies.
March 1992	Acquired Hayashikane Shipyard (later renamed Evergreen Shipyard Corporation).
February 1993	Opening of Evergreen Laurel Hotel (Taichung), the first of a world-class chain of hotels created and operated by Evergreen International Corporation.
August 1993	Established Evergreen Star Hong Kong Ltd to control operations in Hong Kong and China.
October 1993	Established Evergreen Sky Catering Corporation.
March 1994	Opening of Evergreen Laurel Hotel (Bangkok).
April 1994	Established Evervoyage Transport Corporation to provide passenger coach services as well as transportation for employees of the Evergreen Group.
12 May 1995	Conferred the Honorary Doctor of Business Administration by the University of South Carolina.
February 1997	Established Evergreen Philippines Corporation to handle the operation of Evergreen's and Uniglory's services in the Philippines.
July 1997	Commenced construction of Evergreen Laurel Hotel in Paris, completion expected in 1999.
October 1997	Published *Memoirs of Dr Chang Yung-fa* in Mandarin.
December 1997	Opening of Evergreen Laurel Hotel (Penang).
January 1998	Established Taiwan Terminal Services Corporation Ltd. to operate dockside loading and unloading of containers.
	Established Evergreen Aviation Technologies Corporation to provide maintenance services for EVA Air and other airlines.
25 February 1998	Conferred the Honorary Doctor of Shipping and Transport Management by the National Taiwan Ocean University.
June 1998	Established Evergreen Security Corporation to provide security protection, electronic security systems as well as security escort services.
October 1998	Opening of Evergreen Laurel Hotel (Keelung).
2 October 1998	Acquired Lloyd Triestino, Italian state-run carrier.